Love in Motion

REIDAR DUE

Love in Motion

Erotic Relationships in Film

WALLFLOWER PRESS
LONDON & NEW YORK

A Wallflower Press Book
Published by
Columbia University Press
Publishers Since 1893
New York • Chichester, West Sussex
cup.columbia.edu

Copyright © Reidar Due 2013
All rights reserved.
Wallflower Press® is a registered trademark of Columbia University Press

A complete CIP record is available from the Library of Congress

ISBN 978-0-231-16732-1 (cloth)
ISBN 978-0-231-16733-8 (pbk.)
ISBN 978-0-231-85051-3 (e-book)

Contents

Foreword	vii
Introduction	1
Ego Love and Melodrama	9
Categories of Film Love	13
Making Sense	25
The Ontology of Love	37
Eros in History	49
The Social Paradigm	69
American Cinema of Choice	79
French Cinema of Place	95
Hitchcock and Lang	109
Love in the World	123
Conclusion: On Method	155
Filmography	167
Bibliography	173
Index	179

Foreword

This book has been a long time in the making. It started its life as a graduate seminar at Oxford University in 2003. My thought then was very simple: why have so few philosophers after Plato written on love? I also had another thought, which was that Hollywood narrative style imposes on couples a very definite, very rigid structure of meaning or content, a structure, which can be spelled out in long lists of moral and social dichotomies.

I thought that love is something fundamentally different from this sort of meaningful transaction, that love is something that for very deep and inscrutable reasons escapes meaning, even the meaning of non-meaning that we call passion and desire. In the course of writing, these initial thoughts have led me to the thesis that we moderns who pride ourselves on our individual freedoms, have in fact witnessed a decline of love. This book defends a kind of freedom that modernity was about to lose sight of but which, I think, cinema for a sort time recaptured.

I regret that this is a very Western book. This is not because I don't think that classical Indian, Arabic or Japanese poetry and novels, or indeed epics and poetry from any other people on Earth, present compelling thoughts on love. Yet, ignoring the languages and cultures in which these texts originate, it seemed hazardous to try and incorporate fragments of those cultures into the Western story I am able to narrate. Over the years I have discussed these topics with all my friends and I found that everyone had something to say on what love is and isn't, whether love is a word, an idea, a moral ideal, whether love is universal or culturally specific and so on. I am grateful to all of you for these interesting hours of self-examination.

I am grateful also to my editor at Wallflower Press, Yoram Allon, who showed interest in the project many years ago as we met at the BFI National Film Theatre in London. His patience and persistence have been exemplary and encouraging. The Magdalen College library has been an ideal working environment, both because of its inspiring collection, but also due to its friendly staff headed by Christine Ferdinand. My views on aesthetics have benefited from a long and ongoing discussion with Larry Dreyfuss, Jas Elsner, Clare Harris, Andrew Klevan, Emmanuele Gragnolati, Nikolaj Lübecker, Lizzie Fricker, Tiffany Stern, Shami Gosh, Felix Budelman and Dimitris Papanikolaou.

I dedicate this book to my parents.

Reidar Due
Oxford
July 2013

Introduction

This is a book about love, about the philosophy of love and the aesthetics of love in film. One of the difficulties in thinking about love is that one very quickly begins to think about *something else* – about sexuality, or marriage, or morality; what loves are good, what less good, for what reason; or one thinks that the desire for beauty and sex is perhaps a veiled desire for God. This book presents a philosophy of love according to its universal essence, that is, a theory of what love is in itself. This theory does show that love *involves* many different things – desire, social relationships, feelings, thoughts – but *in itself* love is not identical with any one of these component features. This philosophy of love is both ontological and ethical. It is a theory of what love is and it is a conception of what love should be. Love is a relation and this relation is free. Love is an erotic relation prior to being a feeling or a social arrangement. As relation, love escapes definition, both by the lovers and by their surroundings. Because love is thus indefinable it contains a germ of freedom. This freedom is not a mere subjective experience. Love plays itself out amidst other social relations. Love is not private: it takes place *in the world* and has the potential to invade or influence all other social relationships. This worldly freedom is the ethics of love, what love ought to be.

There have been almost no philosophical theories about love since Plato's dialogue, *Symposion*. This may be because love travels across all the different areas of philosophical enquiry: love is metaphysical and ethical, biological, psychological, political. Plato recognises as much in the *Symposion*. Each of the speeches given in honour of Eros is presented from a particular point of view, motivated by the profession, talent and temperament of the speaker. Each situates love within a different *domain of reality*. Plato makes us believe that the last part of the dialogue, the speech that the priestess Diotima gives to Socrates, is the philosophical *truth of love* – and this is a spiritual truth. But perhaps the multifaceted nature of love reflected in the dialogue as a whole is closer to the essence of love than the spiritual theory presented at the end. If that is so, *the unity of love is itself of a particular kind*. The unity of love is of a different kind, that is, from phenomena that can be very clearly defined within a particular domain of reality by the philosophical or scientific theories that investigate that field.

If we return to the question of how experience and theoretical reflection relate to one another in enquiries about love, we could assume, as a hypothesis at least, that love must be something that *corresponds to the experience* of love – love is not a theoretical phenomenon like atoms, that is, a phenomenon that appears only within the experience of a scientist. But it is not clear that first-hand experience would be the best guide to understanding love: for if love is a phenomenon that moves between different areas of reality and which therefore also can turn up in different kinds of discourse, a reflection grounded in experience might not be able to circumscribe love in all its constituent parts.

A further difficulty in thinking philosophically about love is that love is both a familiar experience that most people have and an abstract idea, a topic of philosophical reflection. Love is complex and banal, universal and – for most lovers – more or less unique. Love is not like any other object of reflection in that it is not simply an *object* – even an abstract one. Numbers are abstract objects, but they are objects nevertheless. Love exists as relationships, feelings, longings, desires, sexual acts, thoughts, social conflicts, cultural expectations. Hence, the complex phenomenon that love is always involves two kinds of perspective that are sharply distinct – the subjective perspective of the lovers and the third-person perspective of those who surround the lovers as involuntary observers and commentators. The phenomenon of love – in its full complexity – is not an object precisely for this reason: an object is not simultaneously a subject; it is not also self-reflective.

The first and main principle of this book is metaphysical. It is the claim that love, before it is classified within any particular domain of reality, is a *relation*. It is a relation prior to being a feeling or a desire: the lover who dreams of the beloved, but has never dared to address her or him in speech, dreams of a relationship. It takes two to love. The lover, however solitary, wishes for reciprocity. It is not as subjective feeling but as a reciprocal relation of desire that love fully comes into being. Desires and feelings that motivate love are steps towards love, not love itself. I use the term relation as a metaphysical category throughout this book. A relationship is an empirical, social occurrence. In German and French one has words for 'relationship' that do not carry the word 'relation' in them – '*Beziehung*' and '*couple*'. This treatise on the metaphysics and ethics of love is not a book about relationships, about *le couple*, about *Beziehungen*. It is not a study in the sociology of love or the psychological interaction of lovers within a couple.

The method of this enquiry is phenomenological. I claim to identify the *universal and invariant structure of love*. To say that love is a relation prior to being a feeling is, for this reason, a metaphysical claim. It concerns the fundamental being of love, prior to any other categorisation.

We shall see that love as it escapes classification also eludes the grasp of the social arrangements that give a determinate – and determining – shape to human relations, arrangements such as *hierarchy* and *contract*. For this reason, love may be seen to include a dimension of freedom. By the same token, love may seem to involve an element of equality. In the love relation the lovers become to some extent equal – because sex is an equalising force. Sex may of course be infused with violence and power, but the intimacy that sex invariably brings in its wake is an equalising force even if it does not always, or with necessity, produce equality between the lovers in the social world that they live in.

Love relationships do not exist in a cultural void. Love is not confined to the bedroom. The lovers inscribe their relationship within their surroundings. Hence the love relation has to define itself – or allow itself to be defined – according to some conception of what a love relation can be. We shall see that the problem of freedom in love plays itself out in this arena of definition and description. I call this the 'intelligibility' of love.

Returning to the problem of cultural intelligibility, the categories that are available to lovers are finite in number, historically specific and relative to social structures of power. Categories of love are distinct from social *constraints*. Categories are ways of describing something. They are forms of predication.

Western philosophy since Plato has been interested in love mainly from a theological viewpoint. If we return to the *Symposion*, it ends with a metaphysical treatise on love. This discourse is ascribed to the priestess Diotima, allegedly a friend of Socrates, and it is this metaphysical treatise that entered the subsequent philosophical and literary tradition as a 'Platonic' conception of love. The core of this conception is the view that there is a psychological continuum in the lover leading from erotic desire to spiritual knowledge. Along this continuum, the beloved is invested with a series of superimposed meanings, being at first a sexual object, but ultimately appearing as the depository of a spiritual truth. This truth may not otherwise be knowable or may not be disclosed within other forms of experience. According to this 'Platonic' spirituality, love is the object of a double movement of praise and transformation. Love is a fine thing, it is noble and elevated, and more so than one could think if one thought there was an absolute opposition between desire and the intellect. This elevated nature of love is only grasped, however, once one has transformed the beloved into a kind of *sign*. This sign is not just referring the lover to truth; as a living symbol the beloved embodies a special kind of truth and brings the lover into direct contact with this truth. The most compelling poetic elaboration of this Platonism of love is no doubt Dante's *Divine Comedy*, but it is echoed all the way through Western literature into English Romantic poetry and beyond.

One can say even that Romanticism as a cultural attitude in everyday life, a strand in Western culture that has been essential to the articulation of modern individualism, repeats a certain version of this Platonic spirituality in the affirmation of the uniqueness and unsubstitutability of the beloved. Because we are so used to this Romantic language of love, we tend to cast love in a dualistic battle: either love is Romantic, ideal, and associated with feeling – or love is sexual desire and social convention combined.

Theoretical conceptions of love in modernity – in Hegel, Stendhal and Freud – investigate the social manifestations of sexuality. This enquiry is connected to the problem of subjective intelligibility, that is, to the problem of how the lover gains access to her or his own feelings and desires and comes to understand them. Film is able to present a different, less rational perspective on love. Film is able to present love as a special kind of fact, the fact of an erotic relation that manifests itself in the world. Film is able to do so in virtue of its language of expression.

The film image is a frame that presents a number of things existing simultaneously and in relation to one another. Film editing is a device that creates open-ended relationships between things that do not coexist within one space. Owing to the relationship between frame and editing, coexistence and separation, film is an art form ideally suited to reflect upon relationships. Film is particularly suited to articulating relationships as they exist both in time and in space, in spatial coexistence and temporal distance. Through framing and editing, film is able to present erotic relations with an immediate moral, social and psychological complexity, and it can do so while remaining true to its intrinsic form, which is elliptic rather than explanatory. In this, film differs from another dominant modern aesthetic presentation of love, the nineteenth-century novel.

Nineteenth-century novels of love such as Stendhal's *Le rouge et le noir* provide a refined and detailed analysis of amorous reciprocity extended over a long temporal arc. The realist novel arrives, however, at this fine-grained analysis through a psychological dissection of *individual* characters. Thus, in Tolstoy's *Anna Karenina* the character of Anna is depicted painstakingly in her swift gait, her exemplary decency, her fall into disrepute and her trajectory from passion to dejection that culminates in her suicide.

Introduction

This sequence of events is made causally plausible in that each step is spelled out psychologically and socially, in terms of character, class, micro-social interaction and the relationship between different psychological agencies: desire, duty, reflection, affection, and so on. The realist novel thus succeeds in accounting for love in its social and psychological complexity, yet in this very success, in its very plausibility, the realist novel produces its own blindness. For the ground of this subtlety and this complexity is always the individual character, with its moral, psychological and social traits, its gradual evolution in time and its minutely recorded interactions with others. The realist novel thus misses what film is able to capture, namely the sheer fact of erotic relationships as they assert themselves in the world.

In the realist novel, the reader is persuaded that nothing of substance is left unaccounted for. But precisely this total discursive embrace constitutes an explanatory *objectification* of love relationships. Film, which necessarily depends on ellipsis and discontinuity, is always more suggestive and metonymic in its presentation of love relationships. Film narrative possesses a lacunary and fragmentary nature. For this very reason, film has the capacity, less accessible to the realist novel, to present relationships concretely, with a wealth of determinations, yet to leave spaces open within that web of determination.

The minimal, phenomenological definition of love is this: love is a relation of reciprocal erotic desire. This relation is articulated in language with respect to time and with regard to other social relations. Love further possesses an essential metaphysical and ethical quality of freedom. This freedom consists in the difference between love and any social arrangement, such as marriage. The freedom entailed by the love relation is not identical to the Romantic freedom of feeling, unlimited emotional subjectivity or rapture, since it is not the subject of love that is free but the relation itself. *The love relation is free to the extent that the lovers create distance from the cultural predicates that would normally apply to it*. Desire is fickle: the subject can never determine the duration of the other's desire. Hence, love is for the amorous subject a source of intellectual unrest. The lover can never make the freedom of the relation disappear, because he or she can never possess the other. She can never completely know or own the other's desire, or indeed know her own desire, whether in the present or in the future.

Film has in its history developed a variety of narrative forms in which love has been framed and articulated in quite different ways. By looking at prototypical examples of these different narrative articulations of love, one can see that love has also been subject to very different sorts of moral and psychological interpretations in the course of film history. A more specific aesthetic idea, guiding this study of love in film, is that the arena of aesthetic variation in film consists not so much in the ideas that love is associated with – ideas of family, sex, heroism, social ascendance, individual identity, and so on. That which varies is the degree to which love is presented as intelligible.

The classical film sought to minimise the difference between film and the realist novel. It sought to emulate the determining technique of the nineteenth-century novel and leave the viewers with an impression of closed fictional worlds in which the characters, and their feelings and actions and relations to one another, might all be more complex than the viewer could immediately grasp – owing to the density of film narration and spectacle – but which as coherent fictional worlds would ultimately be intelligible.

A thesis of this study is that film moves close to the freedom of love by moving away from its literary predecessors, showing erotic relationships which are only incompletely intelligible but which are nevertheless shown to exist in the midst of the social world. Modern cinema is able to oppose the modern-bourgeois, essentially emotive and marital conception of love. The aesthetic and ethical claim that is at the horizon of this book is thus that cinema has *the vocation of describing love as a relation that takes place in the world rather than on the stage of emotional subjectivity*. (Melodrama is a challenge to this view. I discuss melodrama in the next chapter.)

A more worldly view of erotic relationships could be the political articulation of love that we find in the medieval German war epic the *Nibelungen Lied*. Here a woman's sense of her man having been betrayed triggers a chain of violence that consumes not only her and those who were part of the initial betrayal, but the entire social group to which they belong. Another, opposing but equally worldly, view is encapsulated in the refrain of a tune that is hummed throughout René Clair's anarchic film *A nous la liberté*: 'partout on peut aimer et boire' ('everywhere you can love and drink'). In the first case, love is worldly because love relationships, in the warrior class of the *Nibelungen* society, are political relationships; in the second, love is worldly because the possibilities of flirtation, infatuation and lovemaking are ubiquitous and permeate the social fabric across all strata of society.

When love is pictured as a force and a relation in the world it is pictured as a relation that is first of all erotic, before it is marital or emotional. It was in being able to encircle the worldly and erotic nature of love relationships that film, at a certain period of its development, was able to encounter love, and the freedom of love.

The lovers that we are would not be the same without film – our ideals of beauty, happiness and sexuality are animated by film's depictions of love. But film's relation to love is not limited to being a mirror and a model. Love has been essential

Introduction

to film's expressive ambition throughout its history. The history of love in film is the history of film's expressive forms and the types of meaning that film, in different periods, has sought to articulate. This book is therefore both a philosophy of love and a history of film form. At the point of their intersection is the question: how is love interpreted by film narrative?

From a certain point of view, love and cinema can be said to be identical: they display the same structures and tensions. It takes two to love, and the film image is ideally suited to portraying relations between two people. The film image always shows several beings co-existing in one space. Love relations are, on the other hand, always hedged in by cultural definitions. Classical narrative cinema defines its characters through sharp contrasts, highlighting the position that each occupies in terms of gender, ideology, social hierarchy, moral virtue, and so on. Relationships are clearly defined in moral terms and in reference to marriage as an ever-present dramatic possibility. Film has in its history displayed different alternatives to this structured narrative form. It has thereby been able to explore expressive potentials that lie outside the analysis of character, morality and social relationships.

To sum up: cinema is able to highlight the difference between a conception of love as a free reciprocal relation and love as a socially and culturally defined relation.

Ego Love and Melodrama

Film melodrama is an aesthetic interpretation of a subject that is first of all concerned with itself, with its feelings and self-esteem. It is constantly given to itself in introspection. Following the phenomenology of Jean-Paul Sartre we can call this 'subject-object' the *ego*. This psychological ego is never completely accessible. In other words, we are not completely conscious of and masters of the ego. But the ego is also not unconscious. It is a web of emotions, volitions and character traits that presents itself to the subject as a constant enigma, and a source of intrinsic psychological interest, indeed fascination. In film melodrama, different moments of a complex personality structure, different temporal phases, emotional and moral possibilities are presented within the arc of one condensed narrative sequence. This sequence is, by definition, an order of temporal succession, but the short time span of a film and the elliptic nature of film narrative contracts this temporality and offers to the spectator an extended image of a complex personality. Modern cinema is characterised by its battle with melodrama. Overcoming melodrama in cinema means challenging a certain conception of sequence, emotion and the ego. At the horizon of this process is a liberation of love as a worldly relation, a relation that can, by definition, not be incorporated into the moral and emotive space of the ego.

The Brazilian historian of melodrama in film Ivete Huppes suggests that melodramatic films are concerned either with the undoing of past injustice or with amorous self-realisation, and often with both in conjunction:

> If we wish to identify the predominant content structures of melodrama, we find two recurrent narrative themes that frequently appear in conjunction with one another: the reversal [*reparaçao*] of injustice and the search for amorous fulfilment [*realizaço*].[1]

Love in Motion

The elegant verbal symmetry between *reparaçao* and *realizaço* is suggestive of a strong moral and psychological affinity in the melodramatic subject between its desire for past wrongs to be undone and its desire for a love that would fulfil its existential longings. At the intersection between the two – between *reparaçao* and *realizaço* – emerges the notion of a love that compensates the subject for past suffering, and fulfils its wishes in the sense of filling the 'void' in its psyche – caused by past suffering. This would be fulfilling in a very complete way indeed.

Love is always at the heart of melodrama. The melodramatic subject wants to be loved because she believes that love will redeem her from the shame of poverty, or save her from solitude, or reverse the effect of past decisions, once and for all. Love is a site and a tool for the melodramatic subject. It is a site because it is in the realm of love that regret, rejection, redemption and its cognates form a happy alchemy of self-transformation. It is a tool because for the melodramatic subject there is only I and me. The other is the alluring woman or the knight on the white horse, an object of fantasy and desire who intrudes into the life of the subject to cleanse it of the stains of its own past. The other is thus important, but important in relation to the subject. I love you because you make me different.

Melodrama obeys a theological temporality of conversion. The structure of this schema is a juxtaposition between past and present, where the past constitutes a burden which the present obliterates, thereby opening up a new future, which is not the future of the subject's past but the future of its transformative present. In film melodrama, love is then typically an arena for the subject's redemption – or yearning for redemption. Jean Renoir's *Woman on the Beach* is one of the most perfect and beautiful films of melodramatic redemption. The narrative subject is from the start shown to be overwhelmed by a past that pacifies him and isolates him from the company of others. Renoir's film depicts, from the lush evocative images of its opening scene, a man battling with a war trauma that has a complete grip on his emotions, his sexual desire and his relation to women. The film opens with a dream sequence which is aesthetically significant in that it is more dramatically clear than dream sequences normally are – and certainly more dramatic than the realistic dream scenes in Bergman or Fellini. From this opening sequence, the film asserts the principle of a melodramatic aesthetic: the visual image aims to absorb the energies of the unconscious, whereas the emotional and unconscious life of the protagonist will be shown to be entirely and without any remaining obscurity expressible by the film image. The lushness of spectacle supports a dramatic tone that is at the same time radically subjectified: the opening scene establishes the narrative domain of the film as being the narrative subject's own mind. Other characters, and in particular women, will be significant to the extent that they occupy a place in the subject's own semi-conscious drama. In fact, the film breaks with this expectation and extends the domain of the plot as the story develops: the story turns out to be concerned with the mental and erotic salvation of its protagonist, his struggle to break the spell of trauma and guilt. The process that leads to this redeeming end is a story of cathartic self-exposure enabling the subject finally to leave his past behind. This story is dramatic in both structure and expression. It involves violent conflict and emotionally charged choices. But at the end, in a manner that betrays Renoir's own view of life, the emotional drama is revealed to be just that, a kind of theatre that the characters have played for each other and which is without consequences in the social world – but which has nevertheless been effective psychologically. The other participants in this drama are similar to the protagonist in that they, too, are emotionally complex, burdened by the past, slightly cut off from ordinary life. This similarity and the tension between dramatic events and an overarching subjective focus on the protagonist's psyche produce a fundamental aesthetic ambiguity in the film: to what extent is this a drama unfolding between independent characters and to what extent is the dramatic story itself an externalisation of the character's mind? Perhaps this is not the right question to ask of a melodramatic film, but pondering that problem will bring us closer to an understanding of the melodramatic aesthetic of love in film.

The protagonist is a marine officer stationed at a coastal base in the US during the later part of World War II. He is suffering from war trauma and this is no secret to those around him. There is his devoted subordinate, who appears as a sort of brother, caring for him and giving him commonsense advice; and there is his very decent and hopeful fiancée, living in a fantasy world of her own. They will, in good time, marry, she believes. He will overcome his problems. They will be cleansed of all the sordidness of war. Already at the first meeting between the protagonist and his fiancée in the film his manifest unrest encroaches upon this scenario of hope. She wants them to marry only when the war is over, when he is cured of his nervous illness. He on the other hand wants to precipitate the wedding. The scene demonstrates a great distance between the two lovers, as he appears not to acknowledge her motives. Later the same morning, he takes a walk along the beach and meets another woman. She is dark haired, sexually alert and appears intelligent. In their conversation she shows that she is experienced and that she knows the protagonist – perhaps even knows more about him than he himself does.

Throughout the film, he plays a wholesome, slightly awkward soldier, trapped in a large body. The 'woman on the beach' conceals dark and interesting secrets. She lives with her husband, a blind painter who no longer paints but who seems, when the soldier meets him, endowed with uncanny powers of intuition. The soldier engages in a tentative courtship of the woman, instantly provoking the jealousy of her husband, who stages two psychological tests for the young soldier, scenarios where their rivalry may be acted out. They go sailing in a stormy sea and embark on a riding tour at the edge of a precipice so steep that the blind man is in obvious danger of being killed. They come out alive from these tests and it then transpires that the blind mind is, in fact, not blind at all.

From this point on, the melodramatic intensity of the film moves towards a climax: the woman and the soldier agree to run away together. The painter burns his paintings. The woman decides to stay with the painter. All three meet and part as friends on the beach, the painter and his wife departing in one direction and the soldier returning to his waiting woman. All three, we are led to assume, have been liberated from past ghosts.

The philosophy of film form and of love that I go on to present follows modern cinema in its effort to overcome melodrama and in its imaginary, egocentric rendering of the love relationship.

There is on the other hand in modern cinema also a non-melodramatic yet egotistical conception of love. It is to be found in theological filmmakers like Bergman and Chabrol. The sublime comedy *Smiles of a Summer Night* appears to be Mozartian and playful. It appears to be concerned with a multiplicity of characters. In fact it is only concerned with the vanity, longings and failings of its male protagonist, a provincial lawyer who considers himself very attractive. The plot of the film explores and exposes his vanity as his teenage trophy wife runs off with his own son. Chabrol's film about Platonic love, *The Butcher*, presents a similar subjective scenario. The prim school teacher's love of and loyalty towards a paedophile murderer is sexual yet chaste. She lives this love in her mind. She loves this man in spite of, or, as Proust would say, *because* of, his vices. She loves him in an absolute sense, and the Catholic undercurrent in the film suggests that this absolute commitment is possible only because their relationship remains mental or spiritual and does not become physical. For Bergman and Chabrol love is a prism through which we can perceive the ego, its aspirations and its finitude. Such a view of love is diametrically opposed to the relational view of love as an erotic force in the world that I propose here.

NOTE

1 'Se quiseremos identificar as matrizes tematicas predominanates no melodrama, encontraremos dois núcleos principais que freqüentemente aparecen entrelaçados: a reparaçao da injustia e a busca da realizaço amorosa' (Huppes, 33).

Categories of Film Love

Morals

Michael Powell and Emeric Pressburger's World War II film *A Matter of Life and Death* opens dramatically and in Technicolor with a fighter pilot, played by David Niven, talking to a woman in a control tower. Assuming that he will die in the next few minutes, he addresses his last words to her. As if by a miracle, he does not die but is washed up on a beach in England. He wakes up close to the airfield where the woman works. When he discovers that he is not dead, and not in heaven but alive, he also realises that a woman walking by with a bicycle is the woman he talked to on the radio. He runs to her and she recognises him. The proximity to death which they shared made them fall in love before they met and they immediately embrace.

Meanwhile in heaven, Niven's character, Peter, is reported missing and an emissary is sent to earth to fetch him. When the emissary and Peter meet, the latter argues his case: he is now in love and cannot meet his appointment in heaven. He cannot leave his earthly existence since love now binds him to it – with a bond different from, and stronger than, that of his own existence. The film culminates in a scene in heaven where Peter is allowed to defend his case more fully, before a court of angels. He employs his friends as witnesses. In the end, love wins over death and he is allowed to return to earth.

The film spells out a metaphysical conception of love: its germ of transcendence, its status as an absolute and non-negotiable value and a gift to human beings, allowing them to become a little better than they otherwise are. If we look closer we see that love here has a further property: it is immediate. The situation of shared terminal danger and the uncanny intimacy of the radio conversation make the two characters love each other mutually, absolutely and instantaneously.

Love in Motion

Love is therefore a causeless event, similar to passion in Racine's tragedy *Phèdre*. Passion strikes suddenly and irrevocably when Phèdre one day discovers that she is caught in an incurable sexual obsession with her stepson Hippolyte. Racinian passion is destructive and a sign of man's fallibility. Love as mutual desire and amorous feeling in Powell and Pressburger's film is on the contrary a quasi-divine gift: it has only positive qualities. The fact of love, accentuated by the situation of war, is here an existential dimension of human life. As such it is outside of culture and social complexity. It is a morally ennobling force. Love is not in itself morally complex. However, in the course of its history cinema has encountered love at the site of its moral complexity.

In the early 1930s, Josef von Sternberg made a series of films with Marlene Dietrich. These films are stylistically innovative in their subtle blending of shadow and light. They situate Dietrich in erotic and amorous situations where she is challenged to move beyond the limits of a given situation and claim autonomy against the odds of a hostile environment. The flamboyant *Devil Is a Woman* and the exotic travel narrative *Shanghai Express* both have Dietrich as their dynamic centre. In *Blonde Venus*, a marriage narrative is the frame around a story that is essentially a study of the character embodied by Dietrich and her capacity to undergo successive transformations. *Morocco* revolves around the emotional shifts in her character as she is courted by two men, a poor soldier in the Foreign Legion and a wealthy aristocrat.

Moral complexity expresses itself as moral ambiguity in Sternberg's films, in *Shanghai Express* in particular. Marlene Dietrich excels in modulating her voice and posture in gradually shifting ways, so that in one scene she might pass through a stance of strength and defiance, followed or preceded by an expression of vulnerability or tenderness. These subtle transitions suggest that different psychological and moral postures coexist – not just in the character but also in the situation that she is in. *Shanghai Express* may cynically be seen as a variation on an age-old theme, the virtuous courtesan, but it is really a film about love. The two protagonists love each other. They have split and seek to overcome their own hurt pride so as to become a couple again. The fact that in the meantime Dietrich has become known as Shanghai Lily, one of the most sophisticated courtesans of China, does, obviously, pose an obstacle, since he is a tight-lipped British officer dreaming of a little house back in England – but Sternberg does not allow this moral obstacle to count *in the last instance*.

Shanghai Lily is capable of the noblest moral actions and she is able to live a love that transcends the obstacles of difficult historical and psychological circumstances. Yet, her virtue and capacity for love coexist with her social role as a courtesan. Her lover is a paragon of English military nobility. He is courageous, intelligent and courteous. Until the reversal at the end of the film, he indulges in self-pity and cynicism, preferring to the difficulty of loving Shanghai Lily the melancholy pleasures of thinking himself the most betrayed of English officers.

Ultimately, the dynamic of desire and amorous feeling follows a psychological trajectory that is indifferent to social and moral criteria: each has to overcome in him or herself a vain pride that hardens him or her towards the feelings he or she has for the other. Just as Dietrich slides in and out of different emotional postures, the film slides in and out of different moral perspectives on love, alternating between a Romantic tender attitude and a cosmopolitan tough stance.

Marlene Dietrich brings to the flamboyant roles that Sternberg designs for her a hint of no-nonsense northern German tough-mindedness which she elegantly – but completely realistically – alternates with a range of delicate erotic, sensitive and emotive expressions. It is not hard to see that this subtle range of expressions is quite different from the melodramatic style presented by, say, Bette Davis or Barbara Stanwyck: the moral tension that we find in Sternberg is generative. It encloses a set of relations that cannot be tied down within a common moral framework or easily correlated with a social world of pragmatic decisions.

Within a pragmatic and melodramatic outlook, moral ambiguity and moral disgrace can be overcome in the future through corrective decisions taken in the narrative present. Sternberg's films seek, on the contrary, to *maintain* moral ambiguity, to keep it alive within an ongoing present – shifts in the story notwithstanding. In *Shanghai Express*, we are thus forced to make a moral judgement that is not supported by the category of decision. This is indeed a different kind of moral judgement from the sort of judgement that discriminates between good and bad actions, laudable and blameworthy characters.

This is not a melodramatic moral world in which people have to become better or leave past sins behind, but a world in which self-reliance obviously and unproblematically implies cruelty and vice – and this does not exclude the highest moral virtues. There is a moral in Sternberg. In this profoundly anti-melodramatic universe, challenges to morality or happiness cannot be overcome. The past cannot be eradicated, but the characters can overcome their own limited point of view and love their beloved not on the condition that the beloved changes, but in full awareness of the challenge that the beloved represents to the subject's morality. This is also the plot of another Sternberg film, *Blonde Venus*. The scientist protagonist does not accept that his wife should work to earn money for him so that he can be cured of a life-threatening illness. She overrides his objections and goes back to her former work as a cabaret artist. He finds the distance between her choice and his values to be more than he can bear and leaves her. She, meanwhile, cannot sustain her choice on her own and enters a process of moral and psychological degradation. Her husband eventually changes his mind, sets out to look for her and in the end finds her. She accepts his offer to return to their home. This change in the husband's attitude is possible only because he no longer attempts to change her. In Sternberg, the temporality of love is suspended within a moral space of reflection. This reflection is not that of understanding (in Kant's sense of the term), that is, it is not a reflection upon alternatives, but on ambivalent individuals as they pass through life.

Comparing *A Matter of Life and Death* with the Dietrich-Sternberg films, we can draw some conclusions as to the potential that cinema has for expressing, and reflecting upon, love. We can make, at least, the following three points. Film can portray love as a simple but overwhelming fact, as something that happens suddenly and irreversibly, or it can portray love as a complex human situation extended in time, subject to social constraints, embedded in cultural conceptions of what a lover or a spouse should or could be. Second, love can be articulated as a metaphysical or as a moral phenomenon. The significance of love can be measured against the entire life of the lovers or set in the context of moral reflections upon the lovers' behaviour. Third, love is in all these films defined by time, but the temporality of love is different when it is articulated in relation to doubt, as in Sternberg, and when it is shown as the temporality of the irreversible event, as in Powell and Pressburger's film.

Simply noting these parameters of reflection that the films involve in their dramatic and visual depictions of love already suggests that love is not something that can simply be named or depicted, in the manner of an object. Instead any depiction of love in film involves some kind of categorisation. This insight does not inevitably lead to a sociological or textual conclusion. It does not follow that films are social facts or texts, or texts about social facts. For the aesthetic singularity and productivity of a film makes a difference. For instance, I doubt if there is any other film than *A Matter of Life and Death* that depicts love in exactly this way. The perspective on love in film that is presented in this book takes account of these two principles. Love involves categorisation; film is not a social text. Another way to formulate this thought is to say that films do not 'represent' love if by 'representation' one means something like a visual and narrative rendering that corresponds to a pre-existing cultural discourse. The semiotic perspective presented in this book differs also from the aesthetic formalism of the French tradition of film criticism in that it focuses on content, and on the *form of content*, rather than on visual expression. A third theoretical position that this book could become associated with, because of its theme, is the moral philosophy and film criticism of Stanley Cavell. He has written philosophically on marital love in film. His philosophy is based on a moral idealism which leads to a subjective and implicitly rational understanding of love relations. The theory of erotic relations that I develop here is diametrically opposed to this idealism and this rationalism.

Class

In an essay on *Brief Encounter*, the English film about post-war lovers who prefer decency to sexual pleasure, Richard Dyer analyses the emotions evoked and elicited by the film's narrative of unfulfilment. He opens his essay by quoting his mother, who distinguished between *good* films and *lovely* films. *Brief Encounter* was a lovely film. The loveliness of the film nests in a fold of compressed emotional potential, that sense of deserving more than one is given, of being somehow ennobled by the love that is not lived. Such masochistic pleasures of self-negation are at the heart of cinematic melodrama.

Melodrama carves out, within the projection of an introspective emotional space, a realm of dreams and self-pity, of passivity and abstract desire. This emotional mode is epitomised in one of the last scenes of *Brief Encounter*, in which the female protagonist, who is also the voice-over narrator, comments on the perfect politeness of her beloved. At this last encounter, in a railway café, only a few minutes before their ultimate separation, a 'friend' of hers intrudes upon them. An unloved middle-aged woman, the 'friend' enters their space with a clutter of hectic conversation. The man elegantly accommodates her, swallowing his anger and appearing to his lover dignified – but he does so by symbolically sacrificing his and their feelings.

Film melodrama has tended to take one of two forms. Either it depicts, in the manner of *Brief Encounter*, Romantic feelings and desires crushed by social obstacles, or it holds out – for the lovers in the film and for the viewer – the prospect of a love so strong that it crushes the weight of social or moral obstacles. The melodrama of *tears* and the melodrama of *hope*, we might say.

The French director Marcel Carné is one of the most lyrical and precise analysts of melodramatic hope. His films fuse a spectacle of emotion – engendered by the contrastive play of light and shadow used to accentuate the sentiments expressed by the human face – with an existential drama of despair. This drama is upheld by stylised character types: the renegade soldier, the lecherous old man, various beautiful and idealistic young women and their down-to-earth pragmatic male counterparts. In dialogue, performance, psychology and plot, Carné's love dramas are always stylised and theatrical, self-referential and self-aware. His characters make their own roles appear self-referential, as they always seem to be chained to a particular moral-social position allotted to them by destiny. Their individuality is subsumed under the general characteristics of a type that is both social and theatrical.

The drama of these films results from the clash and intersections of destiny-types. In *Quai des brumes*, *Le Jour se lève* and *Hotel du nord*, a romantic world of hopes and disappointments is extended between characters who, as types, are all marked by a negative destiny. They are all morally and socially doomed, but love extends to them the promise of a new start. Yet this promise is only rarely fulfilled. The male lovers who fight over the same woman in *Le Jour se lève* kill each other – the younger man kills his rival and waits through the night for the police to find him and kill him. *Quai de brumes* describes a desperate couple fleeing from past difficulties – only for him to be shot down by a resentful enemy at the end. *Hotel du Nord*, however, has an interesting plot: a young woman romantically and destructively loves a sensitive young man. She cannot, for reasons that I will come back to, be with him and seeks to escape with another man. The escape does not work. She escapes from the escape, so to speak, and returns to her sensitive alter ego. Her transient lover then chooses a conflict that is certain to lead to his death. In this film, the tragic and the happy outcomes are both kept in play.

Poetic realism drew its dramatic force from social tensions in contemporary French society. The existential themes of hope, dignity and a leap into the unknown are fused with the theme of social shame in these films. Yet, the prospects of escape and redemption, confined as they are to the realm of fantasy and emotion, remain largely imaginary. This is typical of film melodrama. All the heroes and lovers in these films want to overcome a shameful past. Love extends the hope of a new start that would annul the power of their past. Poverty, sordidness, crime – the reasons for shame are varied, but the dream is always the same. Carné's films enact a melodramatic philosophy of moral reversibility: my sins and my shame, the temporal baggage of my ego can all be cancelled through the transformative power of reciprocal erotic desire.

In *Hotel du Nord* this vision is exaggerated to the point of parody. The slow-moving pimp, hiding from a fellow criminal he once betrayed, reveals unexpected resources of goodness when he falls in love with a young and beautiful woman. She on the other hand has a pact with death, having failed to commit mutual suicide with her boyfriend. Melodrama here thrives on murky emotions where good and evil enter a dark alliance. Carné's films in fact often display unconventional erotic situations. The usurer in *Quai* keeps his innocent niece as a captive and sex slave. The young woman in *Le Jour se lève* is inexorably drawn to an older man whom she does not love, but rather is addicted to. The young beautiful lovers in *Hotel du Nord* open that film with a suicide pact.

In film, love may also be articulated more directly with social and political reality, independently of the lovers' moral aspirations. I will now compare two different aesthetic presentations of love as a social phenomenon. One, a spy film, presents love as an emotional event that is both intertwined with and separate from concrete political circumstances. The other is a self-reflective political film which makes love appear as an illusion crushed under the economic and social necessities of class conflict.

Escape

The Russia House is a spy film and a romance, evoking a gentle sense of adventure. It is one of those films in which danger is never really dangerous, at least not to the protagonists. The performances by Michelle Pfeiffer, Sean Connery and Klaus Maria Brandauer and the location footage of Moscow and St Petersburg are sufficiently elaborate and fine-tuned to anchor the film in a realistic frame of reference. The constant tension between a spectacle of romance and adventure and the social and political realities of Yeltsin-era Russia lends the film a unique aesthetic texture, a tone of light and suspenseful Romanticism.

The story is typical of John le Carré's fiction, with its histrionic individuals cast by fate on a collision course with powerful state institutions. Connery plays Blair, a virile, charming drunkard – more admirable than the eponymous character in the novel since Connery makes everyone around him appear duller than he is, whereas in the novel the protagonist is a subdued character, impressed by the supposed grandeur of British intelligence. The plot places him within the force field of a mysterious and charismatic Russian mathematician, Jacob Sevaliev, operating under the code name of Dante and played by Brandauer. Sevaliev attempts to pass on to the West information about the Russian nuclear defence system. He is assisted in this by his long-time friend and former lover, Katya Barishovna, played by Michelle Pfeiffer. Katya is courageous, determined and idealistic, and she also expresses a spellbinding sensuality. The romance that the film steers towards is an alchemy of the archetypical forces of virility and sensuality. This structural, and hence non-sequential, element organises the story and is presented in a natural and seamless way through the acting personae of Connery and Pfeiffer, with their contagious charm and physical aura. The mutual attraction of the protagonists is expressed in an emotional language of small gestures. A turning point in the film, indicating that they are falling in love, is a phone conversation in which nothing much is being said, but the words exchanged serve as substitutes for tender gestures. Blair calls to tell her that he is about to return to England and Katya tells him to sit down. She explains that it is a Russian custom that travellers who are about to embark on a long journey sit on their luggage and 'say a little'.

All other elements in the film appear to support the advent of their romance, even though the film is not on the surface a romantic drama – let alone a romantic comedy – but a spy film. The mutual seduction of the virile and the sensual, the modern myth of archetypal erotic forces blending within an everyday world, is supported by a seductive *mise en scène*, musical score and editing rhythm which slowly ensnare and include the viewer in an ideal romantic realm where emotions seem to matter more than material conditions, geographical distance or political power. The spectator is thereby gradually and relentlessly drawn into a closed universe of romantic expectations. The romantic hope at the centre of this seduction – of Katya by Blair, of the spectator by the film – is not, on the other hand, melodramatic. There are no moral or social obstacles to the lovers' union. There is no sense of a shameful past: Katya is proud of her love for Sevaliev; Blair is proud of his past as an anarchist musician. The film's happy end does not signify the death of an enemy or the conversion of the protagonists. The end is the outcome of a political bargain. Blair makes a deal with Russian intelligence, selling British intelligence in return for the possibility of Katya and her children and father being allowed to leave the country. It is true that both Katya and Blair seek an escape from loneliness, she as a single mother, he as a man whose love relationships tend to end badly. The film suggests that his relation to Katya will be different. This is made dramatically plausible in the film on a psychological level. It is not love, in the abstract, as infatuation, hope and desire that presents him at the threshold of their relationship. Rather, his own courageous and treacherous actions concretely demonstrate his commitment. These acts move him from the shadows of his own private existence into a world of conflict and risk, a world in which he is exposed to, and at the same time involved with, powerful state institutions. He becomes a twisted incarnation of Corneille's romantic hero Cid, who has to prove himself to be worthy of love. Here the ennobling deed follows the line that runs through the film as a motto, two sentences that Blair utters at a meeting at the writers' colony Peredelkino, near Moscow: 'these days everyone must betray his country' and 'one must be a hero in order to be a merely decent human being'.

Here we see that love in film is not limited to the moral sphere but includes a wider political world. Or to put it differently, the morality that love involves is now articulated within a world of political relations. Love is now articulated as a dialectical relationship between private feelings and public constraints. Love is defined as feeling independent of anything that takes place in the public sphere, but it is only enacted by the subjects' use of force and intellect to remove obstacles within the public sphere. Let us now look at a very different, more conceptual interpretation of the relationship between love and politics.

Power

Peter Greenaway's *The Draughtsman's Contract* is a theoretical essay in visual form. Its style is formal and aestheticist; the topic of its underlying theoretical discourse is the relationship between sex, marriage, material property, class, lineage – and Englishness.

The film is set in a very specific period of English history, the end of the seventeenth century. A mood of hesitant cosmopolitanism mixed with racial and religious tension runs through the film. The film portrays a starkly Hobbesian world in which all human relations are based on power and all human motivation is an expression of a particular material, erotic or social interest.

The main character is an Irish draughtsman who is hired by the wife of a country nobleman to make 12 drawings of his estate, which is named Anstey. In return for his work she consents for him to see her 'in private and agree to his requests concerning his pleasure with me'. This sexual and economic contract appears at the start of the film, and for a long part of the film's duration it appears to put the draughtsman in a position of dominance in relation to the other characters in the film. As the story progresses, however, this privileged position is gradually undermined. With his brusque and arrogant manner, he attracts the envy and hatred of all the men who live on the estate as guests or members of the household. Hence rumours begin to circulate that he might be complicit in the death of the proprietor of the estate, who mysteriously disappeared shortly after the draughtsman's arrival and who eventually turns up as a corpse. The daughter of the house, unhappily married to a German nobleman, then engages the draughtsman in a second contract which obliges him to have sex with her in return for her providing him 'protection'. He accepts this second contract only to realise that her promise of protection was merely a rhetorical gesture and that the purpose of the second contract was to produce an heir, since her husband is impotent. She admonishes him: 'Do you think I would have done so much for pleasure alone?'

Love in Motion

She then goes on to say: 'You seem to have accepted rather a lot on trust.' In fact, the draughtsman, who at first appears to be a master of speech, is strangely trusting of the words of others, and is completely unsuspicious of the machinations that are being prepared against him. From being a strutting young man, putting everyone else in his place, he becomes a tame ingénu, trailing the decisions made by a series of other characters in the household. Part of his naivety is that he appears sincerely and genuinely to fall in love with the mistress of the house. After the completion of his assignment, as he has already moved on to another engagement, he returns to Anstey on the pretext of an invitation that turns out to be spurious. He returns in the hope of sleeping, again, with the mistress of the house, a wish which is in fact granted. Unfortunately, the intimacy that they share is of only brief duration. As they recover from lovemaking, the daughter enters and invites the draughtsman to a conversation with a certain Mr Seymour, one of the draughtsman's rivals and enemies. It is now evening and Anstey is plunged into darkness. The draughtsman finds himself in the garden and sees a procession of masked men with torches approaching. He soon realises that the group consists of all the enemies he has made while staying there. They announce that they will draw up a third contract. The conditions for this contract are that the draughtsman should be blinded and killed. They swiftly and brutally carry out what they have announced.

The draughtsman dies, one might say, of ignorance, but his ignorance is social. He believes in the truthfulness of contracts, in salaried labour, in the value of acquired skills. He is, in other words, *bourgeois*. His employers and enemies on the other hand are aristocratic. They follow a different logic, uphold different values and share different relationships of trust. They operate according to a logic of secrecy and uphold the values of lineage and violence. They believe not in public speech but in the power of personal loyalties. The film is a visual essay on this contrast between two incompatible, class-based principles of action and thought. Across this range of possible behaviour, love is either impossible or other than what it seems. *The Draughtsman's Contract* is filmed in an extravagantly anti-realist style that highlights this content: the relationships between class, sex, property and speech that the plot gradually unfolds form a structure which makes sense of all the characters and events in the film. This logic is not justified by anything that one might say about the characters' *psyche*, inner life, or moral qualities. This meta-reflective film thus stages within the film image the content that otherwise would be left for the spectator to discover. In a conversation between the draughtsman and the daughter, she says of him that he is both innocent and conceited. He retorts with a question: 'Which weighs more heavily?' Her answer is surprising:

'Your innocence is always sinister.' Hence innocence weighs more heavily, is of greater consequence than conceit. How can this be? How can innocence be sinister? The plot of the film explains this remark. The draughtsman is innocent of knowing his own role. He is innocent of knowing the implication of his own presence in the manor house that he has been hired to draw. This knowledge and this implication have two levels. He is implicated in the house as a rival to its master, the unfortunate, soon-to-be-killed nobleman, and to the suitor of its mistress, Mr Seymour. He is also implicated in a plot of which he is not himself the author. He is innocent, in particular, of knowing the distinction between aristocratic and modern power, and this innocence is sinister since it makes him a willing pawn in any scheme that mother and daughter invent in order to preserve their patrimony. In the clash between aristocratic and modern power, love is entirely epiphenomenal and exists only in the brief moment of pleasure shared by the draughtsman and the mother after his return. But even this moment of reciprocal affection is interrupted by a conversation about Persephone that symbolically alludes to his imminent death – since Persephone is a goddess of the underworld. The extreme formalism of this film makes explicit an allegorical method that has been prominent in many love films since the early 1970s (films by Rainer Werner Fassbinder, Bernardo Bertolucci, Pedro Almodovar) but which is here carried to an absolute high point of abstraction.

Through this brief survey of films that encounter love aesthetically in very different ways, employing different narrative and expressive means to interpret love, we have also come to see that love is not a stable entity in film. Not only does love evolve as a cultural notion through film history, but the aesthetic and narrative differences between schools of filmmaking and between individual directors lead to radically different categorisations of love.

Making Sense

Love enters cinema as a material for stories and as a domain of expression in all periods of cinema, but not in the same way. Film has known two fundamentally opposing presentations of love: love as *determination* and love as *self-determination*. Semiotically, this difference can be defined in the following way: the love relation can be presented in relation to a surrounding world according to different kinds and criteria of intelligibility. Now, these kinds and criteria of intelligibility do in fact vary and evolve in the course of film history. To put it crudely, *it is not the same things that make sense in different kinds of film*. According to its form of intelligibility, a film can present a relation as more or less rigidly determined and the amorous subject can be presented as more or less self-determining.

Considered as determination, love is a relation that is defined and made recognisable according to robustly presented moral, social and psychological categories. Love as self-determination, on the other hand, is an erotic relation presented as a field where the amorous subject articulates concrete relations with its social and cultural environment on the basis of its desire, but these concrete relations are not manifest within clear moral or social categories of intelligibility.

Due to this dual possibility of film, the cultural significance of film's depiction of love is dialectical. Film is able both to enact and to resist dominant cultural categorisations of love. Film encounters love in the middle. Film is part of culture and thus may exist in continuity with other cultural forms of intelligibility that seek to make sense of love – but film is also, as we shall see, a particular aesthetic form, and in virtue of this form it is able to withdraw the erotic relationship from dominant cultural forms of intelligibility.

Through its aesthetic form, film has, at certain moments in its history, been able to move backwards, back towards the erotic relation in itself, before it became fully articulated within or with the use of cultural categories. This is surprising, since film as a narrative art form exercises a pull towards psychological clarity and dramatic explicitness. Yet film always moves towards ontological purity *from* a position of narrative articulation. In film one begins with characters, a story and a social world and then, perhaps, one moves towards the presentation of something that is not yet categorised in psychological, moral or social terms.

The film image carries meaning according to where it places the centre of intelligibility of the story and of the film image: *that which must make sense for the rest to signify and which the other elements of the film support*. There can be more than one centre of intelligibility and there can be a mutual relation of support between bearers of intelligibility, such as mood and character. The essential moments of love are located at a specific place in the fabric of a film in relation to these basic carriers of meaning.

This book views cinema through the prism of love: it aims to see, in other words, how film looks in the light of love. It does so by following through film history the aesthetic opportunities that love has given to film. A framing theory of film form contributes to this aesthetic history. The notion that film history has a structure and that film form itself has an aesthetic history is conventional among many film historians and has been discussed for instance by Noël Burch and David Bordwell. The perspective proposed here suggests that it is not only film that evolves historically but also the relationship between expression and signification, that is, the force that relates the film image to some type of content. This constitutes its *form of intelligibility*. Meaning and the relationship between form and meaning are not, on this view, natural and universal traits of the film medium. The relationship between style, story and meaning changes in the course of film history.

At stake here is more than the questions of visual reference, sequence and internal coherence of style that have dominated much of film aesthetic theory from Balázs and Eisenstein to Bellour and Deleuze. The aesthetic topic of this book is a particular *nexus* of expressive elements. These elements have to interact and display a specific kind of coherence and an appropriate reciprocal weight in order to produce a particular form of intelligibility.

Love in Early Cinema

Love is interwoven with the history of film from the early silent days to the present. Few narrative films can do entirely without the prospect of a love plot and few films renounce the spectacle of attractive and beautiful people who fit perfectly within a love entanglement.

As silent film developed a visual grammar of film narrative, the archetypal situations of love plots, as one would know them from vaudeville theatre, offered a resource of immediately graspable, visually tangible themes: a woman attracting the attention of a handsome young man, a jealous husband raging against his young wife, the desperate lover, crying after having been left by him or her – such infinitely repeatable narrative and visual situations have the aesthetic power of imposing structure on the visual space of a scene as it unfolds around the emotional gestures and dramatic action of one or more characters. At the same time, these dramatic archetypes intrinsically refer to either past or future events, but the dramatic situation is nevertheless self-contained within each individual scene.

When film form and film narrative tend towards theatrical spectacle, the character and the actor are the main bearers of meaning in the film. They are supported, often in a contrastive way, by landscape and architecture. The kind of meaning that is carried by the actor's gestures and expressions tends, both in silent and in early sound film, to be fully developed within individual scenes, whether the type of situation displayed is dramatic, comic or based on a realistic observation of daily life. As in popular theatre, the story may well embody a clear moral content, both in the depiction of a social setting and in the outcome of the story. Filmmakers in this period who innovatively explore love and eroticism include Pabst, Borzage, Vigo, Ophüls and Sternberg. Some of the most iconic individual scenes and images of erotic and amorous sentiment in the history of film are to be found in films by these directors.

In these early masterpieces of cinema, when film language had reached a certain sophistication but before the norms of classical narrative cinema had fully settled, in films like *Pandora's Box* by Pabst, *Liebelei* by Ophüls and *Blonde Venus* by Sternberg, a narrative movement unfolds within a spectacle that is both at the service of narrative and the purpose of narrative. In these films, say in Sternberg's *Shanghai Express*, discussed earlier, the close-up is an independent semiotic unit. The iconic backlit portrait of Marlene Dietrich that is inserted into the film's narrative – and which is the basis of the most famous posters of the star – is only loosely motivated by the story and detaches itself from it, producing its own aesthetic effect that is at least as powerful as the rest of the film. In the early films of Pabst, close-ups of characters, dramatically expressing feelings and reactions that are themselves highly dramatic, form the main thread of the narrative, the stations that the story runs through, with surrounding situations and scenery forming merely the sustaining background for these expressive moments. Ophüls' *Liebelei* is a masterpiece of dramatic *mise en scène*. This is a conventional Austrian story of an officer having an affair with the wife of his superior, while also loving a marriable woman his own age, only to find himself forced into a duel in which he dies. The alternations between snow-covered landscapes, sordid student lodgings and the grand house of the superior officer have a dramatic power that is based on photorealistic specificity and sharp discontinuity on the level of tone. The drama provides coherence while the tone of scenes is discordant, and this adds both to the realism of the film and to the dramatic power of each scene. One such scene is a confrontation between the officer and his superior in the latter's house. His superior, played by the legendary Gustaf Gründgens, appears as a natural extension of his palatial staircase that underlines and gives a sinister ring to all his gestures. The film image here achieves a sculptural plasticity that is entirely at the service of the emotion that it develops – the image is not expressionistic; it is not made to shock or produce awe in the audience, but to condense emotional qualities sculpturally within the image.

There is a psychological and plastic naturalism in Ophüls at this point in time that is very different from the melodramatic emphasis in early Pabst. For instance, in Pabst's *The Love of Jeanne Ney* the expressive centre of the film and of each scene is unambiguously the face, the face expressing all the vivid emotions that this wild political melodrama depicts and transmits. Siegfried Kracauer was critical of the film because he found that the original novel by Ilea Ehrenburg – depicting ordinary people caught up in the Russian Revolution – to be historically and politically superficial. In purely cinematographic terms, the film nevertheless reaches a high point of melodramatic purity in its insistent use of the expressive human face as a main vehicle of meaning and of spectacle. It is also true, however, that since this film by Pabst is more episodic in its narrative form than his more conventional and for some reason more famous *Diary of a Lost Girl*, it does show the limits of his expressionistic style. After a while the emotive effects become repetitive as the peripeties of the dramatic action seem increasingly arbitrary. This serial quality of narrative is indeed characteristic of all Pabst's early films, but in his masterpiece *Pandora's Box* he develops the serial principle into a thematic signifier and an independent source of aesthetic momentum. This film, the drama of a young girl fighting to secure a place in society and at the same time defend her own sexual freedom, involves not so much emotion as *feigned* emotion. The tone of the film is one of never-ending murky transactions and desperate erotic projects. Plunged into shadows from which they only barely emerge, the characters seem like puppets in a plot that appears to have very few winners and many losers. Based on two plays by the decadent Viennese playwright Frank

Wedekind, the story involves a number of sexual and political transgressions. The seriality of the story is invested with a mixed quality of rebellion and aimlessness as the protagonist, Lulu, moves from one tenuous situation to the next. She is a young showgirl courted by many men and some women. One of her suitors is an influential newspaperman, Dr Schön. He is at the same time planning to marry a respectable girl. Lulu succeeds in impeding their marriage and marries Dr. Schön. On the wedding night they fight, and she accidentally shoots and kills him. She is condemned to five years in prison but escapes with her new lover, the son of Dr Schön. From this point onwards her life is a series of unsuccessful escapes ending in London, where she commits another murder. Seriality and erotic anarchy acquire a rare but also intensely unhappy grandeur in this film, as sexual attraction appears as a force that knows few moral or social bounds but which is also barely containable by the individual subject or within an erotic relationship between two subjects.

In the two films by Pabst, *Jeanne Ney* and *Pandora's Box*, in *Liebelei* by Ophüls and in *Blonde Venus* by Stenberg, *mise en scène* is celebrated as spectacle and drama, one through the other. The serial narrative of *Pandora*, the decline narrative of *Venus* and the formalised adultery story of *Liebelei* all present a dialectic of spectacle and drama. Drama enhances a spectacle that at times becomes the only purpose of the film, while at other times it is at the service of drama. Thematic, and especially moral, content is staged and unproblematic, consisting of story materials that pose few surprises as vice, transgression, emotion and erotic intrigue are treated as stock themes, only in some cases, such as *Pandora's Box*, granted a more extreme and shrill manifestation.

These films invite us to engage emotionally with the image as it has been invested with intensity by the drama. It is not the kind of cinema that invites us to reflect upon the characters, upon their moral dilemmas, psychological depth, hidden motives. This, as we shall see, will be the specific achievement of classical cinema. Rather, according to the dialectic of spectacle and drama, the iconic film image becomes invested with affect in a manner that can be well captured by Hans Blumenberg's concept of projected wish-fulfilment, or *Wunschprojektion*. It is the iconic image that absorbs the film rather than simply being justified by its narrative. The film is there only for the sake of the iconic image, which is what remains in the mind after seeing the film. Hence, *Shanghai Express* is a film that is made in a retrospective mode, not in the temporal mode of forward-moving sequence. It is made to be remembered, to be condensed in memory as a photograph more powerful than any photograph, since it is the synthesis of a moving image.

Love in Motion

Classical Hollywood Cinema

The next period of filmmaking, known for its continuity editing, depth of field, plasticity of spatial representation and highly developed genres and star personalities, is also, from the point of view of meaning, characterised by more complex and also more rigid structures of thematic content.

In order to make the film image evocative, one had to make it speak, and in order to make it speak one had to limit its semiotic, expressive potential, and make it thematically clear. Visually, the structural requirement for clarity was to materialise as aesthetic norms that can be summed up as a universal need for coherence of tone. This is the requirement that the film's style corresponds to what we can call its moral atmosphere.

The American novelist F. Scott Fitzgerald expressed this notion precisely and vividly in his Hollywood novel *The Last Tycoon*. Here a film producer talks about a 'type of film' as a norm that has to be evident to the director and the producer at all times during the making of a film. A type of film is both more and less than a film genre. The type of film is a moral atmosphere supported by an appropriate style providing for the viewer a definite conception of the characters. In the fictional example discussed in the novel, the producer says of a certain film that it is a love story in which the audience must be convinced that the heroine would never dream of sleeping with the male lead before marriage, but on the other hand sleeping with the male lead is always on her mind – and the audience should never be allowed to forget that. In other words, the audience knows both that the heroine is good and virtuous and that she obsessively and sexually loves the male lead. The tension within her caused by her desire and her virtue is what gives rhythm, atmosphere and wit to the film. The aesthetic theory that Fitzgerald suggests but does not, of course, develop as a theory entails a nexus between style, tone, morality and character, which is well attuned to the problem of how love is captured in film. Thus any film has to possess a certain coherence of tone – but the equilibrium produced to achieve this coherence may be of very different kinds.

I shall use the term 'classical' to refer to *a tonal equilibrium created around moral content*. The film history that I suggest at the horizon of this study emerges from the following question: how is moral content rendered in film spectacle and how does film subsequently move away from moral content in its depictions of love? In the classical film, love is a privileged cause and arena of affect. We can think of how characters are defined both in terms of the character's psychology and in terms of the dramatic relationships between characters. Dramatically, plot structure in the classical film situates the character very clearly within a categorial space of age, sexuality, class, temper and beauty (or lack thereof).

Hence, classical *mise en scène* depicts love as a *positional* relation: in individual scenes, in the drama, in the thematic structure of the story. Just as characters are assigned clear positions in the film image and in the story world, so the love that happens between them is defined as a relationship between very well-defined characters. The love relation itself is defined along a series of distinct and clearly identifiable axes, such as desirability, social difference and moral hope. The classical method of systematic integration of theme and spectacle presupposes, within film production, a very high degree of formalisation of all the aesthetic components and themes of the film – and this was of course the aesthetic impact of the industrial mode of production practised in the Hollywood studio system. This is a mode of production that pushes towards standardisation as well as variation, both on the level of individual elements – actors, stories, directors, themes, genres, techniques – and on the level of their aesthetic integration in individual films. The two aesthetic processes of integration and differentiation go hand in hand. This duality also determines, on a semiotic level, the relationship that we may identify in any given classical Hollywood film between spectacle and content. Hence, robust structures of moral content are a prerequisite for the clarity of narration in many film genres in this period, but moral content is not necessarily the aesthetic or semiotic *telos* of a given film. In other words, we may find that a given film displays a clear and rigid structure of moral content but that this structure is merely incidental to the film, considered as a particular kind of generic spectacle, geared towards evoking and eliciting particular mixed emotions such as fear or erotic thrills mixed with social anxiety or, inversely, a whimsical sense of lightheartedness.

Yet, even when content structures are not foregrounded, they constitute an essential architectonic element in the construction of narrative in the classical Hollywood love film. Therefore, their visual qualities notwithstanding, these films tend to possess a certain *discursive* quality. The classical Hollywood love film has the pleasing effect of immediacy and complexity. We are struck by a unity of tone and atmosphere, yet we can talk, and go on to talk, about the characters in the film, because, precisely, they are upheld by a network of moral significance that makes them interesting, makes them into questions and signs requiring psychological interpretation and moral empathy. (This is why Cavell finds an echo of ordinary language philosophy in classical Hollywood comedies and melodramas.)

If we now turn to the semiotic figure of the *character* and consider him or her as an isolated psychological figure, we note that the dramatic development of all classical love films is destined to compel the viewer to ask certain pressing questions concerning the protagonist and his or her feelings. Depending on genre, the focus on emotion in these films is more or less explicit, and the main character becomes interesting to the extent that we wonder about his or her inner world. We are often induced to asking these questions already at the level of dramatic exposition where the situation that triggers the story also involves a character whose desires or feelings will evolve in the course of the story. At the same time these questions are allowed to be left unanswered. The tight dramatic and thematic structure of the classical film gradually constructs a web of interpretation around the character, and through this web of interpretation the viewer is able to understand, perhaps judge and certainly empathise with that character.

The very aesthetic form of classical *mise en scène* is also positional. It is a form of plastic composition that aims to position characters in dramatically effective ways within a dynamic visual and social space, such that their place within the scene and within the story is determinate rather than indeterminate. It should be determinate both with respect to intelligibility – their acts and gestures are articulated in relation to recognisable social, moral and psychological themes – and with respect to their dramatic relation to other characters. To illustrate this notion of determination we can mention the technique of shot/reverse-shot – or to take a more interesting example, return to André Bazin's discussion of deep focus. If we compare the function of deep focus in *Citizen Kane* by Welles and *The Little Foxes* by Wyler, we can see immediately that Wyler's film is classical (positional) and Welles challenges the language of classical cinema (and positionality). Wyler uses deep focus to accentuate dramatic and psychological relationships. A memorable scene shows the evil mother peering down at her daughter from the top of a staircase. Welles by contrast uses deep focus to open up a space of symbolic and temporal signification that is not fully determined by dramatic interaction within the scene. What is at stake in the distinction between classical cinema and various kinds of 'modern' cinema is thus the extent to which characters are granted a determinate place and function – spatially, thematically and dramatically.

Modernity

In classical cinema, the worldly implication of emotion, the way that emotions are placed in a concrete social reality, depends on morality. Morality is the vehicle of content through which emotions become determined as a response to the world; the character is individuated with his or her emotions through the moral implications of those emotions. In other words, emotion becomes articulated within classical film narrative within a conceptual space, and this conceptual space is organised by moral categories. This can be a space of choice. This is typically the fable structure of classic Hollywood films. But this need not be the case. The conceptual moral space can be one of moral alternatives presented discursively but not explicitly related to choice. We can say that the love films that display a very sharp moral structure and a thematically dense exposition of the characters tend to have a melodramatic undercurrent. We might say that classical American (and French) cinema creates a fusion of realism and melodrama. The lush moral universe of the classical film, always threatened from within by the operatic temptations of melodrama, and hedged in, at the same time, by the strictures of psychological and social realism, is one aesthetic and semiotic pole of cinema. The other trend I shall refer to as the *reflective form*. I argue that the reflective form is prepared by an intermediary tradition, which I call 'fantasy spectacle'.

In the historical narrative of this book, the history of love in cinema is characterised by a dialectical movement that regains the power of the visual image through the indirect route of fantasy and generic formalism. The core of this dialectic is the aspiration of many modern filmmakers to find a means to overcome melodrama, either by transforming its expressive potential or by replacing its resources with other kinds of narrative and stylistic means of expression. Alfred Hitchcock, François Truffaut and Luis Buñuel are some of the filmmakers that develop the opportunities of what I call the fantasy spectacle to interpret love outside the framing devices of moral categories, melodramatic choices and social constraints.

On the other hand, love achieves its perhaps most complex realisation in film in directors such as Maurice Pialat and Michelangelo Antonioni, who return to realism and morality but who seek in so doing to grant an equal weight to human emotions and to the social world. Films by these and similar directors possess a form of intelligibility and expression that I call 'reflective'.

The Legacy of the 1960s

In the historical passage leading out of classical cinema and melodrama, the New Wave movements of the 1960s presented a range of aesthetic resources: psychological realism (Ingmar Bergman, Claude Chabrol), surrealism (Buñuel, Jiri Menzel), allegory (Jean-Luc Godard, Pier Paolo Pasolini), conceptual documentary (Agnès Varda, Antonioni). The politicisation of Western culture that followed in the wake of the '68 movement further seemed to impose a political perspective – also on depictions of love. By using psychoanalysis to show that sexual relationships are scripted by desire and power rather than romantically free, one could inscribe the whole love experience in its full intimacy within a social fabric of power relationships. Hence Bertolucci made *The Conformist* about the erotic psychology of a fascist and Fassbinder traced in each of his films a particular nexus between erotic desires and personal – at times overtly political – relationships of power.

The long and still continuing history of 'modern cinema' is thus inflected by this particular political and cultural development, beginning in the wake of '68 and achieving a new life in the mid-1980s. This development of political cinema (in the 1970s) and post-modernism (in the 1980s) is characterised by a popularisation of the avant-garde techniques developed by Pasolini and Godard in the early 1960s, in films like *Accattone* and *Vivre sa vie*. Pasolini and Godard invest the visual image with allegorical meanings that then determine how we interpret the story and the characters. The next generation of Fassbinder and Bertolucci continues this allegorical method within the frame of a history of national emotions – Fassbinder with his films on the emotional history of Germany from the Weimar period to the 1970s and Bertolucci with his films on the psychology of fascism. The fusion of this kind of allegorical realism with flamboyant spectacle can be found in other significant directors of recent decades, such as Emir Kusturica and Almodovar. In these directors either sexuality is a primary allegorical sign for political relationships (Kusturica) or sexuality in all its cultural implications is itself a political field (Almodovar).

Whereas love continues to be an important theme for Godard – if only because of its prominent role as a cultural *topos* that can be reinterpreted and filled with new significance – love is only marginally a problem in the work of the homoerotic filmmakers Pasolini and Almodovar, who describe sexuality and its place within a field of social forces but do not seek to describe homosexual love relationships as they exist over a temporal arc. The political allegories of sex in Kusturica and Bertolucci are likewise indifferent to the questions of what love relationships are in themselves and how they exist over time. An exception to this political-allegorical approach could be Kusturica's *When Father Was Away on Business*, depicting the life of a couple under Tito. Yet also here the allegorical gaze absorbs the description of everyday longings and desires into a political and social fresco of Cold War Yugoslavia.

Bertolucci's *Last Tango in Paris* is an ambiguous and interesting film in this respect. Apparently a romantic love story, it is also a psychoanalytic allegory, structured by conceptual distinctions: the space of the flat where the lovers meet to have sex and the world that their relationship is entirely cut off from; Oedipal desire and the flight from death. The lovers' attraction to one another, their escape from reality, their pleasure at being together and the impossibility of their relation lasting are all motivated in the film within a structure of Oedipal desire and foreclosure of the social world. She seeks a father, he an imaginary relief from the death of his wife, who has just committed suicide. The middle-aged man and the young woman seek to enact a sexual relationship outside of the symbolic sphere, in the regressive, imaginary uterus-like space of an empty flat. The sinuous *Jugendstil* curves of the flat, accentuated by the brown and yellow chromatic universe of the film, serve as a direct allegory of the regressive and imaginary nature of their relationship. Rather than being a film about two lovers seeking to define their relationship against social convention, this is a deeply conservative and Freudian film, insisting on the normative power of social reality against the claims of desire. If desire is not integrated into some form of social reality, its claims are not real, the film seems to be saying. If desire is nevertheless pursued as if it were real, its regressive nature becomes morbid and its only possible endpoint is death. *Last Tango in Paris* ends with the young woman murdering her lover. The story and the film's chromatic and spatial register are over-determined by a theoretical structure that the film evokes as a code or its own intelligibility. There is nothing to *interpret* in either the characters or their relationship, as the film presents us with a conceptual frame that seems to make any further analysis superfluous. The classical film, by contrast, is eminently interpretable, as characters are presented, through plot and *mise en scène*, as positional figures within rigidly defined moral and social categories that invests them with moral significance and hence invites us to produce an interpretative discourse about them.

The Reflective Film

There was more than one response to the question of how cinema could show that personal relationships, feelings and aspirations are intertwined with a social and political environment. There is a strand of post-1970 filmmaking that I call the 'cinema of reflection' which seeks to show how erotic freedom is articulated with the world. The cinema of reflection is neither a school nor a movement. It is not defined by a particular style. The filmmakers I will discuss are in fact completely different in their aesthetic aspirations. I shall focus on the following five: Antonioni, Pialat, Eric Rohmer, David Lynch and Wong Kar-Wai.

What they have in common within the framework of this study is first that, in relation to classical cinema, fantasy spectacle and the political cinema of psychological over-determination, these are films that assign a generative and meaningful relation to place. The function of place in these films is not reducible to its narrative, social or symbolic implications; rather, place gains a powerful generative force in the shaping of the mental universe and the conditions of erotic relationships. Second, these films present an entirely different relationship between speech, subjectivity and erotic desire than is characteristic of a classical or allegorical film. The two vectors of speech and place are conjoined 'reflectively' rather than 'categorially' (in a determining way): they are not coordinated with a view to supporting a moral – or for that matter political – discourse about the protagonist, against the background of an implicit structure of moral alternatives.

The reflective form that results from this coordination of speech and place constitutes a position on intelligibility that differs from the narrative perspective characteristic of classical cinema. Classical cinema strives to synthesise the point of view of a subject with the objective perspective of social analysis and moral judgement. *The cinema of reflection problematises the very question of the perspective from which the characters and their feelings could become intelligible.* Therein lies its reflective quality.

The Ontology of Love

Love is a universal and intimate, a banal and interesting part of human life. Universally longed for, often the subject of gossip, banter and mockery, love is at the core of all social life and a pervasive theme in world literature. Yet the immense literary tradition of love stands in a strange asymmetry to the extreme poverty of philosophical reflection upon love. As much as love has served as an inexhaustible material for poetry, drama and novels, love has for philosophy remained a sort of afterthought. Why should this be so? Plato formulated a nuanced account of love in the *Symposion*, as we have seen, but after Plato philosophy almost entirely lost interest in love as a separate phenomenon. Many philosophers discuss phenomena that are akin to love or a possible component of love, but very rarely do they discuss love as a *separate kind of thing*. Aristotle theorises friendship. Augustine formulates a theological and psychological theory of erotic desire. Thomas Aquinas presents a detailed psychology of the passions. Spinoza and Hegel formulate theories of marriage as a relationship based on equality. Sartre provides a phenomenology of sexual intercourse considered as a relationship of power.

Several late twentieth-century moral philosophers see in erotic gestures or relationships or in amorous affect a privileged source of moral ennoblement. Levinas writes a spiritual phenomenology of the erotic caress. Irigaray theorises an ethical relation between the amorous subject and its desired other. Nussbaum sees the emotional bond of love as a moral good. Cavell in a similar vein contrasts the subjective attitudes involved in marriage to the subjectivity that is championed by rationalist modernity. Some of the finest contemporary sociologists have written on love. Luhman has written on love as communication in French classical culture and Illouz has written about the ideology of love in American consumer culture.

This recent philosophical and sociological interest in love has not, however, resulted in any satisfactory and encompassing definition of love, since each author

Love in Motion

has pursued a very particular philosophical or theoretical motive, related either to the notion that love is a source of moral goodness (the subject's overcoming of its own egotism) or to the notion that love – whatever it might be in itself – is a social fact that is fully embedded in a wider set of social interactions and that obeys norms that are certainly specific, but that are not *essentially* different from norms governing other kinds of interaction (communication, self-interest, consumption, and so on). We should look a little further afield.

Love is an existential universal and not something that any subject can be indifferent to. Thus along with money and death, love is one of the few things that almost everyone is, or needs to be, concerned about. However, whereas money is the object of an enormous scientific discipline, economics, love and death form part of no particular discipline. Death was an important theme in existential philosophy, and love has been one of the main themes of literature and film. Yet, both phenomena remain at the margins of what one can rationally talk about – with the obvious difference that death is spoken of relatively little in everyday life, while love on the other hand is spoken of a great deal.

Julia Kristeva opens her book on love with a fitting anecdote in this regard. She overheard a conversation among young girls talking about love in the sense of sex, that is, in the sense of a very significant domain of experience that they were about to discover or had yet to conquer. In the life history of each individual subject, love is indeed a domain that awaits discovery. Love is banal, only barely escaping the natural biological development of human beings. At the time when in adolescence one is a sexual being in biological terms one begins to fall in love. Only, this is not exactly right. Both sexuality and the capacity to fall in love predate adolescence. Furthermore, there is a component in the act of falling in love which is not biological, and that is *imagination*. In adolescent experience imagination plays a prominent role. Whether innocent or precocious, the young subject will spend some time picturing the other and try to figure out the intentions, wishes and tastes of him or her. Of course this exploratory imagination is itself quite predictable, banal even. Also, the further portions of the individual life cycle can be rendered in the key of predictability, at least within a relatively limited social horizon, as most societies will present some variety on the cycle: courtship, the formation of couples, domestic life, children, maturity, old age, death. This life pattern, itemised at such a level of generality, is not yet incompatible with romance and passion, the ambition on the part of the loving subject being to create its own happiness or live its desire on its own terms, but only a small step suffices for the *generalising* gaze to become a *cynical* gaze. For the cynical gaze no event is new. This is, in fact, the essence of the cynical gaze. The lover's gaze in itself is never cynical, although the lover may find the cynical gaze soothing and apply it to herself in order not to feel exposed to its own feelings. For the subject of love it is irrelevant, at least initially, if there have been countless others preceding him or her. The fact that the subject's love is not new in the history of the world and may not even be new within its own personal history – it may have had other lovers before – does not itself damage the subject's belief in the uniqueness and importance of its own love. Let us call this self-confidence of the loving subject the 'first-person perspective'. This perspective has been material for poetry in the Western tradition at least since the Middle Ages. The first-person perspective, the subjective point of view that lovers have on their own love, is an intrinsic part of love. There can be no love without the lovers' subjective awareness of their love. Opposed to the first-person perspective is the external point of view, the third-person perspective that originates in a general perspective on human life patterns and culminates in a sort of cynical denial of the importance or uniqueness of any particular love.

Now, what is or is not *immediately given to experience*, or philosophical observation, is love itself in so far as it contains in its being, as a particular *kind* of being, structures that support both a first-person point of view and a third-person point of view. The two perspectives, the first-person and the third-person, are, we might say, 'transcendental'. They correspond to different layers of structure in the phenomenon itself, that is, in the phenomenon of love.

The relationship between a first-person and a third-person perspective exists in a permanent tension. This is captured, forcefully, by the French moral and psychological concept of vanity. The moral psychology of vanity was developed in French philosophy and literature in the seventeenth century and returned in the nineteenth century. The French Romantic writer Stendhal defended the freedom of love and demonstrated love's social complexity in his treatise *De l'amour* and in his novels. A follower of seventeenth-century psychology, Stendhal sees the problem of love as one of vanity: love can only flourish when the subject can protect the first-person perspective that it has on its love against the interest that it has in being seen favourably by others. In other words, erotic infatuation can only become truly reciprocal if the sexual subject is able to relate to the other as being more desirable than the image that the subject has of itself as being ennobled by the other's desire. According to Stendhal, only imagination is able to pierce through the veil of self-interested vanity and make one love the other more than one loves oneself. By imagining the other as loveable, and hence in a sense creating the other, the subject of love forgets itself, and forgets to nurture the image of itself that it wishes to produce in others. This theory is subtle and original, showing both the possibility and the fragility of love. Stendhal is original also in articulating a distinctly modern problem of individual freedom based on the categories of spontaneity and imagination, filtered through the psychological vocabulary of classical French theories of love. The importance of Stendhal from my point of view is that the moral dichotomy between good and bad loves in his theory in no way coincides with a Christian-Platonic distinction between mind and body. Genuine love is for Stendhal imaginative and erotically passionate, whereas weaker forms of love remain spellbound by the subject's vain interest in itself and in the image that it can produce of itself in others.

The focus of the present book is not the subject and its relation to itself, but a realm where the erotic subject confronts its own perspective on its desire with a third-person perspective on that same desire. At the same time, I seek to show that love is not social in the way of being *reducible* to underlying causes, interests or conditions. The seventeenth-century psychological theory of vanity that Stendhal modernises can also be interpreted in a different, less subjectivist direction. The French classical theory of vanity entails a sophisticated reflection upon the relationship between the erotic subject's self-knowledge and its exposure to being known by others. This is an insight that is largely lost in modern, that is, post-romantic, conceptions of love but which – I claim – cinema rediscovers.

The subject of love moves within an equilibrium as within a distribution of speaking positions. Following these shifting speaking positions its relationship can be spoken of, now in this way, now in that way: the subject may address its own desire, the desire of the other, the nature of their relation or its relation to the surrounding world. In each case, the subject situates itself differently, takes up a different position in relation to and within the relation.

An underlying obstacle for thinking of love as a relation is a particular kind of ontological common sense. This common sense consists in saying, as Aristotle does, that to think is to make propositions about things. In other words, thought is structured as predicative sentences, and those things which have being, the only things that truly exist, are the sort of objects that can receive predicates. The only thing that has being is the thing that exists separately from others, which is not itself a predicate, which can be defined, and whose shifting properties I can describe. Kant idealises this model and talks not of what *is* but of all the logical and categorical components that are *involved* in predicative sentences, categories like unity, number and identity. Relations do not fare well in such a common-sense theory of knowledge or being, but it is noteworthy that both Aristotle and Kant obsessively return to the question of relations and their status. Aristotle discusses numerical and physical relations throughout the *Metaphysics*. Kant's notion of a free play between sensation and logical categories in the experience of beauty evokes a scenario of pure relationality prior to the constitution of knowable things. Yet, their shared common sense constitutes a very powerful bulwark against the being of relations. In Aristotelian terms, relations are not properties of things, since they are, we might say, a property of two things. It is their property in so far as they are related, but it is not the property of either. Relations are also not things or substances, since they don't have their being in themselves. We can speak about a relation, but we cannot see the relation as the ultimate substance that we speak about since it presupposes the underlying substances that it relates. Similarly, for Kant, relations cannot really be a fundamental component of the predicative sentences that we produce about the world, since all the fundamental, categorical, components of those sentences contribute to the formation of sentences that have individual things as their content and reference. Another reason for Kant's rejection of relationality in the social and moral sphere is his belief that the subject's self-consciousness and moral consciousness constitute a locus of ethics that has priority, in the order of reasons, over any given actual human relationship.

In order to grant a being to relations it is therefore necessary to gain distance from the ontological category that structures both the Aristotelian and the Kantian account of things and of predication. This is the category of determination, the process by which, simultaneously, a thing acquires properties and is described in thought as being a certain kind of thing with definite traits. Love is never determined in this way since it is not one kind of thing.

The love relation is *self-determining rather than determined*. The subjects of love carry out this self-determination against the background of the relation as a phenomenon or reality that already exists: the subject of love is a subject that *emerges* within a relation. Hence, the subject of love is not constitutive of the love relation in the sense in which the relation would merely be a *property* of the subject, something that could be said about it, even if it is also true that there cannot be a relation without two erotic subjects entering into a relation. Ontologically, there is a priority of the relation over the subject. The amorous subject is not someone who has certain feelings or desires, but someone who *finds* him or herself within a relation – whether real or imaginary.

The being of love as a relation consists of the following necessary component elements: a reciprocal erotic desire between two lovers; the articulation by the lovers of their relationship in language, with regard to time; a relationship between the love relation and a surrounding cultural and social space. These are the elements that cannot be removed from love. Without erotic desire, or without the reciprocity of desire, there is no love. Love requires a discourse on the part of the lovers as to the nature and duration of their relationship. Hence, if two subjects have sex once, or have sex regularly without speaking to each other, no *question* arises, for either of them, about the nature and duration of their relationship, and it is only within the intellectual, emotional and temporal space projected by that question that love separates itself from or becomes more than sex. In other words, love is sexual, but it needs a certain duration in order to become something more and other than a sexual relation, and it is necessary that this duration is taken by the lovers within language as posing a question: for how long? What is this relation? Where does it belong in society? Hence, it is not feeling that fills out the gap between sex and love: feelings may arise in relation to someone one does not know or they may remain unconscious in a long-term relationship. Feelings are neither sufficient nor necessary for describing a love relation. Hence, it is not feeling but the subjects' articulation of their relation in language in relation to time that marks the difference between sex and love.

Now, when the subjects of an erotic relationship seek to articulate in speech the possible duration of their relation, they have to situate their relation within a logical and cultural space that is quite complex, and which implies, on the one hand, social constraints and, on the other, a range of cultural categories, expectations, norms and ideas that the lovers have access to when seeking to articulate what their relation is.

Let us pause for one moment. Every love relation conforms to the being of love as relation. The subject of love describes and addresses its relation within the cultural categories that it has access to. Now, what is the relationship between these cultural categories – which by definition are historically specific, hence relative – and the universal, transhistorical structure of love in its being? The universal structure of love is not concrete, it is merely the formal ontological articulation of love. The *relation* in itself is culturally indeterminate, not defined socially as marriage or any other specific bond. The relation in itself is the *being* of love, the underlying *something* that all feeling and all cultural contents gravitate around. On the other hand, culture exists for love as the range of things the lovers and their observers find it possible to say – about the quality and eligibility of the lovers, about the durability of the relation, about this or that gesture, choice, act or feeling. Love is interpretable only within the conceptual space that is opened up by available cultural categories. The relation in itself, the *being* of love, is not spoken of because it is not manifest as such in experience. As primary being the relation in itself is the formal condition for the concrete relation, which in turn is felt, socially specific and culturally intelligible.

The *being* of the love relation is *pre-categorial*. It is not yet articulated according to specific (cultural) categorisations that would determine what sort of thing love is. When Aristotle says that being has no genus and Heidegger says that being is not an object, they point to this minimality of being, a formal trait that was defined by medieval philosophers as the *transgeneric* nature of being. By definition, the being of love as relation resists aesthetic presentation – since being is not articulated. Its concrete manifestation, on the other hand, love, is a kind of cultural fact, and we, the lovers, find ourselves as subjects of feeling, but also of thought, within a relation that allows us to take up various attitudes with regards to the relation. Hence, to the subject of love, the erotic relationship is always concrete, and takes place within a structured cultural space. Love is then fully articulated, and the subject, with his or her thoughts and actions, is bound to this articulation.

Thus, in *itself*, the love relation is not yet categorised and not yet articulated, for on the level of being, love is simply a relation. The love relation is a particular kind of relation, but it is not articulated *as* relation. In actuality, on the other hand, as a phenomenon within experience, love is always concrete, that is, articulated.

This also means that any love relationship takes place within a specific historical and cultural setting. This setting moulds love from the inside. The norms that govern love are not merely coercive; they do not just govern sex and marriage: who is eligible as a marriage partner and when it is permissible to make love. Any culture has tacit rules that subtly govern courtship, flirtation, seduction and the like. Desire is always a component of a larger conceptual whole to which it is thought to contribute in a specific way, depending on what this whole looks like.

What this whole looks like in turn depends on the predicates that can be said of it, the sorts of things that we may relevantly think about concerning love, and especially the areas of reality that love concerns. On the basis of such an articulation of love, an assumption arises as to love's place in reality and the kind of totality that it is in itself. Against the background of a conception of the whole that love is, one may formulate thoughts as to what it means for a particular love relation to be or not to be intelligible, and what it would be to give an intelligible account of such a relation, what, in other words, it would mean to 'make sense' of a given love relation.

When love is articulated in cultural space, and becomes intelligible, the love relation can receive predicates and is thus interpretable. Such an articulation is the cultural condition of love. It is a condition of its discursive intelligibility. On the other hand, in so far as these categories can be seen to be constitutive of the very life of love, the condition of its discursive intelligibility turns out also to be a condition of its existence. The being of love is articulated, then, through specific cultural categorisations, but no one categorisation can exhaust love. In the next chapters, I discuss three such categorisations: the ancient Greek and medieval conception of love as cosmic erotic energy; a conception of love as an object of judgement, present in French literature from the late seventeenth to the late eighteenth century; and a conception of love as the socialisation of sexuality through marriage and emotion, a view that has been wide-spread in the last two centuries. None of these conceptions exhausts the phenomenon of love.

Love is always culturally articulated in a partial and limiting way, but if we try to grasp love universally and philosophically beyond these particular categorisations, while not staying on the purely formal level of being, we must acknowledge that love is what we may call categorial. On the level of being, on the other hand, love is category-neutral, since its being supports categorisations of very different kinds. Within experience, love exists within cultural categories, and these categories do not exhaust the full range of the phenomenon. This full range can be represented as a kind of existence that stretches across or moves through a range of very different categories. This aspect of love is its 'transcategoriality'. The essential transcategoriality of love poses a challenge to any cultural categorisation, since love is always more than what any particular categorisation allows for – and this might be a reason for the poverty of philosophical reflections on love. It is because love is always simultaneously sexual, social, moral, emotional, at times political, and perhaps spiritual that philosophy has found it difficult to turn love into a separate object of study. This is also true of modern authors, as they each seek to frame love very clearly within a sociological or moral framework. Cinema can approach the transcategorial: cinema can present love as a relation that immediately connects desire, speech, thought, feeling, power, place, class relations and spirituality.

As a phenomenon within experience love is not transient or fleeting, even if its duration may be indeterminate. Love thus manifests itself with its own kind of *assertiveness* and resilience. Love may be difficult to grasp and define, but it also has its own special kind of persistence. Hence love is a claim against cynicism, and this claim is situated in the world. Love sets up a separation between itself (the love relation) and the causal flows that surround it. Love has a binding power, but the nature of this power is elusive. Erotic reciprocity is not exactly a contract; the reciprocity of desire is not only a reciprocity of promises, intentions and expectations. Love is also the experience that in the world there is a particular location where the other exists, and it is not immaterial to the lover that this is so. The beloved occupies a part of the world, a point in space that makes a difference to the subject's plans. It is the point that the errant knight returns to, but it may also be the place where the estranged spouse is waiting. In *Un amour de Swann*,

Proust vividly describes the spatial imagination of a jealous lover. He highlights the phenomenological feature of the amorous subjectivity, that is, the realisation on the part of the lover that the location of the beloved is never immaterial. Proust describes the lover's concern for the other's whereabouts in hyperbolical terms as an obsessive desire for control, leading the subject to be deluded about its own intentions. Swann's lover Odette is going on a trip with a group of friends to a small town outside of Paris, but Swann is not invited. He then decides also to take a trip, to the very same town on the very same day, and he manages to persuade himself that there is nothing untoward in his going there on that day. In this satire of the lover's capacity for self-delusion, Proust demonstrates that the lover's thoughts, imagination, desire and perception are not only directed towards the other or towards the feelings that the other inspires, but are oriented towards the beloved as being *somewhere* specific, in the world.

It should be noted that neither the precategorial being of love nor its articulated cultural reality entail that lovers are happy or that love is a form of kindness or that lovers are not self-destructive. The medieval proto-romantic myth of *Tristan and Iseut* identifies the lover's quest for absolute self-determination with their willingness to die for love. When the freedom that love entails is posed in this absolute sense, the potential for self-destruction that love also contains is made evident. This destructive potential is not simply due to an underlying affinity between desire and death – this was the thought of romantics of transgression like Emily Brontë in *Wuthering Heights* and Nagisa Oshima with his film *In the Realm of the Senses*. It is caused by a particular capacity of the love relation to pose itself as a separate realm, cut off from the rest of the world. This capacity for separation and withdrawal is ambivalent: it is a source of freedom but it also harbours the potential for a closed circuit of emotion that can be destructive in different ways. I shall later discuss a French Romantic novel by Benjamin Constant which describes this predicament.

Against this negative and transgressive conception of amorous freedom, I argue that love is a kind of freedom but that, as it takes two to love and *I can never possess your desire*, the freedom that love brings with it belongs not to me but to us, or more abstractly, to a relationship of reciprocity. The relationship is free in so far as it is essentially indeterminable. The indeterminability of love is both real and conceptual. It is true both that all love relationships contain an element of indeterminability and freedom and that no love relationship can be exhaustively described, either by the lovers or by a bystander.

The lover's subjectivity is determined by the essential impossibility of knowing the other's desire, and the effect of this unknowability is the freedom of love.

Love in Motion

Freedom as indeterminability does not mean, on the other hand, that love exists in a void. Rather, paradoxically, love is free precisely to the extent that it is worldly, to the extent that the world is its stage. Domestic love, secret liaisons, ritual encounters, chance meetings, and so on may be love relationships, but a fully free love relationship is one that an external observer may see as existing in the world. It is by confronting itself with this external perspective that the love relation shows its assertiveness as a free force in the world.

In its being, love is a relation prior to the manifestation of feelings within experience. A subject emerges within the relation, finds him or herself to be in love or to be within a reciprocal relation. A phenomenological description of this subject in its most essential acts yields a structure of experience that we may call the *amorous cogito*. This is the awareness that there is another person whose existence is of relevance to me, and this significance potentially manifests itself across the full range of my mental acts and life activities. The awareness that this is so is similar to those acts of consciousness that Jean-Paul Sartre describes, where one is aware of something without thinking explicitly about that thing (non-thetic awareness). It is also akin to the sort of non-reflective self-awareness analysed by Maurice Merleau-Ponty in that the object of awareness of the amorous *cogito* has potentially very many ramifications and implications in the subject's memory and mental universe, ramifications that may be more or less intertwined – or on the contrary insulated from one another – but which, as such, as implicated thoughts, are manifest only as a sort of sedimentation, or shadow, impinging on the beloved when he or she is an object of awareness.

The amorous *cogito* has the specific nature of being precise in its reference (this person thought about in a specific way, not in a generic way) and encompassing in its manifestation in consciousness. One is struck by someone as a singular being, but the fact of being thus affected has the potential of invading all one's conscious and unconscious life. The thoughts one may thus have are not devoid of rationality – they may be deliberative, scheming, or argumentative – but they are not rational in their basic premise. For the basic premise is that one is struck by the other and one doesn't know why. One may enjoy spelling out the lovable qualities of the other, all the reasons why the other is lovable, but one also knows that these reasons, these predicates, are not the explanation of one's desire or infatuation. Sociologists and psychoanalysts may offer their explanations of a particular relationship, but phenomenologically the other-as-lovable appears as a primary given or fact. The amorous *cogito* then is the awareness that I am struck by someone and that this means that his or her existence and whereabouts matter to me. This is a subjective attitude but it is subordinate to, secondary to, a reciprocal relation of desire – for even unrequited love is a relation, and it strives to become reciprocal. Now, this relation is related to other social relationships. Hence, the subject of the amorous *cogito* soon passes from the simple act of awareness of the other to more complex emotional and intellectual acts. These acts are configured in a space of distribution across a range of *topoi*, or speaking positions. The subject can seek to articulate its own desire, to understand the desire of the other, to determine the duration of the relation and to situate the relation in relation to other social relations. If one thinks of these acts epistemically, in terms of knowledge and acts of the intellect, it is obvious that the amorous subject is dispossessed of its access to rational certainty, since it cannot know the duration of its own desire, let alone the duration of the other's desire.

The articulation of love is not, however, primarily epistemic and intellectual. Grief, jealousy and infatuation may engage the intellect very forcefully, but the basic relation that the subject has to its own amorous and erotic relationship is of a different kind. It is not simply the intellectual expression of a strong feeling. It is a thinking relation to be sure. It is conscious and not just instinctual. But the subject's activity of thought manifests itself first of all in predicative speech, that is, utterances of language that use available cultural predicates within specific *topoi* or positions of speech without thereby seeking to produce knowledge. That is, the subject describes either the relation, the other, or something the other did or something the subject felt, and it does so either to itself or to the beloved or to a third person, and in each case it does so through available cultural categories. Hence, love is a relation, but it becomes articulate through the mental activities of the subjects that form part of that relation. They position themselves in relation to one another and in relation to their surroundings and seek to articulate, within cultural categories available to them – or possibly in resistance to those categories – what their relation is. The philosophical question that love poses to the lover, to the subject of love, is thus whether it is the subject's desire and feelings or the categories that she has appropriated from her culture that constitute the ground of intelligibility for the relation. Amorous freedom resides in the subject's capacity to carve out a space distanced from the cultural predicates that she or others would be able to apply to her. This freedom of love is grounded in its transcategorial nature. If love is transcategorial, it is always in excess of any available set of cultural predicates and categories. Hence it is also something that the subjects of love can appropriate and define for themselves. Against the background of the amorous *cogito*, the cultural articulation of love across the distribution of *topoi* presents the subject with a choice, which engages her freedom: to what extent will she articulate the love relation within the mould of available categories, and to

Love in Motion

what extent will she seek to pursue her desire and sustain her relation with indifference to these categories? It is impossible to live outside of culture and society, but it is possible to make the space of predication porous rather than rigid. This would mean that predicates, within certain given categories, are certainly available – as a promise or menace or fact – but that the applicability to one's own case is in question.

Eros in History

The history of love is the history of its articulations and categorisations; the articulations of love in literature, philosophy, theology and science always imply a possibility of discourse and therefore a categorisation of some kind. We shall now, in this and the following chapter, look at three broad categorisations of love: love as eros, love as an object of judgement, and love as marriage and Romantic feeling.

Eros

A modernist conception of history would suggest that love was invented quite recently, that in earlier times individuals would have defined their erotic choices primarily in terms of family interest and not on the basis of subjective desire. Yet, love has been analysed psychologically, morally and socially from Sappho through Roman and medieval literature to modern and contemporary literature, and in each epoch love is recognised as a violent emotion and desire and as a problematic social phenomenon.

Pre-Socratic philosophers used the same word for sexual love and for natural fertility. This word is *eros*, and it is associated with harmony as opposed to strife. Here love is granted a cosmic spirituality quite different from the individual search for knowledge celebrated by Dante and other Platonists. I wish to retain from this Pre-Socratic view the insight that love is a *force in the world*. From Plato we should preserve a sense of humility in the face of love's multiple nature. Taken together, this insight and this humility lead us to see love as a force in the world that ranges across a great number of domains, from biology over psychology to ethics, politics and spirituality. Let us now turn to the historical development of eros. The concept of eros involves two questions: the relationship between the human and the divine and the relationship, within the soul and within society, between desire and its impact.

In the Greek mythical and philosophical discussions of love, a tension between the human beings and the Gods is prominent. In Godard's *Le mépris*, the character Fritz Lang says about Homer's *Odyssey* that it is a tale of man's battle against the Gods – this remark encapsulates the treatment of eros in Greek myth as well. In Greek philosophy, however, in Plato and in Hesiod in particular, eros is the site not so much of a battle with the Gods as of a tension between the human and the divine spheres of existence. This notion of division is the ancient Greek approach to love's being. But let us dwell on eros in its most basic Greek meaning. Plato suggests in a throwaway remark that midwives are the best matchmakers:

> SOCRATES: And have you also observed this characteristic of theirs: they're the cleverest of matchmakers, in that there are no gaps in their wisdom as regards which sort of woman should consort with which sort of man in order to produce the best possible children?
> THEAETETUS: No, I didn't know that at all.
> SOCRATES: Well you can be sure that they pride themselves more on that than on cutting the umbilical cord. (*Theaetetus*, 149e, translation McDowell)

This remark belongs to the Greek eros conception of love as a natural process in which attraction, reproduction and birth form part of the same physical cycle of eros seen as a force of attraction. Midwives become experts in eros; they know the laws of attraction. Following this naturalistic analogy between cosmos and human sexuality, ancient Greek myth correlated the sexual maturity of women with the social status of being marriable. The adult woman is someone who is ready to reproduce, and who therefore attracts suitors.

At the same time, Greek myths would also challenge the misogynist conception of women as merely reproductive creatures. Hence, the Goddess Atlas demonstrates an inversion of this expectation. Instead of presenting herself as sexual prey, she is a huntress, chasing men. In Greek myth, the motifs of hunt, rape, speed and surprise are in fact pervasive. They are endlessly varied in the erotic stories about the gods and their intrusions into the human sphere. Here, sexuality thrives on physical and imaginary distance – a distance that can be overcome, if one is a god, through very quick movement. Eros is in these tales a connecting force, spanning large distances.

In Greek cosmology, on the other hand, as we saw with Plato's midwife, eros is a connecting force in the sense of being a power of attraction, copulation and reproduction. Straddling the two realms of myth and cosmology, of divine action and natural process, the poet Hesiod presents myth as cosmology and vice versa. Eros is here a generative force that lies at the origin of the natural world, but the world consists of earth and sky and these are personified as Gaia and Ouranos. The erotic relation between Gaia and Ouranos is then both: it is a sexual relationship between anthropomorphic gods – and it is a force of equilibrium in the natural world. Now, in the story of Ouranos being castrated by his son, we witness a passage from a primary realm of order in which eros is a physical element providing proportion to other physical elements, to a human realm constituted by specific acts, intentions and objects:

> And great Sky (Ouranos) came, bringing night with him; and spreading himself out around Earth in his desire for love he lay outstretched in all directions. Then his son reached from his ambush with his left hand, and with his right hand he grasped the monstrous sickle, long and jagged-toothed, and eagerly he reaped the genitals from his dear father and threw them behind him to be borne away.
> (Hesiod, 175–180)

The act of castration performed by his son has a complex mythical significance. It juxtaposes and joins sexuality and violence, but it also confronts a divine realm of cosmic balance with a human realm of specific objects: 'the monstrous sickle, long and jagged-toothed [*karcharódonta*]'. In Hesiod, then, myth is human and psychological, thereby taking authority away from the Gods. Nietzsche's opposition between myth and psychology may well apply to the writers of tragedy, as he says, but it does not apply to Hesiod, where human desires and emotions are integrated with all their specificity into the cosmic-divine game of harmony and strife.

In his multifaceted discussion of eros, Plato is likewise able to capture a tension between the human and the divine realms of being, but his philosophical predecessors depict eros in abstract non-psychological terms. When we pass from mythical genealogy to philosophical cosmology in the pre-Socratic philosophers, eros is depicted as a physical, cosmic reality, a primary generative and structuring force – but we lose the sense of rivalry between a human and a divine sphere.

Hence in the writings of the cosmological philosopher and poet Parmenides, the eros analogy between natural fertility and human sexuality serves his search for a perspective on thought and being that is entirely separate from human experience and consciousness: 'the Gods thought of eros before they thought of anything else', he writes. Eros regulates reproduction but from the outside of experience:

Love in Motion

'The Goddess who is present at birth also induces the male and the female to unite' (this is the same thought that we saw in the quote from Plato concerning midwives as matchmakers). In Heraclitus, whose thoughts on eros are similar to those of Parmenides, we find the following evocation of eros as a cosmic force of attraction and separation: 'eros disperses and also assembles, and unites and separates' (*skidesi kai palin sunagei, kai proseisi kai apeisi*). Note that the Greek phrase is constructed around two pairs of parallel sounding words: *skidesi/sunagei* and *proseisi/apeisi*. This construction evokes the notion of a cosmic rhythm of eros.

The natural philosopher Empedocles develops this image of reciprocal dynamic movement. His use of the eros analogy is reflective. Since the analogy goes both ways – nature is like sexuality, sexuality is a cosmic process – to think about eros and about nature involves a circular metaphorical process of reasoning in which beginning and end might coincide, a process in which it is more important to picture intuitively the harmony of the whole than to understand the exact nature of its parts. This philosophical intuitionism earned Empedocles the scorn of Aristotle, who seemed to think that Empedocles did not understand the nature of his own metaphors, that, in other words, he took literally what could only be understood metaphorically. Now, Empedocles formulated elements of a philosophy of love, something that Aristotle certainly did not do. It may well be that love requires something closer to Empedoclean intuitionism than the classificatory rationalism of Aristotle.

In Plato's *Symposion*, we hear that no-one has dared to praise love according to its due. This would involve acknowledging that the person taken over by erotic desire is as if *possessed by a god*. As we progress through the *Symposion* we are taught the values of seduction and of amorous sacrifice, but these values remain within the human realm. However, we also learn that the person who loves is granted a freedom by both gods and men. Hence, Plato moves back and forth between a social, naturalistic conception of love as a kind of relational behaviour and a metaphysical and religious idea of eros as a sort of gift that has a divine origin. Within the scheme of this oscillation between the worldly and the other-worldly, Plato leaves behind the older cosmological model of attraction and reproduction common to Hesiod, Parmenides, Heraclitus and Empedocles.

Plato's famous theory of reciprocity-as-complementarity, which is attributed to Aristophanes in the text, bridges these two realms. The mythical image of masculine-feminine beings cut in half, seeking their missing half, is invoked in order to give an account of the lived experience and psychology of love, to answer the question of why lovers enjoy each other's company. Plato moves beyond the conventional Greek horizon of theories about love in that he insists that it cannot just be physical pleasure that binds the lovers together. In other words, it is not enough to invoke erotic desire in order to explain why lovers seek each other's company. Here Plato asks a very good question about love, a question that resurfaces centuries later in the French philosopher La Rochefoucauld, but that neither thinker is able to answer.

With the poet Sappho we stay within the orbit of erotic desire and infatuation. Sappho is one of the first writers in the Western tradition to analyse amorous sentiment and erotic infatuation in detail. Perhaps the fact that she as a woman writes about other women gave her a freedom of reflection not available to those who wrote about male relationships or relationships between men and women, since those kinds of relationship were all strictly codified socially and morally within the surrounding culture.

Two stanzas from one of her surviving poems (Poem 2) in an early twentieth-century English translation illustrate the directness and precision of her images:

Then in my bosom my heart wildly flutters,
And, when on thee I gaze never so little,
Bereft am I of all power of utterance,
My tongue is useless.
There rushes at once through my flesh tingling fire,
My eyes are deprived of all power of vision,
My ears hear nothing but sounds of winds roaring

It is difficult to surpass Sappho in descriptive force. She depicts erotic desire and infatuation as a phenomenon that is both sudden and complex, involving body and mind, and engaging the subjective faculties of action and perception to the point of blocking them: 'Bereft am I of all power of utterance', 'My eyes are deprived of all power of vision'.

The Roman poets who write about their adventures with real or imagined lovers and courtesans adopt a very different, less direct tone of clever disdain, light allusion and feigned jealousy. Propertius is the most realist and psychological of the Roman, and more specifically Augustan, love poets. His poetry explores in greater detail than Sappho's the temporality of affect, and his poems are more specific in their contextual and physical details than her depictions of infatuation. His psychological descriptions range across different subjective attitudes and emotions: longing, anxiety, anger. They capture these shifting emotions in a mixed tone that is both crude and elevated and which vividly evokes the material temporality of nights spent together. The persona of the poet presents his jealousy and deliberations, his anticipation of future pleasure but also his own social position. These features of his character are finely articulated through realistic metaphors. In book 1, poem 8, for instance, Propertius stages his certainty that Cynthia is not looking out for other richer men, and congratulates himself in terms that are simultaneously erotic and social:

> My Cynthia has ceased to travel strange roads. I'm dear to her, and she says Rome's best because of me, rejecting a kingdom without me. She'd rather be in bed, though narrow, with me, and be mine, whatever its size, than have the ancient region that was Hippodamia's dowry, and the riches that the horses of Elis won. (1 8a, translation Kline)

The point of view that Propertius offers us on the relationship is thus social and psychological rather than cosmological. It is psychological not in the sense of simply being concerned with feelings and motives, but in the sense of individual character. We find here a motive of individuation that is almost entirely absent from the Greek eros conception of love but which will develop and flourish within the Roman middle ages.

Medieval Love: Intellect and Power

It took the talent of a theologian to synthesise the cosmological and the psychological points of view on erotic desire. The Roman African theologian Augustine of Hippo synthesised cosmology and psychology within a theological conception of eros. On the basis of the Greek psychological theory of eros and a Christian philosophy of transcendence, he forges the Manichean dichotomy of *caritas* (desire for God) and *cupiditas* (desire for things in the world). The relationship between caritas and cupiditas in an individual soul is both cosmic in the sense of being an objective feature of that soul, knowable by God, and psychological, in that any soul possesses its own moral and spiritual nature.

This psychological and cosmological theory of erotic energy became the main script for medieval thinking about love. Faith and lust flow from the same source; it is the same energy that we employ when we turn towards the world and when we turn away from it. The dichotomy and unity of earthbound, material desire and spirituality is a powerful structuring concept that is able to map psychological tensions in the desiring subject as well as ideological oppositions between materialist cynicism and spiritual idealism. We find it in the tension between the first and the second part of the *Roman de la rose*, written by an idealist and a kind of 'social realist' *avant la lettre*. We find it in the contrast between the ribald tales of the *Decameron* and Dante's allegory of Beatrice, the woman that he loved, who died, and who from the underworld guides him towards spiritual and philosophical knowledge.

Now medieval convention would have it that a man or a woman is desirable by virtue of traits that all would recognise: youth, beauty, nobility, prowess, elegance. In Boccaccio desirability is so much a premise that his stories are not about who desires whom. The question that his stories explore is rather how sexual desire, which is dormant everywhere in society, in all human relations, and in all human beings, can come to expression and fruition against the obstacles of moral convention. By contrast, a number of other medieval writers are concerned with the intrinsic psychological complexity of amorous thoughts and feelings. For Dante, Chrétien de Troyes and the author of the *Nibelungen*, the thoughts and feelings accompanying sexual desire are the locus of love in so far as love is more and other than lust.

The richness and independence of the inner life, in relation to what is rational and what is socially justifiable, give love a scope of expansion that extends far beyond the categories of sin/virtue and reason/passion. The reason for this is twofold. The sentiments of love are articulated within relations of *power*, and love engages the *mind* of the subject across the complete range of its activities, including perception, imagination and intellect.

In *Cligés* by Chrétien de Troyes, the flow and concatenation of events, objects, clothes and personality traits constitutes one coherent movement, yet the story is far from being couched in merely material relationships of sex and power. It is richly layered with amorous and moral nuances. For Chrétien in *Cligés* the relationality of love is psychologically explicit and reciprocal. However, the two lovers are initially in doubt about the other's feelings and thoughts, but *in this very doubt they are equal* and exist for one another in the space of the text. They are thus presented as lovers existing in a realm of pure love, of amorous feeling, desire and thought, and this space is at one remove from the politics of local courts that Chrétien analyses elsewhere in the same text. Chrétien presents an amorous and courtly conception of love as a *noble* pursuit. Love is for him both a relation and a complex psychological experience, involving a range of feelings, thoughts and acts of language. Once desire has been ignited, love is depicted as a sentimental yearning for reciprocity, and then as a reciprocal relation of feeling and desire. The reciprocity of desire is presented to the 'reader' (listener) before it is actualised as reciprocity in the narrated story. We learn of the feelings that each lover has before they discover that their feelings are reciprocated. In the description of her infatuation for him we begin with a conventional conception of eros as a force that gradually takes over body and mind, but then the text moves into a more psychological register.

> My strength must indeed have failed, and little should I esteem myself, if I cannot control my eyes and make them turn their glance elsewhere. Thus, I shall be able to baffle Love in his efforts to get control of me. The heart feels no pain when the eye does not see; so, if I do not look at him, no harm will come to me. He addresses me no request or prayer, as he would do were he in love with me. And since he neither loves nor esteems me, shall I love him without return? (Chrétien, 53)

The notion of being constrained to love in spite of oneself implies a complex mental state involving an implicit battle of the self with itself, a battle between rational will and desire. In this state, the narrator is given over to worried and sceptical thoughts about her feelings for him. Amorous feeling is here rendered in the psychological mode of intellectual reasoning. If he had loved me he would have behaved differently towards me. Since therefore he does not love me should I still love him? In *Cligés*, we are shown how both lovers entertain such thoughts about each other before their relationship is sealed. Their love is reciprocal before their desires are reciprocated. It is reciprocal even in the lovers' solitude, because love is here more and other than a mere physical force.

The *Nibelungen* present a different picture. Here erotic relationships are immediately, thoroughly and irreversibly political. There is no such thing as a sentiment that is separable from social status, power, intrigue, and clan politics. The love that Kriemhild has in her heart (*minne*) is intentional; it is love of a particular man, a particular, loveable hero and half-godly nobleman, Siegfried. The man she loves does not so straightforwardly or transparently reciprocate her feelings. Neither the 'listener' nor she is able to forget that Siegfried is a half-god, that he is, therefore, a supremely powerful man endowed with exceptional physical force and magical powers, that he is therefore the justified object of *universal admiration*. Siegfried is thus at one remove from Kriemhild and that is the source of the plot of the *Nibelungen*, but this remove is not itself amorous. Yet there is a sense in which *Nibelungen* is a deeper statement not only about love but about the power of love than the idealistic 'romantic' novel of Chrétien. Love in the *Nibelungen* is an articulation of desire, reciprocity and power with deep-seated ethical claims on the other person, claims on his honesty, his willingness to give himself up wholeheartedly to the beloved, and thus not only desire her and feel for her but be loyal to her – in every respect. The claim on behalf of love in the *Nibelungen* concerns the ethical bond that durable, socially recognised sexual relations are supposed to entail. In the *Nibelungen* love becomes real, is realised as a concrete union rather than as a subjective feeling or longing, in circumstances that are so intricately political that no amorous sentiment can be seen to be autonomous or self-sustaining in relation to these surrounding political circumstances. This is so even if *minne* in itself, at least in Kriemhild's love for Siegfried, has a purely psychological origin.

The complex mythical-political intrigues that form the plot of the *Nibelungen* situate one woman, Kriemhild, in a situation of doubt. She has the notion that she has been deceived by her friend Hagen, who has in fact killed her man, Siegfried. This murder follows from a social rivalry with Brunhilde, and this rivalry is itself caused by amorous betrayal. Brunhilde, who is a warrior, married Gunther on the premise that he had conquered her in battle and in bed – but in fact it was Siegfried, masked as Gunther, who conquered her in both instances. According to the official social hierarchy, Siegfried is Gunther's vassal and Gunther is the king, but Brunhilde suspects this to be, somehow, untrue. Tormented by her suspicions, she courts strife with her rival Kriemhild, who reveals the truth to her and in so doing humiliates her in public. Following their acrimonious dispute, Hagen then kills Siegfried with the purpose of securing peace. Kriemhild plots revenge and after a certain time has passed manages to orchestrate a catastrophe in which all the major characters of the story are extinguished.

As a love story, the *Nibelungen* is highly ambivalent. On the one hand, this is a hymn to the power of love. If Kriemhild had not been overwhelmed by grief at the death of her man, she would not have embarked on a course of action that was to unleash the total destruction that takes place at the conclusion of the story. On the other hand, love is always already political in this exceedingly violent world of clan warfare. Within the history of love the *Nibelungen* is a liminal text that shows the extreme point of political ambition that can be claimed on love's behalf.

Dante's *Vita Nova* presents a different end of the spectrum in medieval thinking about love. This text is remarkable for the rich conceptual register that Dante uses to describe the mind's shifting states and thoughts. Following the conventional medieval conception of love as an affection of the soul, Dante describes these thoughts, by extension, as intellectual affections. Dante the rationalist stages a psychological scenario of introspection in which he accompanies the amorous mind over a long period of time, itemising and analysing not just the *affects* of this mind but also, and especially, its activities of reasoning and deliberation. Love's intelligibility is not, as it might be in modern culture, inscribed in the interpretability of the lover's gestures, but presents itself to a neutral, godlike observer as a process that the soul passes through. In *Vita Nova* Dante figures both as character and as narrator. He recounts his amorous experience and in so doing dwells, in particular, upon the thoughts that erotic love gave rise to. 'I was often distressed when memory stirred my imagination to consider the effect which Love was having on me' (XVI, 3). He initially presents the effect of love in negative terms: 'From that vision onwards my natural spirit began to be impeded in its functioning, for my soul was wholly given to thoughts of the most gracious person' (IV). A more specific and concrete impact of love on the mind is that it propels the intellect to entertain conflicting thoughts, stopping it from reaching definite conclusions or finding definitive answers to its questions: 'After the vision which I have described [...] a number of conflicting thoughts began to contend and strive one with the other, all of them, it seemed, unanswerably' (XIII). All he can say is that thoughts of love are about the beloved: 'I cannot comprehend the place to which my thought takes me ... I understand this at least that this thought of mine is entirely concerned with my Lady' (XLI). For Dante in *Vita Nova*, love imposes a particular temporal form on the subject's psyche and thought processes. He finds that love mobilises all his intellectual capacities. The rapid succession of these acts and states of his mind is not reducible simply to their content. It is not this or that feeling that is significant. Rather, the fact that they succeed each other and are in conflict with one another is what defines the love experience. This discontinuity makes love a teacher, but in a negative sense. Love induces us to let go of our belief in the intelligibility of our inner life. This is not, on the other hand, just a matter of a single passion whose sheer strength would carry us away. Rather it is the diversity, the inconstancy and inventiveness of amorous thought that overpowers and tests the subject – even as it seeks to demonstrate complete lucidity in its own account of that amorous thought. In Dante, a negative epistemological claim is thus made on love's behalf. Love has a formidable power to solicit our mind even in its most rational capacities, but to do so in a way that is not at all rational. This thought may appear overly familiar to us, as we find it for instance in Proust's *Recherche*, where it is developed at great length in the context of sexual jealousy – and we saw an example of this earlier. Dante, in his terse and subtle language, expresses this thought with an even greater phenomenological sense of nuance than Proust. When we read *Vita Nova*, we realise that being in the grip of a passion is not like being subjected to a powerful force, or moving in one's psyche as on a stormy sea – to quote a conventional metaphor. The challenge to reason and tranquillity that love brings in its wake is much more pervasive, insidious and hard to grasp than any such metaphor would be able to capture.

Judgement and Classification

In the domain of love, French classical (i.e. late seventeenth-century) culture is one of the rare moments in the history of humanity in which the normally tacit norms of courtship become the object of philosophical reflection.

In this cultural moment, love is for perhaps the first and only time in Western history elevated to the status of a philosophical object in its own right and not treated as a gateway to theology (the medieval view) or an appendix to social morality (the modern view). It was only within classical French culture that it was possible to achieve this, and one reason for that accomplishment is a particular genre of prose practised by French aristocratic philosophers and writers.

The scholar Marc Fumarolli has coined the phrase 'diplomacy of the mind and wit' – 'diplomatie de l'esprit' – to describe the prose rhetoric of these writers. The French word *esprit* means both wit and mind. If mind and wit are closely related, this means both that wit is a social exercise of thought, a means to provoke the mind into new feats of thinking, and, inversely, that mere thinking without the test of conversation and the challenge posed by other quick-minded interlocutors is like a wheel spinning alone; it is thinking in a void. Writing is then an imitation or continuation of conversation, whether in the form of aphorisms, letters or conversations recorded in a novel. Such a conception of intelligence and social life is ideally suited to grasping the fluid and manifold depictions of love in the writers of the period. Madeleine de Scudéry, Le Marquis de La Rochefoucauld, Mme de Lafayette and Mme de Sévigné were thinkers who were also accomplished writers, and in the case of the latter three they were also connected to each other in friendship.

The classical view on love presupposes, then, a social concept of thought that the notion of diplomacy of spirit suggests. Its focus lies in the intimate relationship between the lovers and a person who observes their gestures and interprets their motives. Infatuation is at the basis of an erotic relation, but the main significance of sexual desire is not that it has causal power *but that it differentiates between objects of desire within the perceiving erotic subject*. Men and women do not indiscriminately desire all men and women who can or could be defined, socially or by nature, as desirable. This is a difference to the conception of objective desirability that we saw was a common thought in medieval literature. A further focus of analysis in this paradigm is *gesture* and its meaning. Gesture must here be taken both in a wide and in a narrow sense. All the words, movements and social acts by which a friend, husband or admirer may testify to his or her intentions and to the nature of his or her desire are *social objects of judgement*. Anyone present can observe, remember and comment upon these gestures and their meaning. The only person who is not well placed to do so is the author of the gesture – unless that person has trained herself or himself in social behaviour to the extent of being thoroughly aware of how his or her acts are perceived by others. In this late seventeenth-century French culture, love is cultural in a dual sense. First, love is a kind of behaviour that falls within a cultural space in which it can be evaluated. Second, as it manifests itself within this cultural space, love is conceived according to its being *in cultural terms*. In other words, according to the language of phenomenology, love is *constituted* as a cultural phenomenon. To say that love is a cultural phenomenon means that it is not merely a sexual, social, moral or emotional phenomenon. Within this classical paradigm, love contains elements from all these categories. The attraction may be erotic, the experience emotional, the gesture social and the choice moral, but the essence of love is something other than these constituent components, in the accounts given by these writers. When love is determined and categorised as a cultural phenomenon, this means not simply that it is possible to make judgements about it, but rather that making judgements is the activity that love calls for.

Love is a being that is cultural to the extent that it invites and even requires judgement by a third party, who may or may not be personally interested in the duration or interruption of the love relationship. About a sermon, a musical performance, a person's dress or manner of entering a room one can have opinions, one can make a judgement. Love is for these writers a phenomenon on a par with other such cultural facts of behaviour and performativity. There is a further philosophical implication of this culturalist view. When love is determined and classified as an object of judgement it is at the same time acknowledged as transcategorial. It goes without saying that the term and concept of culture is anachronistic here, as it arises only a century later, but it is presupposed by the way in which these writers discuss love.

The cultural thought space of love established by classical French culture is paradoxical. Amorous behaviour, feeling, gesture and activity are analysed with precision and nuance. Yet the phenomenon itself is maintained in a kind of *indeterminacy*. The feelings and the acts are not vague, but the discourse on love that classical French culture produces is rarely explanatory. It is not, in other words, concerned with causes. Nor is the judgment that one can make of amorous behaviour simply an application of social and moral norms. In their cultural and non-causal conception of love, these thinkers were closer to grasping the ontological nature of love than any philosophers before or since, and any philosophy of love – as was the case with Stendhal's modern theory of amorous passion – must follow in their footsteps. My concern in this book is to reformulate the French classical writers' insight that love is a phenomenon that takes place in the world and to do so within the conventional philosophical terms of metaphysics and ontology. But let us return to the classical French discourse on love.

There may be many complex and specific rules that a spouse needs to conform to in relation to her husband or his wife – not to be physically remote, not to be unfaithful, and so on – but many of the things that one can do wrong would be so also in relation to a third party, that is, as the infringement of a commonly endorsed norm. It is wrong for instance of the Princesse de Clèves to refuse to go to parties where she is afraid of meeting the man she has involuntary fallen in love with. This is wrong, according to her husband, who does not know her reason for refusing to attend parties, because it angers him, and it angers him because it makes him look weak in the eyes of others to appear in society without his wife. It is thus not so clear what comes first: the obligations that arise within the marital relation or those that arise from rules of social behaviour particular to a certain social class. Rules governing marriage are social rather than amorous, whereas the realm of amorous feeling and behaviour is thought about within a register that is at one remove from the mere application of social norms.

Mme de Sévigné spends much of her many letters to her daughter describing her states of mind. In these letters she says very accurately what her own obligations are, what causes her pain, what causes her pleasure and what she admires. In the universe of these letters, many different things are worthy of attention. They all concern the writing subject that is Mme de Sévigné, but they form an open-ended non-hierarchical list in which family matters, friendship, gossip, affairs of state, literature, religion, introspection and moral exhortation alternate and compete for space. Mme de Sévigné writes little on the subject of love but reveals much about a manner of thinking that she shares with her friends Mme de Lafayette and La Rochefoucauld.

According to the classical French conception of amorous feeling and erotic behaviour, love is a social and not a personal phenomenon, in so far as the lover has to live his or her feelings, acts and desires in a world shared with others. And in this shared social space the acts that the lover performs in order to seduce, to please, to maintain a relation, to abstain, to conquer or to enter into an emotional intimacy – all such acts are available to public scrutiny. They fall within the public domain. The feelings of the lover are, we might assume, private. Mme de Sévigné would disagree. In a letter to her daughter she writes about her son's sexual infatuation with an actress, entering into some physical detail. She cannot generally be accused of prudishness. Her judgements and opinions are generally far reaching, specific and self-assured, she has no qualms about criticising the behaviour of her friends, as she is never afraid to criticise behaviour that she finds worthy of criticism, and her scorn is often bigoted. Certainly she criticises her son's infatuation. She criticises it precisely *because it is an infatuation*, an obsession that seems to distract him. But there is nothing about erotic activity that *in itself* would be shameful and hence constrained to remain hidden and private.

In a more philosophical vein, Madeleine de Scudéry presents an idealistic and ethical perspective on amorous behaviour and feeling. In her salon and in her novel *Clélie*, with its famous allegorical painting *La carte du tendre*, a map of amorous sentiment, Madeleine de Scudéry promotes an ideal of friendship that is tender to the point of resembling very closely an erotic relationship, but which is not sexual and thus maintains the distance that usually – in Aristotle and Montaigne – is thought characteristic of friendship. She uses the notion of tenderness, 'tendresse', to identify an affectionate disposition that can exist in friendship but which does not include sex. The word *tendresse* in French has a range of meanings. In the domain of love relationships, it designates a particular shade of sentimental love, which is complementary to sex and chiefly consists in a concern to be pleasant to the beloved. On the other hand, Scudéry defines tender friendship as a category that is sharply distinct from erotic love, but she also considers how the virtue of tenderness can be applied to erotic love. In Scudéry's novel *Clélie, histoire romaine*, Clélie ends her praise of tender friendship by saying: 'there is such a significant difference between a tender friend and an ordinary friend, that there scarcely is one bigger between a tender friend and a lover'. As the conversation continues, another character, Aronce, retorts that the virtue of tenderness is even more necessary to love than to friendship, since it hedges in the potentially limitless force of sexual desire and adds to the selfish pursuit of pleasure a concern for the well-being of the other.

> In fact, love without tenderness knows only impetuous desires without limits nor restraint; and the lover who harbours such a passion in his soul only considers his own satisfaction and does not consider the glory of the loved one; for one of the main effects of genuine tenderness is that it makes one think much more about the interest of the beloved than about one's own. (Scudéry, 76)

Scudéry's ethics of love seeks to civilise the brute force of desire and distil from love and friendly affection a range of moral virtues. This is thus a reflection upon love and amorous sentiment that is highly discriminating when it comes to analysing both the motives of the lovers and the nature of their union. In *La Princesse de Clèves*, Mme de Lafayette presents a psychological and philosophical reflection on love in this spirit of discrimination. The novel dwells on the shades, kinds and degrees of attractiveness of the characters at the French royal court of a century before. At court, there are so many young and beautiful women of noble birth and so many handsome and powerful men that the amorous gaze becomes highly discriminating. It may be that the ideal lovers desire each other for reasons that are universally recognisable, that is, that each is desirable also in the eyes of many others. But whereas a medieval author of romances would be content to enumerate superlatives, the language of praise receives a different inflection in Madame de Lafayette's text. It becomes reflexive, as it is the language with which the narrator reflects on human difference and it is the language with which the characters reflect on their own motives and those of others. *La Princesse de Clèves* is further a study in amorous behaviour, and it goes into great detail in the study of how gestures reveal thoughts, and how they can be interpreted by an observer who comes to know the person producing the gesture better than he or she knows him or herself. The heroine, who was married young to a man who she esteems but does not love passionately, subsequently falls in love with a handsome nobleman, a certain Duc de Nemours. She does not admit to herself that she has these inappropriate feelings. Her mother, however, carrying the title of Mme de Chartres, is a vigilant observer of her daughter. Hence, she discovers her daughter's infatuation before she does. Let us look at three passages from the novel that concern the development of the Princess's feelings towards Nemours and her mother's scrutiny of her feelings and behaviour. At the threshold of the love story that unfolds between Nemours and the Princesse de Cleves, Mme de Chartres is convinced that her daughter, only recently married to the Prince de Clèves, remains chaste of heart, that is, protected from violent emotion and amorous sentiment.

> Madame de Chartres marvelled at her daughter's great frankness, and with good reason, for it was unmatched in its spontaneity. But she marvelled no less that her heart should remain untouched, especially as she saw clearly enough [*voyait bien*] that the Prince of Clèves had touched it no more than her other suitors. (Madame de Lafayette, 21)

Love in Motion

The mother sees clearly (*voyait bien*) that her daughter's heart has not at that point been captured by erotic desires or deep amorous feelings for a man exceeding the pleasure of being courted or the friendly esteem that a wife may have for her husband and that social convention requires. As M. de Nemours falls in love with her and begins to court her, without nevertheless declaring his love, the narrator comments that his desire and sentiments (*inclination violente*) find expression in a particular gaiety and tender attentiveness that is produced by the wish to appear attractive:

> It is true, too, that the violent inclination M. de Nemours felt for her gave him the engaging, amusing manner [*cette douceur et cet enjouement*] that flows from the first impulse to please the beloved; he was thus even more charming than usual. (Madame de Lafayette, 25)

Just as Mme de Chartres is fully able to judge that her daughter has not yet experienced erotic love, so the love felt by M. de Nemours is clearly evident to her in his vivid charm, his gallant behaviour and the intensity of his presence. When his desire is reciprocated, the Princesse de Clèves departs from her usual openness towards her mother, and does not reveal to her the discovery that Nemours loves her, nor the nature of her own feelings towards him. Her mother, nevertheless, sees only too well the love that is growing between this man and her daughter:

> She found herself to be less disposed to tell her mother what she thought about the Duc de Nemour's feelings than to speak to her of the other men who were in love with her; without deliberately intending to hide anything, she said nothing about it. But it was all too evident to Mme de Chartres, as was her daughter's liking of him. (Madame de Lafayette, 32)

This literary psychology of characters reading the minds of other characters has an important philosophical implication: it is normally assumed in philosophy that self-knowledge is not relational. But in the realm of love, Mme de Lafayette shows that we may have to assume that self-knowledge is indeed relational, in that the amorous subject is a subject that produces knowledge about itself in a social space, a knowledge that can be enjoyed by another, but that only at a later stage, if at all, becomes accessible to the subject itself. According to La Rochefoucauld human beings are driven by an effort to mould a favourable image of themselves. La Rochefoucauld distinguishes between three levels of social self-love, that is, the interest one takes in the image that one produces of oneself in others: pride (*orgeuil*), vanity (*vanité*) and prickliness (*amour-propre*). One's pride is invested in status. Out of vanity one pursues new goals. One's prickliness is solicited in any social encounter. It is not hard to imagine how seduction – considered as a field of competition where a woman can prove her beauty and charm and a man his virility and attractiveness – provides a rich ground for the development of social self-love. La Rochefoucauld thus does not describe what in contemporary English is colloquially described as 'true love', the idea of an innocent, unselfish reciprocity. His maxims on love are characteristic of the behavioural approach that he shares with Mme de Lafayette and Mme de Sévigné. What is most interesting about La Rochefoucauld's analysis is not his cynicism and humour, but the subtle way in which he portrays the amorous self as a social self, a self that becomes what and who it is within a social space. This is not because La Rochefoucauld would attach particular importance to social things, but because the philosophical problem of vanity entails a distinction between how a person sees him or herself and how that person demonstrates his or her thoughts and feelings in a social space: the assumption that the self is only fully actualised in what it shows through its behaviour and gestures and that the perspective of vanity that we all have when we look at ourselves makes it impossible for us to gain an adequate self-understanding through introspection.

The classical French paradigm of love is parodied and reversed in the eighteenth-century novel *Les liaisons dangereuses*. If gestures reveal emotions and desires, if an observant and experienced subject of knowledge can know the inner stirrings of others better than they know themselves, this knowledge can be used to seduce, to corrupt, to destroy. In *Les liaisons dangereuses* the kind of foresight and insight that we find cultivated by the characters of *La Princesse de Clèves* is here pictured as an instrument of power. Cécile, a young, sensuous woman with a convent education, enters, unprepared, the world of social exchange. Her mother being a less insightful woman than the mother of the Princess of Clèves, Cécile is always intellectually without resources of analysis. She thus falls into the clutches of the scheming socialite Madame de Merteuil, who plans to use her as a pawn to take revenge on a certain Gercourt, whom Cécile is destined to marry. The revenge is simple: if Cécile is seduced and loses her virginity before the marriage, Gercourt will have lost some of his dignity. With the aid of her former lover Valmont Montreuil she carries out her plan brilliantly. The psychological theory that in the seventeenth century served to analyse love is now used to demonstrate the mechanics of seduction. Love enters the novel as a challenge to that psychological model. Merteuil and Valmont are able to analyse others and predict their behaviour, but their own latent love relationship is less transparent to them and comes to challenge their claim to rational supremacy. In the course of the novel they become entangled in a complex game of rivalry, which ultimately triggers their downfall. Love thus manifests itself in Laclos's novel at the exact point where the characters' explanatory resources break down as they apply them to themselves. In this novel, the central character Mme de Merteuil is portrayed as a paragon of self-observation and self-control. She is subject and object in one, self and society united in a prodigious thinking mechanism. In the classical paradigm it is thought to be a virtue to know oneself, to know one's vanities and the foolish things one is prone to do in order to be admired by others. This kind of self-knowledge is not thought to extend so far as to exclude spontaneity. For if one were to lack spontaneity one would be devoid of sentiment. In this later text, the enlightenment notion of autonomous thinking is introduced into the space of moral self-knowledge, producing an extreme figure of alienation, a person who by using herself, her gestures, feelings and desires as tools to gain power, is more a machine than a human being. Love is that vestige of humanity that disturbs the smooth functioning of the machine, inducing Merteuil to pursue actions of rivalry with Valmont that prove self-destructive. Laclos thus presents a paradoxical and, we might say, dialectical defence of love as the reverse side of our material and mechanical nature.

To sum up, in classical French culture, love presents a distinct moral problem of subjectivity: how are we to bridge the gap that opens up between our social (actual) self and our appearance to ourselves in consciousness? This problem of amorous subjectivity is very different from the modern problems of autonomy and deliberate choice that are discussed in nineteenth- and twentieth-century culture. The social problem of vanity concerns the subject as it is very much at stake in its appearance before others and in its possible ignorance of how it then appears. Yet, my appearance is not subjective in the sense that it would be determined within a space of consciousness or remain secluded within an arena of self-control. The lack of self-control that vanity entails is also different from the lack of autonomy implied by the unconscious in Freud. For I may still say to myself that my unconscious is, after all, me. I may not be able to catch up with it and make clear to myself on the level of consciousness what it is that I actually want, but as long as my wishes are presented to me and acted upon by the unconscious, my lack of knowledge is of little consequence. Vanity produces a lack of self-knowledge that is more threatening but also more interesting.

Classical French culture opens up to a worldliness of love precisely because it problematises the evidence on which the earlier Augustinian paradigm of eros as passionate desire depends. The world will be that arena where gesture and action and hence relations, future and actual, are evaluated, judged and interpreted.

The world is then the counterpoint to an ego that is in excess of what the subject needs, an ego that plays itself out in the world, that exists for the world and in the world as it is made of vanity and pride, and hence depends on the admiration, desire and consent of others. Yet the ego exists entirely for itself: its essence is self-love, *amour-propre*. It was Stendhal who theorised, *post factum*, the classical insight that *amour-propre* cannot be *amour*, that it is an obstacle to love. He did so by opposing vanity and the pursuits of the ego to all-absorbing passion.

The Social Paradigm

When we enter the modern period of Romanticism, individualism, the rise of the bourgeoisie and industrialisation, the ancient and classical conceptions of love based on eros or judgement are left behind. The modern conception of love construes the intelligibility of love primarily in terms of the bourgeois family, conceived as a social locus of reproduction and emotion on the one hand and as an obstacle to erotic passion on the other. The family in modernity is ethically and logically a space in which the subject defines and *positions* itself: this is my freedom, this is my desire, this is my husband/wife, these are my duties. Love is always other-dependent within this social paradigm. The other on which I am dependent is also posited by me in a definite logical and moral space. I am not a positional subject if I am arbitrarily, or open-endedly, dependent on another who could abuse me, take my money, or constrain my freedom beyond the reasonable limits of morality and the law. When I position myself, I therefore by the same token position the other, within a *structured* space. The two main theorists of this modern articulation of love are Hegel and Freud. They theorise marriage as a social form that imposes an ideal and moral structure upon natural sexual desire. Thus Hegel prepares and Freud completes a picture of human erotic relationships which can be characterised as 'positional'. This picture consists in seeing *marriage* as a social form that moulds natural sexual desire into an intelligible and rational relation of reciprocity. Romanticism is a reaction to this marital schema. It consists in the claim that desire is radically subjective and remains resistant to discursive representation. Modern categorisations of love, that is, dominant conceptions of love during the last two centuries, exist in a tension between a marital and a Romantic, radically individualist conception of love.

There is nothing specifically modern in being concerned with the social implications of sex, reproduction and marriage. It may be that kinship alliances predate the formation of statehood, as Levi-Strauss says. Clan societies, caste-based societies and different social classes in modern society present different versions of this concern. What is, on the other hand, specifically modern is a conjunction of two ethical notions concerning love: 1) love is ennobling and presupposes individual freedom; and 2) love is defined, positively or negatively, in relation to the bourgeois institution of marriage. Romanticism as a cultural trend or as an ideology permeating our sense of selfhood consists in a set of principles and values: spontaneity, individuality, emotion, authenticity, freedom from social constraint. In Romantic ideology, these values are used in a self-referential, or better, self-celebratory, discourse of, and upon, *modernity*. According to this discourse, love is a privilege of the modern individual who has access to authentic emotions that he can act upon unconstrained by social rules. Romantic individualism is not simply opposed to family values. The original and radical thoughts of German Romantic writers were certainly in conflict with the familial discourse of Hegel. As a broad ideological trend in modern society, on the other hand, Romantic individualism easily enters a complex, and often murky, alchemy with a discourse about social identity that explicitly or implicitly presupposes the family as a locus of personal development. It is this modernism and its cult of personality that I seek to criticise and to oppose to a different notion of freedom, one that finds its way into the world grounded in the erotic relation.

The conception of love and of the subject of love that we find in Hegel and Freud is characterised by its *composite* nature. Positionality is in both Hegel and psychoanalysis the outcome of a very complex process. This process has many constitutive elements, as it is the passage of the human being from a natural or biological being to a fully integrated social and moral subject. Both Freud and Hegel think that love, and specifically marital love, is a privileged site and demonstration of such a social transformation and integration of the human animal, since love has a dual nature: it has sexual desire as its core and it manifests itself as a social relation among other social relations. The term 'positionality' is a concept that I introduce here as a device in order to highlight the similarities between the Oedipus complex and Hegel's philosophy of social relationships. I further use this concept to show, subsequently, the direct inscription of this social and rational view of love into the aesthetic fabric of classical film.

Rational Relations

Hegel comes to the problem of love at different stages of his development. In his early writings, the conceptual context of love is the relationship between erotic love, spiritual-moral love and social community. Love is here pictured as an alternative ideal to that of the Kantian subjective moral law. The word 'love' resonates both with contemporary Romantic, anti-enlightenment theories of man's emotional life and with the moral teachings of Christ. At a later stage, and from the starting point of social morality, Hegel arrives at a moral conception of marital love. Hegel is keen to eliminate from the norms governing marriage any merely subjective and *natural* criterion such as desire, inclination and pleasure. There is thus for him a marked difference between a sensual union based on mere physical desire and a moral union based on mutual *moral commitment*. The justification for this distinction and its importance is two-fold. First, a sexual union based on mutual inclination is not motivated by any rational considerations, since it is merely sensual. There is thus nothing to recommend the union in social and moral terms. The relation is not, so to speak, able to carry itself into social reality. From the point of view of society it thus barely exists. Second, a union based on mere inclination has no internal reason to endure. It may end as arbitrarily as it began. A legally contracted marriage on the other hand has every reason to last. Hegel would not however consider marriage a moral union if its being were constituted by a merely formal legal bond. Let us examine this in greater detail.

We can learn from the two commentators Franz Rosenzweig and Jacques Derrida that in Hegel's works, the intelligibility of love is granted through the intersecting categories that love is covered by. These categories are not static but apply to a process, a movement from nature to society, from desire to self-consciousness, and social identity. This process is intelligible to the extent that for Hegel the acquisition of morality and social identity entails participation in a social-spiritual sphere structured by collective, ethical and religious, notions. Nature is for Hegel a beginning and a given for thought. But nature does not present itself to us in and of itself as the key to our own self-understanding. Nature is a given for us as biological individuals. We are born as biological beings and we become social, moral, religious and political beings. In his commentary on love, family and desire in Hegel, *Glas*, Jacques Derrida demonstrates the structural importance of love in Hegel's philosophy, as love involves all the major categories of his thought: subjective spirit, ethics, religion, the law and, more generally, the relationship between feeling and reason and between nature and society. In the early twentieth century Franz Rosenzweig had pursued a similar path. His analysis of Hegel's early theological and political philosophy, including his philosophy of erotic love, shows Hegel in search of a stance that is spiritual without being Romantic. In his comments on an early Hegel fragment on erotic love, Rosenzweig demonstrates how Hegel from the first instance is keen to translate the sexual basis of erotic love into ideal ethical categories. In the fragment that Rosenzweig discusses, Hegel depicts the relationship between erotic love and the life of spirit, that is, the sphere of ideal ethical objectivity. Rosenzweig says that he is 'hinting towards Plato in the ambiguity of expression between the sensual and the transcendent, yet, by contrast to Plato, he surreptitiously introduces a suprasensible meaning – not in the image of erotic longing – but in that of erotic union' (Rosenzweig, 76). This interpretation is certainly resonant with a general strand in Hegel's thinking, since for Hegel love is primarily categorised as a *relation*, not as a feeling or affect. Love is marriage and sexual consummation, not longing, inclination or subjective desire. Rosenzweig shows how the philosophical and legal conceptions of love, feeling, moral freedom, marriage and family that Hegel confronted as he developed his philosophy constituted a complex web of mutually exclusive positions that he sought to steer between. Thus, the basis of love should be neither feeling and spontaneity nor physical desire, nor should the moral value of love be evaluated according to formal rational criteria. Marriage should be seen neither as a union based on reciprocal inclination nor as a contractual relationship. Derrida argues that for Hegel, love in marriage is a bond of ethical-spiritual reciprocity that is manifest primarily in the minds and lives of the two spouses but which is at the same time hedged in by a legal framework. Marriage is a living morality only to the extent that the spouses freely, reciprocally and perpetually reaffirm their union – but within the parameters of the law.

The structure of Hegel's first mature work, *Phenomenology of the Spirit* from 1806, is determined by this development of moral spirituality and the possibility for the individual subject of living a fully unfolded ethical life. Within this prospect of an ideal ethical life, marriage – which he does not theorise in that text – could be seen to offer the subject an opportunity for moral and social self-determination with regard to its own inclinations and natural instincts. Within the structure of Hegelian ethics, as it is developed in *Phenomenology*, such an opportunity would be structured as *an intelligible position that the subject occupies in relation to its desire, in relation to a spouse and in relation to society*. The positionality of love would be the subject's self-determination in social and moral terms and its acquisition of a determinate identity in the realm of family and sexuality.

The acquisition and structure of such an intelligible relational position is grounded in Hegel's *Phenomenology* in a wider scenario of transition from nature to society. In *Phenomenology*, the model of an idealised individual subject going through human history is situated at a threshold between nature and social being. Having made the transition to social being, this subject enters a dynamic development that leads to the development of modern society in its full complexity. At the centre of this genetic process is a transition between two states of being that Hegel calls desire and self-consciousness. Desire is here an embryonic biological subject that is deprived both of self-consciousness and of the capacity to relate to other beings as equal to itself. Desire is incapable of seeing another desire as another desire, that is, as of the same kind as itself. This incapacity is for Hegel inscribed in desire's lack of self-reflection. Desire is a process of self-satisfaction that runs through cycles of repetition. Nourishment and reproduction follow the same pattern of 'consumption'. One does not eat only once; one's desires are not satisfied once and for all. The object of desire is therefore replaceable. It is destroyed in the case of nourishment. In the case of sex, which he does not directly discuss in this passage, the object is not destroyed, but desire is indifferent to it, as long as desire is not self-reflective. For subjectivity to emerge, desire has to become self-reflective and it has to be able to situate itself socially, to picture itself in relation to others that it can conceive as being like itself and not just as objects to be devoured or consumed.

The philosophically innovative dimension of Hegel's account consists in thinking of self-consciousness and social reciprocity as parallel and interdependent phenomena that come into being simultaneously. One can define these two dimensions of being, reflexivity and reciprocity, as two axes of *relationality*. The subject comes into existence as a social and self-conscious being when a consciousness is able to relate simultaneously to itself and to another, thereby disclosing to itself a logical space of determination and reflection. The subject thus constituted can reflect on its position with regard to another subject. We are the same to the extent that we are both subjects, but we are not the same to the extent that I am me and he is he.

The transition from desire to social self-consciousness illuminates in a prototypical fashion how the modern bourgeois subject sought to articulate the social nature of sexuality as a positional structure composed of a dual relationship between reciprocity and self-reflection. To be positional entails that one is consciously situating oneself in relation to another in terms of generally accepted social and moral norms, hence that one is self-conscious as well as part of a relation of normative reciprocity. Hegel was the first philosopher to emphatically stress that love is a relation and that it is a relation of a special kind, that is, a relation that cannot be reduced to feelings, contracts or social norms. He is therefore an important interlocutor and opponent in the present account. However, Hegel *misunderstands* the nature of the love relation in that he ascribes its binding power to an entirely subjective spirituality within each of the spouses, thereby intellectualising and rationalising the love relation and obliterating its natural, biological basis.

Love in Motion

Sexual Intentionality

If we now turn to Freud, we find that he arrives at a very similar structure of social *positionality*. Elaborating his theory from a materialist standpoint, Freud offers a conception of sexuality that reaches into the spheres of consciousness, social life, culture, art and religion. However, in contrast to Hegel, Freud does not seek to obliterate the sexual basis of love even as he seeks to show that the family as a moral and social institution is the proper place for sexuality. Thus whereas Hegel seeks to show how biological nature is transformed into social relationships, the relationship between the sexual and the social remains for Freud in an inevitable tension and a much more complex, less linear relationship than we saw in Hegel's account of social genetic processes. This complexity is rooted in the epistemology of psychoanalysis. Freud seeks to carve out a theoretical space for categories that neither are completely biological nor belong within self-consciousness. Against the background of this theoretical project Freud is able to categorise love in a way that encompasses its sexual and its social dimension. The non-reductive nature of the relationship between the material and the ideal in Freudian psychoanalysis is thus part of its appeal as a theoretical perspective on love. If all men are Oedipus we all relive an ancient myth. Yet, we do so while we undergo a purely material, sexual development. This development concerns the differentiation of the body's erogenous zones and our capacity to direct sexual energy towards objects other than our own body. Between mythical repetition and the development of sexual orientation, the family occupies a multifaceted role. Desire needs to become *familial*, that is, patriarchal and reproductive, in order for the sexual subject to escape the snares of its own endemic narcissism and hence to enter social normality. This configuration of problems is very similar to Hegel's conception of *recognition* as a trajectory that leads from nature to ethics and social relationships.

Family is in Freud the context of infantile and adolescent sexuality – as the case histories attest. The family is further a stock, or raw material, for the unconscious in its effort to develop, for sexual energy, a logical space in which to identify social characters. The etiology of individual illnesses leads Freud to construe a new concept of causal determination, a structural and temporal causality *situated between mind and body*. Hence the etiological cause is not purely material. It is not merely an organic cause. It is a cause that is embedded in, and stretched out over, the subject's individual life history. Still, this cause *behaves* in epistemological and medical terms as if it were an organic cause. It accounts for specific symptoms and provides a key for the cure of those symptoms; it is a cause that involves experience, unconscious thought processes, unconscious affects and unconscious fantasies. It is thus a cause that also resembles a self-conscious *subject*. Instead of the conscious subject being accountable for its own desires and decisions, it is in psychoanalysis a structural cause which is the primary agent in the psyche. This cause takes up material from conscious experience. It transforms this material within strings of thought and invests these thoughts with affect, sometimes even producing wish-fulfilment fantasies. Now, this powerful structural agency leaves the conscious subject (*Ich*) somewhat in a limbo. The conscious subject haplessly follows a logic of commonsense rationality. It aims to be consistent with itself, to act according to reasons rather than whims and to make emotions count within decisions only when the pressure of emotion can be formulated rationally. The unconscious structural agent by contrast obeys a much more powerful and effective logic of dynamic transformation, in which formal relations of contradiction and simultaneity are used to reorder experiential material. Hence the unconscious can maintain contradictory thoughts without conflict. It can pursue parallel tracks of affect and thought simultaneously. Thereby it can transform thoughts and affects and give them a masked expression of conscious behaviour, thus steering the conscious subject behind its back. This transformative agency operates against the background of the subject's psycho-history, its sexual and social development. This development is, initially, moulded by the infant's relationship to its parents. The Oedipus complex is the representation in the psyche of this relationship as it evolves over time. The theory of the Oedipus complex synthesises a theory of sexual *intentionality* and a theory of *narcissism*. Infant sexuality is not goal-oriented, not intentional. The infant's sexuality is coextensive with its skin; it is as Freud nicely says, polymorphously perverse, which is simply a way of saying that it is not intentional. Normal development moves from this polymorphous desire to genital heterosexuality, which is a kind of intentionality. The object of desire gradually becomes separated from the auto-erotic objects of primary sexuality and is then identified with a member of the opposite sex. The acts that form the aim of desire, the sexual activity in which desire finds release, become concentrated around genital sexuality, hence intercourse. The erogenous zones of the anus and the mouth that dominate infant sexuality are subordinated to the use of the genitals within intercourse. This reproductive model conceives intercourse as a microcosm of a goal-oriented, rational and socially well-defined subject.

Narcissism on the other hand is a necessary stage between childhood and adulthood in which sexual energy becomes invested in an *ideal ego* that is subsequently granted the task of censoring and controlling the rest of the psyche. Once this ideal ego is established, it enters into a dynamic, unconscious and conflictual relationship with sexual desire, a conflict that is summed up with the dichotomy of

Freud's canonical 'topic' model between *id* and *superego*. If the ideal ego becomes too dominant, the individual *does not manage to occupy a stable social position*. The subject then withdraws into its own world of desire. In order to fully complete the Oedipus complex it is not enough, therefore, to establish a genital heterosexual identity. This identity has to be anchored within a social and moral self, and this self is constituted and generated by a successful passage through narcissism and the construction, but also limitation, of an ideal ego. This moral and social self is as if held in place by its precarious relation to the id and the superego.

Positionality for Freud is then not, as it is for Hegel, based on a complete transformation of biological conditions into social structures, but on the channelling of sexual energy into a sexual subject that is simultaneously a social subject. This integrated subject is positional in that it is defined by its position within the family. It is the product of a successful negotiation of its own familial origins and it is able to occupy a reproductive role in a new family. It is further familial in that it leads a fragile existence at the border between the id and the superego.

We can perhaps best picture this Freudian subject through an analogy. The subject is like an anti-hero. A hero coincides with a specification. He is strong, courageous, lucky, virile, loyal, and so on. The anti-hero is defined by his failure to conform to any such set of predicates – he may conform to some, but not to a coherent list: he may be courageous but unlucky, or physically strong but whimsical. The Freudian subject positions itself in relation to an ideal set of predicates that at the same time it knows that it can never conform to, entirely. Its precarious relation to its own self-imposed moral norms is rooted in the tension between its genesis and subsequent sphere of existence. Its origin is sexual, but the life of the subject is spiritual and social. Working out its own role within a positional structure, covering up the discrepancies between its own desire and a prescribed social role, the subject establishes its own incomplete and unstable existence.

Romantic Desire

Romantic idealism defines love as a sexual passion that is at the same time individual in its direction, ennobling for the lover and manifest not primarily in sexual activity but in a wide range of feelings. The German Romantic writers Kleist and Schlegel think about love as the cultural and social ennoblement of natural sensuality. The prospect of finding within primary sensation, pleasure and desire, a germ of moral goodness is by no means discarded out of hand by these writers – as their study of Rousseau, pre-Romantic theological philosophers like Haman and, more remotely perhaps, Scottish empiricism would have presented them with the ethical possibility that virtue and moral goodness arise from our own innermost and most natural instincts. The German Romantics all shared, however, a Kantian assumption that ethics involves a dualistic relationship between nature and culture. They took different views on what this relationship was like – it could be educational, or simply one of antinomy – but they followed Kant in thinking that there could not simply be a continuum between the senses and moral sense. It might just be for instance, as Kleist speculated, that there is an *irresolvable* antinomy between the natural demands of our sensuous nature and the rational demands of practical reason as defined by Kant. In pointing to a gap within moral discourse as the locus of a radical sort of freedom, Kleist presented an alternative to both Kant and Hegel and their common belief in the ultimate intelligibility of man's moral destiny: for Kleist the subject's moral and metaphysical aspiration to achieve harmony between reason and sensuousness is doomed to fail and to remain a tragic aspiration. The German Romantics thus shared the philosophical and ethical assumption that moral and spiritual life is likely to be organised around opposing impulses and aspirations. They therefore also shared the view that moral thinking, and indeed moral individual life, is faced with the vital task of resolving or overcoming these tensions between opposing demands. While Kleist took a negative view on the possibility of overcoming such conflicts, thereby also postulating for our moral and erotic life a nature that is not fully accessible to moral reason, Schlegel experimented in his short novel *Lucinde* with a problematic rather than tragic resolution between the moral value of erotic desire and the moral claims arising from society. Kleist's story *The Marquise from O*, a Romantic tale written in limpid and concise language, describes with utmost clarity the social and moral intransparency of sexual desire. It thus points to a gap within moral and literary discourse. This gap is the place of desire. In a more tragic version of this scenario, the character Werther in Goethe's novel *The Sorrows of Young Werther* gradually becomes disaffected with the world as he fails to fit into the moral picture that he himself endorses and propagates. He falls out of the world that he projects as a moral ideal and has no other choice at the end of the novel than to commit suicide. A French version of the Werther story, Constant's *Adolphe*, is even more radical in its account of the subject's disaffection with the world. Living in the shadow of an austere father, the young Adolphe is unable to choose a path through life. Adolphe is an impressionable and volatile young man. He rashly seduces a married woman, slightly older than himself, and as she gives him her affection and her desire he is overwhelmed. He now loses his sense of orientation, and falls out of love – but he is equally unable to break off the relationship. After sharing a period of intense unhappiness they

Love in Motion

both die. In *Adolphe* the place of desire is a space of deliberation, but the thought process of the amorous subject entertains a destructively ambivalent relation to the social context in which he lives, and this context informs his deliberations at every point. He is unable to identify his purpose in life, his social position, his erotic choice or his feelings independently of social pressures, but he is equally unable to integrate his feelings and actions within the range of roles that society appears to make available to him. Caught in a no man's land of social dependency on and rejection by society, the subject nurtures only negative amorous feelings. Against this background, Barthes's *Fragments d'un discours amoureux* is a late Romantic text. It stages the lover's discourse as a radically first-person account of the affects and thoughts that befall the subject who is at the threshold of love, a subject who is not yet in a relationship but who is in love, anxiously in love, and hopes against better judgement to capture his beloved. Within this staging of the first-person discourse, intelligibility reaches a zero point. There is a continuity between Kleist, Constant and Barthes, between the gap in discourse and the radically first-person subject of enunciation: in different ways social and moral intelligibility are problematised. Love and desire emerge at the margin of discourse, at the limits of society and of intelligibility.

Romanticism defends the autonomy of desire, negatively, in relation to positionality, but by doing so it loses sight of desire's vocation to manifest itself in the world. Authors like Austen and Henry James are anti-romantic and positional. They insist on the social intelligibility of desire and transform the classical culture of open-ended judgement, or diplomacy of spirit, into a positional exercise. In their novels judgement is never disinterested. It is always propelled by social suspicion. The chief ground of suspicion and fear concerns money in the realm of prospective marriage, the disastrous possibility that an attractive woman or a handsome man from a good family *may not be what they seem*. They may harbour secrets that undermine their fortune, their moral virtue and their capacity to love disinterestedly. This potential scenario lends amorous judgement a quality of detective work in these novels.

American Cinema of Choice

This and the next chapter are devoted to classical narrative cinema of the 1940s and 1950s. This chapter examines examples from Hollywood filmmaking. The next chapter studies examples of French cinema. The reason for this focus on France and the US is that these countries were able, during this period, to establish their own style and canon of filmmaking. Both of these styles obey robust norms of narrative clarity. In both traditions entrenched principles of characterisation, style, plot structure and theme cut across genres and are shared by many directors. It is perhaps just this fusion of scope and uniformity which marks a tradition in art as classical.

Through an alternation of semiotic and ethical analysis, I show that classical cinema in France and in the US produced a compelling, yet stifling, perspective on love. This is a perspective that *couches love within rigid content categories in order to make it intelligible*. Love is rationalised as emotion, that is, it is made intelligible as a series of named psychological states with known causes. It is further made intelligible as moral choice. Love is presented within sharply defined moral alternatives in relation to clearly drawn characters. Love in classical cinema makes sense – and it makes sense on a stage of moral subjectivity. Even when characters seem lost and confused, the viewer is invited to understand the causes and moral significance of their confusion.

From a sociological point of view, it is plausible to think that when cinema became a middle-class art, cut off from its roots in vaudeville and the avant-garde, speech became prominent as a source of pleasure. It is a middle-class virtue to reason about all matters of life. Film in the classical period not only celebrated this virtue but flattered the audience in their own inclination to speak. The classical film presents characters that overtly invite interpretation. The pleasure of watching a classical film is only fully realised when, after leaving the cinema, you talk to your

Love in Motion

lover or your friend about the characters in the film.

The style of classical narrative cinema consists in an explicit integration of *mise en scène* and narrative, of character development and action, dialogue and sequence. The semiotic essence of this integrated form is, we might say, the film's *readability*. The film image, however elegant is the *mise en scène* and the editing rhythm, strives for readability. The film image is not merely a spectacle or an image to be looked at but an image that conveys meaning, an image to be read dramatically and sequentially. This presupposes that something in the image is intelligible, that is, 'makes sense'. We can distinguish between the sorts of contents that are thought to constitute meaning in film and the kinds of formal elements that are the main *bearers* of meaning, the centres of intelligibility.

Characteristic of the classic American love film is its moral focus. It is rarely social tension, eroticism, feeling or wit taken on its own that provides the source of drama and spectacle in these films, but an integration of desire, feeling and relationships within a moral 'space'. By 'moral space' I mean a cultural universe of judgement and intelligibility. In the classical American love film, characters, the events that happen to them and the words they say, or that are said of them, gravitate around a moral centre, which can be a *problem* or a *choice*. This moral centre assigns a certain meaning-bearing role to all the other elements in the film. The moral space of the film is the horizon of an implicit thought process that the characters go through – or will have gone through – in order to complete the actions of the story. This thought process is not external to the story, or to the spectacle, but is embedded into the very texture and fabric of the film, into its style and narrative progression. Classical Hollywood cinema depicts the relatively classless American society with strong social mobility as an arena of opportunity, but also as a reality in which moral certainties are problematised and the individual subject has the opportunity, as well as the burden, of defining his or her own moral map. The actual content of moral deliberation is often structured by dichotomies and informed by categories of purity and corruption, innocence and vice. Such moral categories allow the characters to compensate for their fleeting social identity with a strong moral identity. One of the main pleasures offered by the classical film is, as I suggested before, interpreting and speaking about the characters in a film. It is a pleasure which we can call 'deliberative'. As a viewer of these films one is coaxed into thinking about the characters, their motives, desires and choices, after the film is over. Hence, criticism of such films often takes the form of an interpretation of the film's characters and the moral universe in which they act.

The Aztecs, building on a millenarian tradition of theological thinking, devised a sophisticated symbolic topography of the correlation between the earth and the underworld, the world of the dead. In such a *thanatological* topography, location, movement and spatial relationships are heavily charged with meaning. Classical American cinema with its clear moral oppositions and explicit articulations of these themes within *mise en scène* possesses some of the hyperbolical intelligibility of this ancient mythical universe. In Capra's *It Happened One Night*, the story of mutual seduction between an enterprising journalist and a rich young girl is encapsulated in a scene endowed with a high topographical significance. The handsome young journalist played by Clark Gable is a man that many young women might find attractive and would be happy to sleep with. Owing to happenstance, he finds himself sharing a room with a pretty young girl from a higher social class. Moral decorum dictates that, obviously, they will enjoy the thrill of sleeping in the same room from the position of chaste propriety. Hyperbolically enacting this moral norm, Gable divides their space by hanging a sheet on a rope in the middle of the room. This gesture does not only exemplify the thematic structure of the film. One can see it as allegorical of classical American cinema in general: here we find visualised the *dichotomising gesture* that seems to inform all scriptwriters, directors and producers in Hollywood between the mid-1930s and the mid-1950s. The point of this comparison with Aztec theology is to emphasise that structures of content are inscribed directly into, are indeed immanent within, the visual structure of *mise en scène* in classical Hollywood films.

I shall discuss the French and the American classical love film both separately and together. Let us now stay with what they have in common. In spite of different visual and narrative styles, both traditions are classical. Films in this tradition are primarily narrative, and not for example poetic, conceptual, documentary or spectacular. The tone and more generally the visual style of the classical film, its use of light, rhythm, spatial composition and the relationship between speech and image do not simply *express* and extend the emotional semi-conscious realm of a narrative subject. Rather the subject, relativising its emotional attitudes and pretentions, often ironically so, offers itself to a critical interpretation.

Both comic self-referentiality and ironies of plot may serve to assert an objective gaze on the protagonists and their feelings. Hence film noir plots may often present ironies encapsulated in mirror constructions embedded in the *mise en scène*. In Sam Fuller's *Pickup on South Street* an erotically charged scene at the beginning of the film announces a game of mutual transactions. As a woman appears to seduce a man with her gaze he is in fact stealing her purse, but having won the content of her purse, he also loses his freedom, since he unwittingly comes into possession of secret material belonging to a spy ring. In this game of exchange, the characters strive to assert their own autonomy and carve out a space for their feelings against the odds of a plot in which they become the instruments of other characters' stratagems. In a different key, ironic objectification of a character's pretensions can take the form of a satire that relativises the hero's wishes and ridicules them by holding them up against social convention. Romantic comedies like Cukor's *Philadelphia Story*, for instance, alternate between a gentle mockery of the protagonist's romantic aspirations and a romantic empathy with those aspirations. In Fuller's film the acting style is naturalistic, while in Cukor's film it is staged and light-footed, but both styles of acting and narration situate the protagonists in an objective world larger than them, in which they are compelled to acknowledge themselves as objective points.

The classical film is anti-romantic in establishing a basic *continuum of intelligibility* between a first-person and a third-person point of view. When melodrama intrudes into the classical film and becomes dominant, the aesthetic equilibrium is tilted towards emotion and narrative subjectivity. Then the continuum of intelligibility is articulated in terms of, and in sympathy with, the narrative subject. In films that objectify the subject's emotions through dramatic or comic irony the continuum of intelligibility is momentarily threatened through a distancing perspective on the narrative subject and its pretensions. The classical balance is situated between these two modes of subjectification and objectification, between melodrama and irony. It is within this balance of the subjective and the objective point of view, in the continuum between the subject's self-perception and its perception of how it can be seen in the social world, that American classical cinema presents love.

Point of View in Casablanca

In *Casablanca*, Rick, the character played by Humphrey Bogart, is introduced first through the words of others. In the city of Casablanca everybody knows Rick and everybody meets at Rick's café and gambling hall. Visually we see, first, his signature on a cheque: 'Ok Rick', thus signifying not only his personal endorsement of the check but his power as owner of the Café to decide which cheques to accept, whether incoming or outgoing.

Then we see his hand, and finally we see the familiar Bogart face, composed, concentrated and with the trademark mixture of cynicism and sensitivity. The subsequent sequence presents itself as the filmic equivalent of a realist novel. We are shown a typical set of incidents characteristic of Rick's café and of Rick the man: a rich variety of foreign guests, all needing something, all in transit. Most hope to leave Casablanca for Lisbon and America, but they find themselves in different

American Cinema of Choice

financial situations. Some are foreigners making a living in Casablanca, such as a representative of the Deutsche Bank whom Rick denies entry into the gambling hall, while others belong to different categories of thieves, resistance fighters, black market merchants, and so on who make a trade thanks to the transit population. Others are refugees, hoping to leave; some of these are affluent, some are poor. Rick tolerates this diverse population and is aloof from their troubles. We are told he does not drink with customers. He is further the one who makes the final judgements about the customers: who to allow in, who should be sent home. An incident that marks the end of this introduction shows him sending home a young woman who, we are told, he spent the previous night with.

This characterisation is situational. Rick is what he is because of his café and the power he has in the café and through the café. The café gives him a certain reputation and social standing in the city of Casablanca. It is natural for him that his two main interlocutors are the owner of the rival café the Blue Parrot and the chief of the French police. Both men are immediately shown to be corrupt, the first because he runs a black market operation, the second because he takes bribes and profits from his position as a police chief to seduce young women. Rick is contrasted with both in a subtle way. He is shown to be less corrupt than the owner of the Blue Parrot, since he is not himself involved in black market trade. He is on the other hand markedly shown not to be an idealist, but to be politically neutral. Several times he says that he 'sticks his neck out for no-one'. His integrity thus seems to rely on his cynicism. The relation between Rick and the French police chief is neither one of opposition nor one of identity. They are clearly distinct physically, in terms of nationality and profession, but they are more than anything colleagues, fellow operators who could be allies, rivals or enemies depending on the situation.

When the famous resistance fighter Victor Lazlo, who is on a wanted list in Germany, enters the café, a new contrast is established, between Rick and Lazlo. The latter is tall and very well dressed – this is a little fantastical given that he is supposed to emerge from several months on the run from the Gestapo and the Nazi authorities. Lazlo is handsome in an idealised sort of way. He exudes strength and clarity of vision and clearly looks like a hero. Bogart is of course much shorter and he does not look like an ideal hero, nor does he look like a morally ideal person. His face is not simple but complex. It expresses twisted rather than clear motives. This entire characterisation of Rick is embedded in a voice-over and vignette-style description of the city Casablanca.

The city is likewise portrayed through a series of connected comic incidents which precedes the long sequence at Rick's which introduces Bogart. Rick is thus not the initial centre of the action. He is part of a place, in some sense the centre of that place, but given that this place is a corrupt and very complex city, to be at its centre does not correspond to a clear moral or pragmatic position. At the beginning of the story, Rick is portrayed as a survivor and an opportunist, a man who is clever at manoeuvring in an environment that is dangerous and presents competing claims on his commitments.

If we pause to look at the formal narrative characteristics of the sequence at Rick's that introduces Bogart, it is, as we saw, a sequence composed of many small scenes or, to put it differently, a series of small scenes enveloped within one large scene. Now, generally, one can define the narrative unity of a film scene either by location or by a discrete section of dialogue. Here the location stays the same through the whole sequence – since it takes place at Rick's – but there is a succession of short dialogues, with shifting and overlapping characters. The action that drives the plot, the crossing between the Bogart/Bergman love story and the story of Lazlo's attempt to flee from Casablanca arise gradually from this web of relations.

Yet in plot terms the main story is composed of discrete and clearly discernible blocks of action, allowing the film to combine the continuity of the Rick's Café scene with a melodramatic style of editing between scenes. In the course of the story, the Ingrid Bergman character undergoes an important personal development, and this development is shown as a series of clearly distinct attitudes: regretting her past with Rick, refusing Rick, loving Rick again.

The film in fact narrates two parallel and separate trajectories of choice, his choice and her choice. The love relation in the film consists in this reciprocity of a choice situation. They both love the other and they are both, simultaneously, faced with the choice of whether to live this love or not. Her choice is the main source of spectacle in the film. In the retreat of his apartment above the café, in the middle of the film, she breaks down, cries and through her tears confesses her feelings and declares her love for him. His decisive choice is not shown on screen. It takes place in the lapse of time between her declaration and the final scene on the airfield, where he chooses for both of them. His choice is the centre of articulation in the film. He undergoes a moral conversion from cynicism to heroism and self-sacrifice – and the preparedness to choose on behalf of his lover, thus sacrificing her desire for him in the name of a moral cause.

This is stylistically a very classical film. His conversion is thus neither dramatically explicit nor melodramatically expressive. His choice takes place off screen. His decision is declared in a moment that is dramatic within the story, but his own speech is restrained and economic. She is the emotional centre of the film. Not only an object of desire but also a subject of amorous agency, she is a full-blown subject of love – but her agency very quickly encounters real obstacles. She first has to overcome her hurt pride after Rick has insulted her. She then has to set aside her moral duties towards her husband. She is able to do this for the sake of the love she and Rick shared in the past, a love that she believes can become their common future. But on the airfield, in the end scene, as she is squeezed between her perfect husband and her interesting lover, a dramatic train of events brings her agency to a standstill. She is here the melodramatic heroine of a non-melodramatic film. She is the centre of an amorous articulation that mirrors, negatively, Rick's choice. In the symmetry of their choices they fully display the stakes of their situation. *Casablanca* is classical not least in this: the reciprocity of the love relation is not enacted and experienced by the lovers but is *only manifest for us*, the third-person observers who have the luxury of appreciating the moral stakes of their amorous dilemma. These two centres of choice also constitute two centres of intelligibility corresponding to two different kinds of film that *Casablanca* blends into one. The film is both a very masculine and witty film about war and exile and a very feminine film, a melodrama of tears and a story of unfulfilled desires.

Choosing Against the Odds

Howard Hawk's Chandler adaptation *The Big Sleep* is a noir with a playful atmosphere and an idealistic moral universe. Yet, the moral setting of the film is a universe of universal moral corruption. In *The Big Sleep*, Lauren Bacall plays Vivian, a morally corrupt member of a wealthy and equally corrupt family. She and her sister, as well as their ill and ageing father, have become dependent on criminals who blackmail them. The family is concerned, most of all, to avoid public scandal. But neither Vivian nor her sister or father are free to make independent decisions about their lives. The plot offers Vivian a solution to her problems in the form of the detective Marlowe, played by Bogart. Hiring him on false pretences and lying to him throughout most of the film, she is offered the pleasant experience of saving herself through her own mistakes, since the situation that she is involved in changes, partly owing to her actions, but not in the ways she initially intended. Love is suspended in the film in this space between intention and unintended consequences.

Vivian's attractiveness and strategies of seduction make Marlowe fall in love with her, and he ventures to save her from the criminals that she seems dependent on. She, in turn, gradually reciprocates his feelings, thereby gaining the moral strength required to step outside of the spell that she has been under and side with him rather than with the gangsters. She is saved, then, by love, that is, by her powers of seduction, by Marlowe's love for her, and by the strength she gains from loving him. These emotions and this bond develop out of and *in spite of* her effort throughout most of the film to mislead him. There is then an interesting moral complexity in this very idealistic film. Since she is not actually herself a gangster she is saved from the rigid morality governing the film noir universe. She is only *dependent* on criminals, not actively a criminal. Love in the film has its own morality separate from that of truth and falsity. Seduction works its ways through the games of manipulation that she has to play, or thinks that she has to play, in order to honour her obligations to the criminals that she depends upon. This moral complexity of love in the film is inflected by the melodramatic premise that her character can only develop through the intervention of an external agency. Love makes Vivian take sides, choose against her family, take a courageous decision. But this decision and this courage are already implicit in her union with Marlowe, since he represents the antidote to the moral corruption of her family.

In a Lonely Place by Nicholas Ray shows a different drama of choice. This is a melodrama of trust. It pushes to a paroxysm the moral tension between hope and hopelessness, between the moral stakes of a situation and the prospects of a happy outcome. The tone of the film is shrill, desperate, bordering on hysteria. This makes it very different from classic films like *The Woman on the Beach* or *Brief Encounter*, where the melodramatic mode is a set of narrative devices that allow the film to evoke powerful emotions within a clear moral setting. In the classical use of melodrama the operatic and excessive impulse is contained, limited to certain scenes of confession or dramatic climax, but not allowed to penetrate the texture and narrative content of the whole film. Ray's film is also different from films that employ the dramatic register of excess formally as a material for experiments in *mise en scène* – one may think of *Letter from an Unknown Woman* by Ophüls or *Macbeth* by Welles. The high-pitched tone of despair that is tangible in every scene of *In a Lonely Place* knows no irony, no distancing effects of formal brilliance, no concessions to social realism. The film is in a sense highly realistic, but its realism is purely psychological, not social or moral.

The story is taken from the world of Hollywood, thus a world that the director is familiar with, and also a world that is socially very different from other parts of American society. This is neither a glamorous Hollywood, seething with competitive energies, nor a seedy world of crime. It is a world in which abject, tragic failure coexists with glamour and success. This is true both of the place and of the individuals who live there. This proximity of success and failure creates a fertile breeding ground for the melodramatic morality of rapid and drastic reversals of fortune. By inscribing the dramatic trope of reversal into a world that is already saturated with surprising stories of failure turned into success, of success ending before it has begun, Ray changes a basic parameter within melodrama and the moral world it constructs. In this Hollywood world, where characters are both cynical and sentimental, prickly and hardened, surprises are no longer surprising.

A note of hysteria that spreads through the film is subtly modulated by a constant note of cynicism. In more conventional melodrama, there is always a background or a surrounding world of established normality, a normality that is economically modest or affluent, but in any case stable, morally and socially. The surprising events of the main narrative can gain their spectacular effect in part through this contrast, which, on the other hand, also provides the moral framework that gives meaning to these events. In this film the notions of success and failure are themselves flimsy and hard to grasp, as there are no very clear examples of either. The representatives of 'ordinary life' are prying, envious, meddling characters who poison the minds of the protagonists with 'sensible' advice.

The melodramatic love choice is here expressed in its purest form. The lovers believe that their love holds out the promise of a complete redemption from past sins. Yet this prospect is cast in an ambivalent light throughout the film. The film undermines its credibility by casting suspicion on the male protagonist and making it difficult for the audience to believe that love could change him. Yet in its tone, in its mode of high-pitched emotion, the film appears to sympathise with his point of view. Melodramatic choice in this film acquires an almost philosophical clarity of abstraction. The story concerns a woman's consideration of the question: is this man that I desire loveable? The answer to this question is presented in the film as a question of belief, a question of whether to believe what everyone says, what common sense dictates, or to believe against all odds, against what seems sensible, that desire is right and common sense has no power over it. A man and a woman fall in love, but the woman has reason to believe that the man is a morally weak and even dangerous man. He is a failed screenwriter and an alcoholic. He is known to have an explosive temper and has a criminal record of physically molesting people in public. To make things worse they meet in the context of a criminal investigation. The wardrobe clerk of a bar makes a late call on the main character, Steele, played by Humphrey Bogart, on the pretext of giving him the summary of a novel she has just finished reading – and which he is supposed to turn into a script. She is eager to stay, but he turns her out. A few hours later, he receives a visit from the police. The woman has been found dead, murdered, a

Love in Motion

few miles away. In the compound where he lives a woman living in a flat opposite his has seen him stepping out on the balcony late at night. Her testimony to the police is in his favour.

Following this forensic encounter they very quickly begin a relation. The scene where they kiss, or rather where he kisses her, is a masterful expressionistic condensation of the whole film. He approaches her with an intense and desperate stare, looking like the vampire Nosferatu in Murnau's film. His body casts a long shadow on the wall and his hands possessively take possession of her face, as if to strangle or suck out her life force. This is indeed his desire: that the young and beautiful woman, who happens also to be in the film business as an actress, will give him back his force to live and enable him to write. Initially this hope is fulfilled; but the criminal investigation intensifies and his old friend, who is now in the police homicide department, plays an ambivalent game with him, appearing to be his friend yet never completely believing in his innocence. Foolishly Steele goes along with this game, even accepting an invitation to dinner at the friend's house with his prying and nervous wife. He brings his new girlfriend with him. The two women later meet on their own and the policeman's wife confides in her what the husband has told her about Steele's past, that is, that he is a dangerous and volatile man. Throughout the film, Steele does everything to confirm this negative image that he knows people have of him. Under the pressures of suspicion and his own paranoia he becomes more and more irascible, at one point almost killing a man that he has an argument with while driving. Naturally, she becomes increasingly unsure herself whether to believe in him. In the criminal plot of the film, to believe in him means also to believe that he cannot possibly have committed the murder, but it is very difficult for her to protect herself against doubt, since there are three powerful reasons that lead her to be cautious: his past life, what other people say and his own behaviour that she has herself witnessed. She is tormented by doubt and this is again encapsulated in one powerful scene, a dream sequence where her mind, or one would like to say soul, is literally torn between two opposing forces.

Steele in his paranoid sensitivity immediately senses that she is slipping away from him and this makes him increasingly possessive – to the point where she only goes along, or appears to go along, with what he says because she fears that he will harm her physically. The melodramatic climax of the film occurs in the last scene: as he discovers that she has 'betrayed' him, that she is not in fact going to leave with him in order to get married but is planning to take a plane to New York on her own, he turns into a murderous monster and tries to kill her. At this moment she receives a call from the police, who have found the murderer and thus definitely cleared him of all suspicion. This phone call comes a few minutes too late, since his attempted attack has destroyed their relationship for good.

Love in the Underworld

The crime films that became known retrospectively as film noir offer a fertile ground for exploring love relations, erotic power and amorous obsessions. The shadowy world of middling criminals, which is the preferred environment of film noir stories, features erotic ambitions that do not have marriage as their inevitable or natural horizon. Here desire is not thereby adulterous, but is presented to the world independently of marital codes and expectations. It was possible for Hollywood cinema after the self-censoring Hays code of 1934 to explore erotic sentiment in a nuanced and sophisticated way in films like *Laura*, *Gilda*, *Out of the Past* and *Double Indemnity* by framing the moral freedom of sexual desire within strict temporal and legal constraints.

Rebelling against the gentle and pragmatic romanticism of Capra and Hawks, who portrayed love as a whimsical but not ultimately irrational or unmanly deviation from the ethical requirements of camaraderie and work, European noir directors like Charles Vidor, Billy Wilder, Otto Preminger and Jacques Tourneur emphasised the specificity and autonomy of erotic desire in relation to conscious wishes and moral demands. Like many other creative people working in Hollywood at this time, all of the above were European *émigrés*. Vidor was Hungarian, Wilder and Preminger were Austrian and Tourneur was French. In any case they do not contribute to the educational programme that forms the core of Capra's and Hawks's filmmaking. Their films do not teach us to become decent and considerate, to minimise our own pretentions and set limits to our sexual ambitions. These are films in which sexual energy, erotic desire and relations that have no other reason to exist than mutual attraction are celebrated in full awareness of the existential price that may be paid for such a freedom in a culture based on the austere and puritanical moral values of rationality and work. The noir genre allows these European Americans to stylise a clash between two kinds of freedom, the American freedom of work and incessant activity, and the self-destructive erotic freedom of desire pursued for its own sake, as an end in itself, answerable to no one and to nothing. Yet, these filmmakers also pay a price, as they have to punish desire two times over. They have to make sense of desire in the terms of a moral discourse, thus robbing it of its freedom to be merely itself, to be merely desire. Second, they have to show that the uncompromising egotism of sexual desire is incompatible with the ethics of communal values: thus it is not only crime that is punished, but the prospect of erotic claims that are not reducible to peaceful life in society.

Gilda is a story of pride and electrifying erotic tension. It is the story of a sado-masochistic relationship and the difficulty that two lovers have in affirming and publically asserting their love. Gilda is an attractive and sexually adventurous woman devoid of economic means and social privilege. She marries a charismatic and wealthy crook, a ruthless casino owner. His assistant turns out to be her former lover, and he was, as he tells her, picked up from the gutter by the very same casino owner. Their love is based on erotic attraction and a relationship of aggressive defiance and mutual humiliation. Their relationship is also shown as being overshadowed by economic and social necessities. In the course of the story, the two lovers gradually manage to carve out a space for their love in the world, but their efforts create a precarious situation. The triangular story with the casino owner is a foil that gives them time to test each other, and to conduct various experiments with each other's limits of self-respect. This dynamic of mutual testing is serial, infinitely repeatable and hence not conducive to a decision. In its structure of sexual ambivalence, *Gilda* presents choice as a counterpoint to moral choice films like *Casablanca*. In *Casablanca* choice is the *telos* of the story; here choice is constantly at stake and constantly staged in every situation, but it is also clear that the characters cannot translate their sexual tension into a choice that could be spelled out in a moral discourse. Yet even this quite un-American film about amoral desire is structured by clear psychological dichotomies that define the characters' relations to one another.

Double Indemnity features an unequal couple. Walter Neff (Fred MacMurray) is an insurance agent of limited experience and modest dreams. His lover, Phyllis Dietrichson (Barbara Stanwyck), on the other hand, is a murderess and a calculating mind untroubled by ordinary inhibitions. Neff embodies corruptible niceness, normality willingly led astray. Within the very small circuit of his insurance work, he can believe himself clever and a cut above the rest, but his sphere of action is limited, and almost entirely legal. She belongs to a different species and a different sphere of action. She obeys her own reason exclusively and disregards all legal, moral and sentimental scruples. It is thus not difficult for her to manipulate Neff so that he acts as her pawn. She feigns love for him so that he will kill her husband. When this is accomplished, she withdraws and takes a different lover. Enraged by jealousy, he arranges a meeting with her and kills her. At the moment of death she confesses that she is 'rotten to the core'.

Double Indemnity stages a relationship between normality, which constitutes the narrative perspective of the film, and a different world: alluring vice, something beyond the male and nerdish world of the insurance business. As a disciple of Lubitsch, Wilder privileges dialogue over psychological characterisation. Stanwyck performs a flamboyant sexuality and we know little else of her character. Choice is here not the outcome of deliberation as in *Casablanca*. It is nested within the protagonist's unconscious. Neff chooses unwittingly and unconsciously to get involved with Phyllis, immediately after their first meeting. We are shown how he drives back after seeing her the first time and we are told in a voice-over narration that he then didn't yet know what he had chosen, what he had got involved with. Choice is here internal to desire. She ignites a spark in him, not just by showing him her attractiveness but by flattering his ego. She makes him feel that he is powerful and seductive, that being an insurance salesman is a potent profession.

Laura depicts the parallel infatuation with an attractive and elusive woman on the part of two very different men. One is an effeminate aesthete and connoisseur of Oriental art. He is a socialite and a snob. The other is an 'ordinary guy' and a policeman, someone who likes to make people ill at ease by playing mini-baseball on a handset. The woman who is the object of these different, persistent and overpowering erotic desires is defined almost exclusively through the words of the men who covet her. We know little of her character and feelings apart from the fact that she is socially ambitious, beautiful, cautious and has good taste. This is a very *male* film about emotion. It depicts male obsession and desire but also a sort of male ignorance and bewilderment in the face of a female universe that both the aesthete and the policeman remain excluded from.

Choice is here depicted as the characters' effort to analyse their own beliefs. This is a story about trust. Laura trusts the aesthete but does not love him or desire him. The policeman has to suspect her within the crime plot of the film, but wants to trust her. Laura comes to trust him because he demonstrates his desire to believe in her. Thus underlying the film's lush and decadent atmosphere – the story takes place in wealthy homes full of expensive art objects – is a puritanical moral structure centred on the category of trust.

Out of the Past is perhaps the most erotic of these four films. It depicts an intense mutual infatuation between a young gangster and a woman adrift. The film creates a noir alternative to melodrama. The lovers do not at any point believe in love or happiness or conversion, but they act as if they did. They know that they exist and operate under adverse circumstances and so are not given the luxury of believing in pure sentiment or uncorrupted desire, but they do their best to assert the truth of their desire in the face of these circumstances. They do not succeed. She is emotionally and economically subservient to a powerful criminal played by Kirk Douglas. He is dependent on the moral purity of a nice young woman. He is able to overcome the pressures that this goodness elicits, but she is less capable of picturing herself as independent of her demonic benefactor.

All these films are structured around erotic choices and binary moral alternatives. In *Laura* this structure is rendered complex by the film's convoluted plot and narrative form. A section of the story concerns Laura's Pygmalion-esque transformation, at the hands of her protector, from an unknown journalist trainee, without connections, to the director of design at a magazine and a successful socialite. This story is told at a double remove from the main story. It is told in *flash-back* through the *voice-over* narration of the man who is the main object of suspicion in the film, the elderly dandy. The plot itself involves a disconcerting shift in narrative perspective. A woman is murdered in Laura's flat while she is out of town, and it is not immediately discovered that it is not Laura who has been killed. For a time the audience and everyone in the film wrongly believes that Laura has been murdered. When she suddenly reappears, this shakes the ontological status of the fictional universe of the film and disturbs the viewer's general sense of reality. Just before that moment, the policeman investigating the murder is seen obsessively rummaging in her belongings, spending an evening in her apartment, gazing up at her portrait on the wall. The dandy caustically remarks that the policeman seems to have fallen in love with a dead woman.

The conventional moral and social opposition between the rich and morally corrupt dandy and the wholesome policeman is not the arena of choice in the film. It provides moral intelligibility to the crime story but not to the field of erotic choice where both men love Laura, equally. The dramatic choice in the film is the policeman's decision to believe in Laura, to believe that she has not orchestrated her own death and thus to allow his judgement to be guided by his erotic desire. The film differs from other noir films in that this willingness to be steered by desire is compatible with social morality, since Laura is in fact shown to be innocent.

In *Gilda*, *Out of the Past* and *Double Indemnity* choice is situated in the relation between one man and one woman. The man has to choose to be with her or to betray her: in other words, to either escape or allow himself to be consumed by a destructive love. In these films, we rarely follow the woman's point of view. We are concerned with the man's erotic investment in his love for a *femme fatale*. Laura appears very much as a *femme fatale*. She is beautiful, young, capricious and a social climber. Yet for all the decadence that Preminger is able to evoke through his sets and the dandy's voice-over narration, this is not a film about universal moral corruption. Moral decay is seated exclusively with the character of the dandy. Other characters may be imperfect, but they are not perverse or decadent. This is why the policeman can remain true to his own moral beliefs while at the same time allowing his desire to guide his judgement concerning Laura.

In *Out of the Past*, both the plot structure and the mode of narration are heavily temporalised, as in *Double Indemnity*. The protagonist's choice between the good blonde and the bad dark girl is coterminous with past, present and future. In the past, there was the dark girl, but the present with the blonde girl is disrupted by the return of the past, which therefore reveals itself to have been pointing to a future, bleeding with unsettled possibilities in the form of incurred debts towards her benefactor. In *Out of the Past*, the *femme fatale* is not an abstract force available to puritan moral judgement. She is human and fragile, in pact with the demon that she cannot flee; she is not evil but weak – weak in not being able to quit this character. This is a structure in which morality is corroded by sexuality, where the energies of the psyche play themselves out on a plane very different from that of present-tense choices and judgements.

This does not point to a structure of repetition, as in *Gilda*, but to the presence of another temporal dimension within the present. Not the past but the inevitable continuation of the past within the present forms the temporal rhythm of this film. It is a rhythm that is permeated by a metaphysics of fate: what agency, what subject, what consciousness or choice could be mobilised against this presentness of the past? The consciousness of the protagonists is reduced to the function of witnessing their own lacking agency, their own subjection to debt and destructive desires. The male protagonist shows a stoic stubbornness in the face of his own fated desire. He displays a numb recalcitrance and cool rationality even as he embarks on the most irrational and self-destructive courses of action: courting the wife of a gangster who he works for, returning to work for that gangster after his betrayal has been discovered. This numbness protects him from impulsive actions but is not powerful enough to make him step out of his fate or provide him with distance from the circumstances in which he lives.

Double Indemnity presents erotic choice as a transgression and a poisoning of normality through sexual attraction. The film is told retrospectively through Neff's voice-over narration. He describes how he met the woman. We first see her dressed only in a towel and looking down on him from the top of a staircase. Their ensuing conversation shows him confident in his wit and clever repartee, and he openly makes advances to her, which she accepts. To fall in love with this woman comes to mean that he embarks on the self-destructive path of murdering her husband. It thus involves a series of moral choices. This can also only be known retrospectively. In the film's narration we are led to believe that all these choices can be summed up in one primary and impulsive choice, namely the choice on the part of Neff to allow himself to desire her and to fall in love with her. This choice however is made unconsciously, since he is not fully aware of the extent of his infatuation after their first meeting. *Laura* and *Double Indemnity* display a narrative structure in which the intelligibility of the plot, and of the erotic relationship, hinges on a superimposition of desire and choice within the mind of the protagonist. In *Laura* this identification comes out in favour of morality, since neither the policeman nor Laura is presented as a morally corrupt character. In *Double Indemnity*, it is the other way around, since Neff's semi-conscious infatuation is itself a corruption of his normal world. He is at the outset a not entirely sincere or honest man. Being in the insurance business, he is well acquainted with fraud, but his behaviour has always been on the side of law. He has only fantasised about fraud. Under the spell of his erotic infatuation he will cross the line and live out his fantasy.

French Cinema of Place

At the core of the classical Hollywood film is a claim to *moral intelligibility*. French classical love films also possess a moral core, but the structure of morality in classic French cinema is very different from that of American films. This morality is rarely dichotomic and almost never related to a significant *choice* that the characters have to make. Morality in French film is often embedded in a social world shown to be more or less corrupt. French cinema also displays a subtler and, most of all, less *verbal* eroticism than that of the classical American film. This eroticism is often sustained by characters and situations that are also defined purely in erotic terms, in terms, that is, of desire, rather than in the more psychological terms of 'emotion'. Many of the masterpieces of classical French film display desires that are not romantic or compatible with any kind of marital solution. For instance Melville and Cocteau's psychological study *La Chambre* from 1951 is the story of an incestuous relationship between brother and sister.

French classical cinema excels in developing narratives grounded in a closed diegetic space that provides something like a laboratory for the enlargement of the human psyche. The closed diegetic space circumscribes the action and dominates its meaning. Plot, action, conflict, resolution and human relations are fully developed within this closed diegetic space, but the dynamism of action is as if *arrested* and gains a static character, an *agitation* rather than an *action*. Through this agitation, layer upon layer is peeled off the main character or characters and we get to know them to the extent that they get to know themselves. They may face choices and undergo intense affective states but they are always tied to a place and to the people surrounding them, and they appear to be incapable of solving their life problems on a different stage. Classical French cinema is, one may say, anti-escapist: it is a cinematic narrative form in which characters are often bound to a place as to their fate.

Love in Motion

One often contrasts the spectacle and aesthetic innovation of Renoir and Clair in the 1930s to the sombre psychological narratives of Clouzot, Becker and Melville in the 1940s and 1950s. Yet the fatality of place is common to *La Bête humaine* (Renoir), *Le Jour se lève* and *Hotel du Nord* (Clair) and *Pépé le moco* (Duvivier) from the 1930s and great films from the late 1950s and early 1960s such as *Touchez pas au Grisbi* (Becker), *Ascenseur pour l'échafaud* (Malle) and *Léon Morin, prêtre* (Melville).

The semiotic dominance of character over plot in these films is served by this aesthetics of a closed diegetic space. Bound to their locations, characters in these films are inseparable from their region and class. The psychological analysis of the main character is therefore interwoven with a realist social characterisation. It is a shared assumption among classical French filmmakers that emotions cannot detach themselves from social condition. Morality is not explicit in the language of classic French cinema just as character psychology is not defined by the characters' actions. It is not what they *do* but what they *are* that matters. It is not emotional attitude such as pure pride or pure hypocrisy that is ascribed to the main characters but character traits that gradually gain in *nuance* as the characters become analysed and at times illuminated by the story.

The proud woman in *Leon Morin prêtre* does not exhibit her flaw in the extravagant manner of Bette Davis. It is not a pride that is easily detected *as* a flaw, although her physical appearance, her gestures and her behaviour signal a kind of strength that keeps her isolated from others. It is no doubt part of the sexual opinions of the time that this reclusive strength is associated in the story with her desire for another woman. The emotional austerity of her life is, however, as the film progresses, more and more inseparable from the severe material and moral conditions of life in a small provincial French town during the German occupation. She is not actively involved in the resistance – but that is where her sympathies lie. Her loneliness and her strength are displayed in tandem, through the story of her falling under the spell of a charismatic young priest who converts her to the Catholic faith of her childhood.

An erotic suspense arises between them and within the story through the sequence of their meetings. The outcome of this suspense seems less important than the moral and psychological development of the heroine. She is introverted, independent but at the same time dependent on her own resilience and resolve – and yet she keeps returning to the priest, who challenges and surprises her. This is a 'woman's film' in that male desire and intentionality are portrayed consistently from a woman's point of view. It is the story of a woman intrigued by a man whom she cannot classify. The erotic tension and exchange that take place between her and the priest in the course of the story are both intense and inconclusive. The two understand each other – but since he is a Catholic priest there is no social space of marriage available to them. There is no sense either of romance or of tragedy, of a positive or negative resolution. The psychological subtlety of the film resides in the build-up of intransparency between them. This is a late classical French film made by Melville, a director situated at the margins of the French production system. Let us now turn to one of the best films made by Continental, the German-French production company set up during the occupation.

The Immorality of Reason

Clouzot's *The Raven* (*Le Corbeau*) is a double portrait. It depicts a small town and a foreigner in the town, a young doctor, called Germain. The film is paced quite slowly. The tensions and themes that circulate within the story are presented one by one, as we follow Germain's daily life. Seen through his eyes, *The Raven* presents us with a detailed social analysis of the morals in a provincial French town under Vichy. The film's binding plot, revolving around a smear campaign, ties the moral destiny of Germain to the moral anatomy of this town. Hence the town and the man come to illuminate each other – even though they are by no means each other's mirror, since the man is and remains an outsider, but for this very reason he offers a privileged analytical perspective on the town's inhabitants, social structure and general moral corruption.

The narrative form of *The Raven* is one of alternation. The visual point of view alternates quite rigidly between that of Germain and that of the town in its anonymous mass. The camera is relatively static throughout and mostly placed at a mid-shot distance to the characters. Germain's outsider quality comes to serve a dual narrative function. He becomes a prism through which the town appears as a unified whole and he appears as an object of observation for the inhabitants in the town. Being different from the people around him already gives him an enigmatic quality. He arouses interest. He is invested with suspense: who is this outsider? Why is he different? Does he hide something? He does in fact have a dark secret, and the gradual revelation of that secret constitutes a source of momentum in the film as well as a key to his psyche.

Beyond these broad narrative features of the protagonist, the film portrays him successively through a large number of specific traits. He is short but he is handsome. He is well-dressed, wearing correct but not over-elegant suits. He prefers not to wear the white doctor's uniform. The story weaves together shifting perspectives on Germain. We see him as a social being and as a psychological being. Germain is shown in the film as attractive to women. Two beautiful women in the film court him: Denise, who is the sister of the school director and who lives in the house where he is a lodger, and the respectable doctor's wife Marie. We also see him as a being haunted by past guilt. He is but a shadow of his former self, eking out with grim dignity a ghostly life in the town he has chosen for himself as punishment.

Germain is shown as a secret abortionist at a time when abortion was illegal. The film's second scene – after a tour of the town – shows him assisting at a difficult birth. He saves the mother but the child dies. In the next scene we learn that this has happened twice already in the month. His manner is from the opening scenes brisk and assertive. He appears indifferent to the opinions of others. He does not engage easily in conversation with his colleagues. He treats a difficult nurse with blunt authority. The content of his statements seems from the start guided by a sort of *moral certainty*. He declines a colleague's offer of having a look at a patient in a very advanced illness, as if for 'fun' or out of morbid curiosity, and adds that he is not very jocular, '*pas très blageur*'. He also shows a streak of defiance. When a superior admonishes him for having saved the mother and not the child during the episode mentioned previously, he is unapologetic, courting conflict. Thus through these different encounters *he is singled out as a man who singles himself out*, as someone who misses no opportunity to mark the distance that separates him from his fellow men. We get the sense that this distance is a moral one, his fellow men *falling short of the clear moral standard that the protagonist has made his own*. This moral and psychological difference is also implicitly social and geographical. The jovial drawl of his provincial colleagues makes his own short and precise sentences appear as gunshots. We later discover that he is in fact a Parisian doctor of high renown who, driven by personal tragedy, has changed his identity and sought refuge in the province. Hence throughout the film, Germain is under the spell of the pressures of a secret and of an unfinished past. His wife died a few years earlier, during childbirth. He was at the time a famous surgeon at a Paris hospital. Mortified with grief and self-recrimination, he changed his name and his identity and withdrew to the small town of Saint-Robin, where the story takes place. He decides never to let a woman die in childbirth if he can prevent it but rather to sacrifice the child.

The town itself is characterised by a particularly provincial blend of narrow-mindedness, sordidness and ideological uniformity. The capacity to gather physically around a few shared fears and passions is the essence of this town, its stamp of dark mediocrity. Politically, this portrait of a provincial town is implicitly pro-German, since it suggests that the inhabitants are incapable of moral autonomy and hence would side with the collaboration rather than with the resistance. Narratively, the film is organised around an opposition between the lonely outsider and the unified town. Most of the city's inhabitants – though not the doctor – follow Church convention. Provoked by a smear campaign, the town succumbs to a frenzy of collective panic and mutual suspicion. This collective emotion finds release in a witch hunt. The town gathers in collective rage to hunt down an innocent but unloved hospital nurse whom the audience by then has also learned to dislike.

Germain becomes the victim, along with other characters, of the anonymous letters that divulge, alternately, hidden truths or invented slander. Everyone in the town is affected by this avalanche of gossip, but Germain is at the centre both of the story and of these accusations. He is pilloried as an abortionist. The poisonous letters also refer to his relations with women. As paranoia and suspicion take over life in the town and at the hospital, Germain comes under increasing pressure. He gradually loses his composure and betrays both of the women who love him, convinced at different times that either Denise or Marie is the author of the smearing letters.

We see Germain as a subject of desire, falling in love with a woman below his status and station, a woman living by different moral standards than his own, the disreputable Denise. As the film evolves, it becomes less clear who is the more deserving of praise or blame, the Doctor or Denise. She may be socially stigmatised but she never allows her human or moral judgement to be clouded by fear or excessive intellectualism. She remains faithful to her feelings and desires and takes responsibility for what she wishes. He on the other hand is easily swayed by reason and doubt, unable to trust either his own feelings or other people.

Love here is sexual and dark, steeped in memory and longings for liberation from personal demons. It is a site of hope, but what is hoped for, social independence and erotic freedom, is portrayed in sharp contrast to heavily constraining social forces. Love is complex. It is created between individuals. It is rooted in subjective desires. It exists in a social space eliciting various pressures. And, finally, love is also a field of competition. Marie and Denise both want the doctor, and they make their rivalry explicit as they fight over him openly. Love thus has a melodramatic component, but unlike Carné, Clouzot focuses not on the fickle and discontinuous nature of desire or the unexpected vicissitudes of fortune, but on the continuity of existence within the protagonist.

We saw that classical Hollywood controls melodramatic pathos by ironically relativising the protagonist's sentimental pretensions. Clouzot relativises the protagonist's thoughts in a less ironic mode. The duality of perspective in this film, whereby we see the town through the eyes of Germain and him through the eyes of different members of the town, serves to objectify Germain in his dignity and his desire but also in his folly – highly strung and socially vulnerable, he is unable to trust his own emotions and thus betrays his love for Denise by suspecting her of being the author of the slanderous letters.

Two films from the same period: *A Matter of Life and Death* and *The Raven*. In both cases, love is sexual and a means for the characters in love to gain something. What is gained in *A Matter of Life and Death* is life itself, as love comes to stand for life in its full dignity; the fact of love is the fact of life seen from an ennobling perspective, life as something that is not merely social or biological but capable of engendering the ideal 'thing' called love. What is gained in *The Raven* is a negotiated peace with the world, a momentary peace with past demons, a respite from inner and external pressures. Love is earthly and earthy, but *The Raven* is neither cynical nor devoid of romance and hope. In the guilt-ridden shameful world of Vichy France that Clouzot depicts, sexual desire is for the main character a means for him to interrupt the circuits of his thoughts and become receptive to the mind and body of another being. This is far from the de-eroticised marriages of classical Hollywood, where love is a sporting partnership, barely involving some necessary sex. In *The Raven* love does not exist outside of or apart from a space of erotic tension. In *A Matter of Life and Death* attraction is immediately idealised, sublimated into a total infatuation, transformed into 'pure love', a love which has desire merely as an internal component.

In *The Raven* the conceptual moral space that mediates emotion with the world is structured around a series of polar opposites – *and these opposite poles are not aligned with one another or superimposed upon one another* as they would inevitably be in a classical Hollywood film. The film thus presents a moral space that is not quintessentially dichotomic or dualistic. The main polarities are purity–fallenness, individuality–community, sexual reticence–promiscuity, solipsism–receptivity and madness–normality. The two women embody the opposition of reticence–promiscuity. The doctor embodies purity, individuality and solipsism. His relation to the fallen woman challenges his purity but also allows him to overcome his solipsism. This is the main and most complex temporal development of the film. Is this a film about the necessity of moral corruption, the doctor finding salvation only in the betrayal of his ideals, or is it a film about the necessary *self-limitation of reason, about the fragility of the individual relying only on reason and refusing to accept love*?

In *The Raven*, the characters move relatively little in each scene and there is a clear distinction between scenes of dialogue between two or three people – the dramatically most significant – and scenes from the town involving many characters. These group scenes include a visit to the hospital ward, scenes at the funeral of a patient who killed himself, some evenings at the club where the town officials meet and exchange gossip, some scenes in the corridors of the hospital where the doctors discuss what to do, as well as a number of dramatic situations connected to the attempt at discovering the identity of the raven, that is, the author of the smear campaign.

This is a world in which people either are free to talk privately or appear within a group, and so are *not* free to talk privately, but engage rather in a semi-formal and public exchange of comments and banter. The utterance of these comments is marked by rivalry and the need of each character to defend his or her own social position and reputation. A few scenes provoked by the anonymous letters introduce this public quality of rivalry into a conversation between two people. Thus a comic scene shows the hospital director confronting his subordinate with an embarrassing anonymous letter accusing him of malpractice, whereupon the latter produces a letter suggesting that the hospital director is having an affair with the subordinate's wife. The exchange that ends the scene marks the reversal of their social roles. The superior retorts that the last letter has convinced him that these letters are a heap of lies. The subordinate answers in a menacing voice: I am convinced too. The alternation and overlap between intimate and public scenes thus shows a different relationship between the private and the public than in *Casablanca*. In that film every character's life appears in a public space of objectification. The public space of Rick's is essentially a bazaar where human lives are traded, and it admits of almost no privacy. In *The Raven* characters seek in vain to preserve their privacy. The smear letters only render visible the hypocrisy that consists in pretending that there is privacy when in fact gossip and rivalry leave a minimal space of action to each member of the town. The crisis provoked by the letters only reinforces pre-existing tensions and rivalries.

Love thus takes place in the social world, but this is a world permeated by secrecy, double standards and collective repressed guilt. The classical Hollywood cinema of the type that *Casablanca* is an example of is a cinema that tends towards an overcoming of melodrama and the ego through the semiotic resources of plot and thematic structure. The subject is not allowed to harbour a secret interiority because the emotions and moral stakes that the viewer can ascribe to him in virtue of the plot are no different from the emotions and thoughts that the characters express in speech and gesture. The first-person perspective that the characters could have on their own emotion would not disclose a content that would be different from the thoughts that other characters or the viewer could have about them – from a third-person perspective. This overcoming of the first-person perspective is upheld by the very robust structures of moral content that sustain narrative in classical Hollywood films. In *The Raven*, the difference between a first-person and a third-person perspective is inflected, rather, by sociological and psychological complexity. The many degrees of publicness and of secrecy, the pervasive sense that people are not *what they claim to be* and that solidarity possesses the corrupt structure of blackmail – I will keep your secret if you keep quiet about me – make it difficult to envisage a character whose motives are transparent. Hence, the happy semiotic prospect of a complete disclosure of interiority in a public space that is so characteristic of Hollywood is here punctured by the sense that since the public space is so corrupted there must be for the characters a different interiority, a subjectivity that remains protected from scrutiny, sealed off and self-sufficient. This is indeed the case for Germain, who, as one says, keeps his own counsel.

The inner life of the doctor is not displayed as a succession of emotions but as a twisted dialectic of reason and emotion. This dialectic is destructive and immoral, as it produces *moral solipsism*, that is, it overrides his own belief in the people he loves or cares for, making him commit violence towards them. This destructive dialectic is not expressed within an expressive semiotic system of facial gesture and mental content supported by plot structure. Rather it can be inferred from the doctor's actions. It is expressed as a kind of Dostoyevskian despair in the climactic scene of the film, when Denise stares pleadingly into his eyes and finds only cold suspicion. The protagonist's inner life remains therefore an irrepresentable yet intelligible place. We can know the kind of thoughts the doctor has, the kind of states he goes through, but they are not directly expressed. The moral stakes of his actions are not external to the erotic relationship as a frame of reference that would give value to love or evaluate his feelings. Instead, it is within the realm of love that the erotic relationship grows, that a sense of moral responsibility takes form – and this responsibility is more *concrete* than any general social values. It is not invested with any other content than the notion of amorous loyalty, demonstrated negatively, the notion that Germain should not have betrayed Denise, the woman whom he loves. *The Raven* is a profound love film because of its psychological precision, sublime acting and photography and extraordinary moral complexity, but most of all it is a film that presents love as an imperfect yet resilient good in the midst of the world.

At the Margins of Sense

Within classical French cinema, Louis Malle's *Les Amants* occupies a privileged place since it contains within itself both the visual grammar of classical storytelling and, in the last sequences of the film, a break with this grammar. Sustained by a solid visual grammar of narration and character construction, the first part of the film presents a refined psychological portrait of a woman, of her marriage, of her friends and of the places she inhabits. At the centre of her life is an absence of love. Neither loved nor seen as an individual by her husband, she takes a lover, Raoul Flores, an Argentinian polo player she meets in the world of Parisian high society. Raoul's perfect courtship flatters and confuses her, but it is with a third man, a man who does not form part of her life, and with whom, it would seem, she has nothing in common, that she experiences an erotic adventure that turns out to put her whole previous existence into question. Through an aesthetic tension between psychological storytelling and the poetic and psychologically *unjustified* appearance of desire, love is situated in this film, subtly, on the border between the social and psychological world of character and the indeterminate, not fully intelligible space of erotic desire. This film is made within an industrial mode of production. The script imposes structure on both the story and the *mise en scène*. It is the second film by Louis Malle, and the story is based on his own background in a large provincial industrial family. The protagonist is played by Jeanne Moreau, a rising star at the time. Upon release the film acquired fame for an erotic scene that was too explicit for contemporary audiences. The main characters in the story are Jeanne and Maggie, friends from childhood, born in Bourgogne; Henri Tournier, Maggie's husband and editor of the *Moniteur de Bourgogne*; and Raoul Flores, Jeanne's polo-playing lover in Paris. Bernard, is, we might say, an emerging character. He enters the story at a later point and is not rooted in the world of Dijon.

We are first presented with Jeanne at a polo match. A shot/reverse-shot sequence and a voice-over narration establish her as a spectator sitting next to her friend Maggie. We are also told by the narrator that both women grew up in Dijon and are thus, in the narrator's words, *'provinciales de naissance et d'éducation'*, provincial women by birth and culture. Whereas Jeanne stayed, Maggie went to Paris and became a socialite. Jeanne is now visiting her, as she has come to do regularly; she has become the mistress of Raoul Flores, the polo player they are watching. In this remarkable scene, everything comes together, everything is integrated, light and landscape, the viewers' and the characters' gaze, desire, cultural background, the characters and the dramatic contrast between them. We see

Love in Motion

what they see and we see them seeing it while we hear what makes them see this spectacle in, for each woman, a different way. A nice detail in the *mise en scène* that gives the final touch to this portrait of Jeanne is that she wears a dress that is pretty, but not fashionable, whereas Maggie wears a chic urban dress, the latest Paris fashion. In this scene we are comforted as viewers, as *there appears to be an absolute correlation between what we see and its narrative meaning*. For a long time this confidence is sustained. The film depicts Jeanne's return to her provincial manor house. At the dinner with her husband that same evening, he speaks to her through heavy cigar smoke in a ponderous, slightly mocking and contemptuous voice. He questions her on the values currently in vogue in Parisian society. Jeanne explains with an expression that suggests she were still in Paris, still gossiping with Maggie, listening to what Maggie says about feminine beauty. Maggie thinks that if one is not a great beauty one has to be a *type*. Maggie also says that the hairdo is the crucial feature of a woman's appearance: '*c'est la coiffure qui donne du chic a la robe*'. Her husband, immediately possessive, asks her who she wants to look beautiful for. This theme of jealousy is gradually built up through the course of the film until a scene where the husband comes home, drunk, late at night and forces her to invite Maggie and her 'friend' Raoul to come to dinner. The dinner scene is a masterpiece of classical narration in which the characters' relationships are described by how they appear together, opposed or separated by framing. At this dinner there are, apart from Jeanne, the husband, Maggie, Raoul and a stranger, Bernard, a man who gave Jeanne a lift when her car broke down on her return from Paris, but who also happens to be related to a family that is well known to both Jeanne and Maggie. The scenes preceding the dinner make up a long sequence showing Jeanne on a country road, her car broken down.

She is given a lift by this young man, who turns out to be very different from the people she knows and is used to dealing with. He offers opinions that are unfailingly at odds with everything she believes in and stands for. She is a social snob and a provincial woman aspiring to be a socialite. He is unpretentious and a nature enthusiast. He has negated the values of his own high bourgeois provincial family. In spite of these differences, he makes her laugh, and when the car arrives at her home, he perceptively describes her husband and the two guests, Jeanne and Raoul, who stand in front of the house nervously waiting, as a great bear about to eat two innocent victims. She finds this so apt that she cannot stop laughing, so instead of excusing herself for being late, as her husband and her guests obviously expect her to do, she laughs insolently in their faces and moves past them.

The shot that introduces the dinner frames the table against a background of two parallel doors leading to two parallel corridors. The stranger arrives along the corridor to the right (in the frame) and the others arrive through the other corridor. This distinction between the stranger and the others is reinforced by the conversation at dinner and by the shot sequence that describes it. Silent throughout, Bernard is only in frame when the shot covers everyone present. All the medium close-ups of individual characters, or couples of characters, cover the four others and serve to analyse the psychological tension and relations of power that unfold between them, as the husband seeks to humiliate his wife and her presumed – and in fact actual – lover. During the dinner, Jeanne is either silent or makes polite conversation, with the occasional remark designed to reign in her husband. Maggie is chatty and mildly defies the husband's authority. Raoul makes conversation in the diplomat style. This dramatic high point in the film also marks a sort of dead end. The husband has managed successfully to ridicule Raoul by pretending to feel great passion for his wife. Jeanne for her part seems squeezed by the claims of these two men, who both cut a poor figure as they carry out their symbolic fight over her.

After they have all gone to bed, the film surprisingly takes a different turn and abruptly changes style. Jeanne wakes up in the middle of the night. Noticing that the moon is out, she goes out into the garden. There she discovers Bernard, who is embellished by the night. He approaches her, recites poems and woos her. They walk through the garden, which is enchanted by the moonlight, and they become lovers. They make love in her bedroom and in the morning they drive away together in his 2CV, while the rest of the characters, who have risen early to go hunting, look on in stunned silence.

Narratively and stylistically, the film thus falls into two very different and asymmetrical parts. The first and longest part is realist, dramatic and satirically crisp. Characters are sharply drawn and contrasted, environments are precisely sketched and the *mise en scène* emphasises both the dramatic contrast between characters and their dependence on a specific environment. The second, shorter, part is a lyrical evocation of love in the moonlit park of the manor house. This scene is romantically idealistic, as it has two characters meeting and becoming lovers *against all odds*.

This idealism is in part broken by a subsequent return to psychological realism. The next morning we see Jeanne, looking at herself in the mirror, as a voice-over narrator explains that the lovers' future is open and uncertain. The two lovers, when shown together, have lost the lightness and magic of the preceding night. The film thus juxtaposes realism and romanticism, social determination and a self-determining erotic relationship. But this opposition is also aesthetic. In the lyrical night scene *mise en scène* is no longer positional. Hence in *Les Amants*, love is *not* something that can be placed within a category – whether sexual, social, moral or romantic. The heroine, Jeanne, is in search of love. As a character she is inseparable from all that makes her what she is: her upbringing in the provincial town of Dijon, her marriage to a local landowner and newspaper proprietor. Her speech is made up of all the snobbish, narrow-minded opinions that come naturally with such a social position. Yet, the erotic adventure that she embarks on is indeterminate in relation to this social position. We could say that the man she is attracted to is desirable to the extent that he is different from what she knows – but so is her first lover, Raoul, the Argentinian polo player. Her decision to let herself be seduced is not an act of rebellion exactly. Rather she is carried away by events, carried off by a possibility that would have seemed completely unlikely, ridiculous and shameful within the framework of her ordinary opinions. Love thus drives a wedge between a social self made up of opinions and attitudes and a different self, emerging directly from seduction and desire. This other self is initially the affirmation of desire and is thus a purely romantic self, but this emerging self does not grow into a romantic subject. Malle's film is careful to accommodate only a limited space of romantic freedom. The day after sleeping with her new lover, Jeanne is in the grip of doubts and appears vulnerable. She does not possess the certainties of her former social identity, and neither does she have the certainty that her desire from the night before carries a future. Love is here opposed to the social world as a poetic element is opposed to the dramatic elements of rivalry, power and social status. Love is not selfless, perhaps, but it is released by the interruption of a certain social game.

This does not mean that the subject's relation to the position it occupies is otherwise necessarily stable in classical French cinema: the drama of *Leon Morin* consists in the ambiguity of the characters' relation to their erotic desire; the depth of *The Raven* resides in the doctor's dialectical relation to his own erotic desire and hence his ambiguous relation to the woman whom he loves, Denise. However, the aesthetic power of *Les Amants* resides in a different logical register than that of ambivalence and dialectic, which are after all *positional* devices, dependent on positions that the subject can be ambivalent about or between which he or she can establish a dialectical relationship. The aesthetic power of *Amants* springs from the sheer *lack of psychological motivation* in the heroine's choice of the third man. The long sequence in the moonlit park and the witty and erotic scene of lovemaking that follows obey a different logic, where visual beauty, expressions of intimacy and the poetic power of speech point directly and non-dramatically to the lovers and the love that they create – rather than towards social, moral or speaking positions that they could occupy in the eyes of others. This love is *presented* – rather than framed through categories of conflict and signification as something that we should understand, interpret and make intelligible. Indeed, the historical and aesthetic importance of this film lies in the relation between the first, classically narrative part and this poetic end sequence: the story told in the main section of the film presents, on the part of the heroine, a reason to be erotically accessible, but nothing that we learn about her and about the man who becomes her lover would make them a *plausible* couple. Thus the two parts of the film support each other and are in tension with one another. This poetics of love is gently upheld by a narrative that leaves the space of that love *undetermined*. Les Amants is a great film about love because it hovers around the line that demarcates intelligibility from visual poetry.

Hitchcock and Lang

Fantasy spectacle is a tradition of film which liberates the erotic relationship from its cultural intelligibility. It develops in parallel with classical cinema. Hitchcock's elegant thriller from 1935, *The 39 Steps*, is loosely based on a World War I spy thriller by James Buchanan. The novel is typical of early spy stories, and is similar for instance to Maugham's *Ashenden*, in that realist detail and nuanced character psychology flood the text to the point of obscuring the structure of the plot. Hitchcock, on the other hand, privileges plot over all other components of the film spectacle and thus substantially transforms the novel.

We can, then, distinguish two opposed ways of conceiving of love and of the film image. *The 39 Steps* is a prototype of what I call *fantasy spectacle*. The fantasy spectacle knows only one emotion and one desire: fear of death and the desire to survive. The narrative subject in the fantasy spectacle is an agent stripped of character traits and inner life. His properties are all relative to his pragmatic situation. It is a subject re-enacting archaic mythical anxieties in a light and playful mode.

The philosopher Hans Blumenberg claims that the human being's knowledge of its own physical vulnerability is the original human characteristic, the trait that qualified the human being at the moment when, in its early species history, it stopped crawling and became a biped, raised up in the air and thus visible from afar as a potential prey. Mythical stories are, according to Blumenberg, humanity's original response to this situation of ineradicable fear. Unable to remove the cause of its vulnerability, the human being playfully imagines scenarios in which the causal connections and obstacles that it encounters in reality enter new and varying compositions. It thereby reduces on an imaginary or aesthetic level the monolithic force of the real. Fantasy spectacle is a remote descendant of this mythical playfulness. Hitchcock's English thrillers differ from later action films in their almost complete absence of depicted physical violence. Spectacle in *The 39 Steps* is temporal and erotic, rather than physical and violent.

In most of his silent and very early sound films, Hitchcock presents erotic relationships as narrative clichés that he could insert into a context of social satire. *The Lodger* is a less ironic film than the others, and in this film the erotic drama is reduced to its minimal sexual nucleus of sadomasochistic ambivalence: the woman desires a man who may or may not be a mass murderer.

In *The 39 Steps* erotic precision and social satire are joined very subtly. The narrative subject is a Canadian visiting London. His Canadianness resides chiefly in his detachment from the hierarchies and geographic stigmas of the British class system. He is socially an outsider, but a well-to-do and smartly dressed outsider. He is not an *émigré*, a spy or a struggling artist, but a figure of English detective novels of the time, quick-witted, masculine but not obviously violent. He is handsome, interested in women – and unmarried. We are introduced to this outsider before we know his identity. We see him enter an entertainment hall in London. Gradually the scene establishes him as the narrative and visual focal point of the film.

During a lowbrow performance by a memory artist – called 'Mister Memory' – a shot is fired in the midst of the crowd. The crowd is panic-stricken and rushes to the door. Our hero finds himself in the street next to a beautiful and mysterious woman who asks him – in a vaguely European accent – whether she can come to his home. As they reach his flat, she reveals to him that she is a spy and that she has discovered a foreign spy network in England that is very close to bringing an important military secret out of the country. After eating a haddock he has made for her she goes to bed – it is quite curious that the supposedly continental European delights in eating this quintessentially English dish, prepared for her by another supposed foreigner. This is just a small symptom of the aesthetic principle in the film already mentioned: the properties given to the characters are purely instrumental, at the service of the plot and the spectacle that envelops it.

In the night, Hannay is awakened by a scream. The woman enters and looks down at him with a large knife sticking out of her back. She utters these dying words: 'they will get you next, Hannay'. From this point onwards, the plot is a contraption. It is designed to present the narrative subject, Hannay, with certain, very clearly defined options for action. These options are embedded in very specific feelings and desires.

The plot premise, when Hannay faces the dead woman in the flat, is that he is himself in danger, since he is also a threat to the spy ring. It is puzzling why those very dangerous foreign spies, instead of killing Hannay right away, leave the flat that they seem to have been able to enter without problems and ring him from a phone booth in the street. The focus here is thus not dramatic but subjective. We are presented with the protagonist's fear and sense of urgency. The visualisation of the threat in the form of the enemy calling from a phone booth that he can see from his window also presents very clearly the parameters of his own pragmatic choice: *me or them*. There is not a choice here between two alternatives as there would be in a classic love film such as *Leon Morin* or a melodrama like the *The Woman on the Beach*. There is instead a more basic situation of choice. Either I act so as to save myself, or I die. This situation is amplified by the fact that Hannay is immediately suspected by the police of murdering the woman. He is thus chased both by the villains and by the police and can, conforming to the narrative principle of transferral of guilt in Hitchcock's films, only save himself and prove himself innocent by revealing to the police the identity of the villains.

The plot has already presented the protagonist with one erotic situation, but this situation did not develop, as the woman immediately died. He soon thereafter meets an English girl. She is blonde and prim, but turns out not to be quite what she seems. At their first encounter he kisses her on the mouth in order to pretend to the policemen chasing him that they are a couple. She immediately denounces him and he narrowly escapes. This initial encounter establishes the pattern of their relationship. She is defiant and sceptical, he is physically intrusive. As chance would have it, they meet again a few days later. The first meeting took place on a train to Scotland, where Hannay is following a lead given to him by the dead woman. He is seen by her during a political public meeting. She is again eager to hand him over to the authorities, and she immediately gets the chance to do so, as two policemen looking for Hannay are also present at the meeting. They ask her to accompany them and Hannay to the police station. Hannay soon discovers that they are not policemen but representatives of the foreign spy ring. He forces her to flee with him and they escape over the moors tied together with handcuffs. They find refuge at a local inn. In the night she gets out of the handcuffs and overhears a phone call by the fake policemen. She realises that Hannay is innocent after all and decides to help him. The narrative of their escape together and stay at the inn is both comic and richly textured by sexual allusions. A bantering relationship grows between them, creating a bond of complicity long before she has discovered his innocence.

This is a depiction of love where coexistence, sex and friendship are intertwined, presented as a continuum that is indifferent to the moral and social categories of erotic choice that we found in the classical Hollywood film. In *It Happened One Night* the journey of the lovers-to-be highlights differences of class and temper. He is a journalist with wits and no money, but equipped with an easy charm and devoid of social arrogance. She is a rich and over-protected girl who lacks experience and is, at least initially, entirely impractical. The temperamental differences in *The 39 Steps* between the strong-headed and intelligent English girl and the dashing Canadian do not map on to any such social or moral grid. *It Happened One Night* stages a slow courtship based on the woman's will being gently crushed by male initiative. This is presented as a kind of education. She learns to love him to the extent that she becomes less self-centred, less rooted in her family and class. The sexual battle between the supposed murderer and his defiant captive in *The 39 Steps* does not involve this sort of moral education. She is not in need of education. The attraction between them is not different from the tension that results from their battle of wills. Capra acknowledges erotic attraction in his famous bedroom scenes, but a purely sexual bond or a dynamic of seduction is never allowed to exist on its own, to exercise its force and its freedom independently of a moral discourse. With a similar narrative of love emerging gradually, Hitchcock is careful to reduce the sexual relationship to its core, just as the detective genre reduces plot to certain basic elements.

In both cases, emotion is treated as a function of other relationships – the suspense plot, sexual attraction – and not as a semiotic key to the interpretation of characters. Hitchcock is in most of his films the most anti-melodramatic of filmmakers for this reason. The history of love in film thus finds a counterpoint to the melodramatic themes of hope, reversal and redemption in the fantasy spectacle, with its geometrical plots of suspense and erotic possibilities. We shall now look at one more example of the fantasy spectacle before examining how it was reinterpreted as a spectacle of amorous purity in Truffaut and Buñuel. The fantasy spectacle is 'mythical', in Blumenberg's sense of playfulness, because the social fabric of class and the biographical fabric of feelings, guilt, desire and hope, with their appearance of solid necessity, are swept aside and replaced by purely erotic relationships. These relationships may leave little freedom of choice for the narrative subject, but as a formal structure existing independently of emotion and class they demonstrate, on a different and more abstract, reflective level, the freedom of erotic relationships that can be formed and exist in the world in defiance of common sense. Let us now look at a minor Lang film that very clearly exemplifies a rudimentary structure of erotic freedom within a fantasy spectacle.

Ministry of Fear is considered by many to be one of Lang's minor American films, and it certainly is less melodramatic and symbolically dense than films like *The Woman in the Window*. Yet, the austere simplicity of its narrative style, supported by the clear lines of the script written by Graham Greene, bring this film close to Hitchcock and show a different sort of exit from melodrama, and a different kind of fantasy spectacle from the suspense and eroticism of *The 39 Steps*. The film is a romantic thriller set in and near London during World War II. The story revolves around one man.

He is tall, shyly affable and a little reserved, kindly yet showing an underlying resilience. This complexity of characterisation is dramatically full of potential. The film starts in a prison, where he is waiting out the last minutes before he is released. The prison warden exhorts him to stay away from crime and he reassures him that he will live the quiet life from now on. He leaves for the train station. As one might expect, events quickly take a different turn. A charity fair organised by local housewives next to the train station is the site of his immediate return to crime; at least, he will soon thereafter be arrested and suspected of a crime. At the fair, he visits a fortune teller and wins a cake in a quiz. It turns out that the cake is the secret storage place of an important object. Later, on the train, he is attacked by a fake blind man who runs off with the cake as the train stops during a bombing raid. In the light of the falling bombs the escaping man fires at him, but is then himself hit by a bomb and dies. The cake and its mysterious content disappear. The rest of the film shows the protagonist attempting to establish who may have been behind the cake scam. He gets to know a pair of siblings who fled Austria after the Nazi invasion. The woman decides to help him, first out of solidarity with someone who is alone like she was when she arrived in England, but soon she falls in love with him, and he with her. Their mutual falling in love is woven into a depiction of his vulnerability. He never loses his composure entirely, but he is always brittle, alone against the world. The two are shown as good and decent human beings adrift together. She is motivated by an idealistic desire to help; he is held up by a tenacious will not to be eradicated, either by those who tried to kill him or by the police, who suspect him of a crime. Love here is not the arena of a redemptive desire or a hope for a new life, as we saw was characteristic of melodrama. Their hope stretches only slightly beyond their desires in the present, erotic desire and also desire for companionship and survival.

The protagonist does not need to become a different human being. He is not ashamed of having just come out of prison. He just wants to go on living and not to be alone. The narrative is presented in a factual tone without dramatic high points, even as the plot contains many violent events and colourful characters. The film mixes situations from English detective fiction – attractive and unreliable women appearing suddenly out of nowhere, making charmingly enigmatic conversation – and situations relating to the setting of war – one of the most moving scenes shows the two lovers staying the night in a tube station that has been turned into a bomb shelter. The houses and flats that the protagonist has to visit on his quest are all slightly artificial. They come to take on the function of boxes, each containing a self-enclosed narrative scenario, each representing an existential possibility, and each corresponding to an unconscious fear or desire. The temporal arc of the film is a succession of these boxes, as if each scene were the enactment of a fantasy, a small dream sequence or scenario of desire embedded within the fantasy quest of the whole story, the quest to survive and to be, at the same time, allowed re-entry into society. The depiction of social integration within a fantasy spectacle differs from a melodramatic representation of a similar theme because it is the movement of the quest itself, the series of situations and incidents, that constitutes the narrative difference between beginning and end, rather than a change taking place in the relationship between characters or a change within the protagonist's feelings and beliefs.

The characters are not pitted against each other in situations of choice, and they are not characterised morally or psychologically, beyond the basic goodness of the protagonist and his lover. Neither is the protagonist himself shown to undergo any substantial change. Love is here a more basic human reality, on a par with anxiety, death and loneliness, than the social and psychological composite that is love in melodrama and in the classical film. We have seen that Hitchcock and Lang use the detective genre to empty love of emotion in order to lay bare a structure of desire (Hitchcock) or of basic human need (Lang). Let us now examine how this project is taken further by Buñuel, and continued in a more amorous vein by Truffaut.

Buñuel and Truffaut

Luis Buñuel is a *nuclear* filmmaker: he is capable of generating a story, psychological characters and a filmic world from just a few objects and sexual ideas. 'Between two pebbles, two streets, two columns I always prefer one or the other' says Tristana, the heroine of the film of the same name. This inclination for choice applies only to options that are of no consequence, either because it matters little whether she eats one pea before another, takes one street instead of another, or because her preference is imaginary. Her preference for one column over another in a colonnade matters little to the columns, which remain where they are regardless of her 'choice'. In matters where choice is of consequence, Tristana shows little aptitude for decision or preference.

An orphan brought up by nuns, she is mentally, and sexually, immature when she is taken under the wings of her kind uncle and invited to live in his house as an adopted daughter. He soon decides to change their relationship and makes her his mistress. In return, she hates him, vividly, but makes no attempt to leave the house. Only when she has taken a lover, a vigorous, virtuous and handsome young painter, is she able to break with her uncle, and the two leave the small town for Madrid. After two years the couple returns. She is seriously ill and wishes to see her uncle. He rejoices, triumphantly telling his housekeeper, 'once she is back in the house she will never leave again'. She in fact does return to stay with him. A doctor recommends that her right leg be amputated at the knee and thereafter she continues to live with her uncle as a cripple, playing the piano and seeing her painter husband less and less frequently. Her hatred now includes him as well, since, as she says, he made her return to her uncle's house, where she became a cripple.

Throughout the film, she has a recurrent dream: she sees the bell tower in the local church, the bell replaced by her uncle's severed head. In the end, she is able to make this dream come true by provoking his death. He is ill and calls out to her during the night. He says that he is unwell and asks her to call for a doctor immediately. She pretends to call a doctor but does not dial the number. Instead she opens the bedroom windows to let in the winter air, presumably to precipitate his death.

The film and the love relation that it depicts are generated from a nucleus of structural elements: the severed head, the amputated leg, the game of choosing between insignificant alternatives. The film does not so much pose an enigma as present a closed constellation. We are not invited to interpret the feelings, motives and desires of Tristana. Catherine Deneuve, who plays Tristana, excels in shifting between innocence and cruelty, virginity and nagging bitterness without giving a hint that these shifting attitudes imply a shift in her personality. Tristana accepts everything. She acts not by confronting her enemy – the lecherous and treacherous uncle – but by creating a new situation: taking the painter as her lover. This *fait accompli* turns out to be a trap for her as well, however. Even this decision dictated by desire is too much of a decision for Tristana and for the film, which undermines its effect, forcing her not only to return and be humiliated by this return, but also to become an invalid, a prematurely aged and bitter woman.

Love is figured here in its nuclear essence at the edge of character psychology, as the fact of a constellation that, once it has imposed itself, creates its own inert power of permanence. This structural narrative form is underlined by other stylistic elements in the film. The hyperbolic and ridiculous figure of the uncle is played with sublime naturalness by Fernando Rey, who says the most monstrous sentences with an air of well-meaning, patriarchal good sense. Thus he calmly says to Tristana when he senses her slipping away, 'I am both your father and your lover and I can always choose which I shall be'. Montage grows out of the film's restricted locations. The house of the uncle, a playing field at the orphanage, the labyrinthine hilly streets of the little town and a few other locations in the town (a café, a church, a train station, the painter's house) constitute the whole diegetic space of the film. Different scenes thus repeatedly take place in the same or similar locations, creating a rhythm of repetition, like a movement within an ever-narrower spiral. This sense of a narrowing spiral is mirrored in the uncle's appearance. The film shows him ageing quite rapidly. He changes from being, in the beginning, a respectable middle-aged man to becoming at the end an old man in the grip of physical decay. A small detail of his appearance underlines this. At the height of his perversion, when he has managed to chain Tristana to the house with her crippled leg, he painstakingly goes to the baker to buy her favourite sweets. We see him emerge from the bakery hunched and obsessive, the cake box in his hand and wearing small sunglasses that give him a slightly deranged look.

The narrow spiral is the thematic and rhythmical counterpoint of the film's structural narrative. The spiral is the concrete texture of a temporality that is entirely suspended between desire and death, within a closed constellation of love. If this is love at its most nuclear, its most basic, it is because reciprocity on the level of pure desire cannot be fully articulated in any discourse that would determine the duration of the relation. Since Tristana hates her uncle, she could say: never, it should never have happened, never have started, but she does not say this. He would say: forever, always. The truth is that their relationship, being purely a relationship of desire, is determined in its duration by his death, a death that she desires and which constitutes the only limit to her own desire for him. In this film it is as if time simultaneously stands still within the factual space of a constellation and moves forwards and inwards in a spiral that makes the distance between sexuality and death ever smaller. This nuclear narrative style liberates the erotic relationship from its conventional moral coordinates and treats the feelings and emotional affects of love as mere effects or properties of the structure. The old man's limitless possessive desire is a given premise. His triumphant glee when, aided by her infirmity, he can again lock her up in the house is simply a natural result of this desire within the circumstances presented by the plot. Her feelings are volatile, like her actions. Her emotional core appears to be an ambivalence that flows directly from the ambivalence of her sexual desire.

In his different mature films, both in the Mexican and in the French period, Buñuel stylises a conventional realist setting – a Mexican hacienda, a Parisian bourgeois flat – and seeks, through this stylisation, to make the location as it appears in the sequence of events into a vehicle of erotic imagination. He thus does not externalise the unconscious as Lynch attempts to do in *Blue Velvet*.

One of Buñuel's minor films illustrates the realist and psychological programme that he subsequently puts into practice in his more famous films, *Viridiana*, *Tristana*, *Belle du jour* and *Cet obscur objet du désir*. The film is called *Ensaie de un crimen* and it is a psychological comedy made in Mexico in the early 1950s. It tells the story of a bachelor and aesthete. He lives off his own money and indulges in the hobby of amateur pottery. His gorgeous villa in a tranquil suburb of a provincial town has large representative rooms with high ceilings, invoking an aristocracy that is otherwise absent from the film. We learn that his life has been spent reiterating a murderous fantasy that he had as a child and which marked him for life, as it appeared to have been fulfilled. As a young boy he ardently wishes for the death of his nanny. She is promptly killed by a sniper's bullet fired by a revolutionary soldier. A particular toy was part of this scene: an exquisite music box with a turning statuette on top. This toy becomes charged with the value of a traumatic-sexual symbol, associated not only with the woman's death but also with the intense pleasure that he felt upon believing her death to have been caused by his own wish. Fatefully, he sees the toy again later in life in an antique shop. He immediately buys it, and in so doing steps on the toes and honour of a gentleman and his daughter who had also wanted to buy this toy. The daughter comes to play an important part in the plot.

He then gets to know an unhappy rich woman who lives in a love-hate relationship with an older man. On the way back from a party she smashes her car into a fence. He stands nearby, accompanies her home and prepares to kill her. Before he has managed to do so, the husband returns and he has to leave without having accomplished what he had planned. The next morning she is found dead, having killed herself after a quarrel with her husband. He meets the daughter of the man who had wished to buy the music box and they strike up a friendship. He invites her to his house alone and just as he has lured her into the perfect location for the crime he has in mind, a group of American tourists arrive, a group that she assists as a guide and that she invited as a backup in case he sought to seduce her. He ends up in a psychiatric hospital. This part of the story is in fact a framing narrative presented at the beginning of the film. Here he tries to kill a nurse with a knife and she runs away, but as she tries to escape she runs into an empty elevator tunnel and dies. He accuses himself before the director of the hospital and before the police but is acquitted of all crimes.

What is real in this story is thus his subjectivity in its imaginary appropriations of the world. The film not merely functions as the evocation of states of mind, or of unconscious wishes, but stages a series of coincidences which allow him and the film to inscribe his imaginary wishes into the world. What then is the world that these desires are inserted into? It is a labyrinthine world. The film's narration, montage, point of view and camera angles are all sympathetic with the careful and obsessive effort of the protagonist to pursue his desires. The film is in solidarity always with his focus of attention, the murderous-erotic opportunity. All the settings of the film are then locations for imagined crimes. But these locations themselves are depicted with a modicum of realism – it is in their concatenation through narrative montage that they become a labyrinth representing indirectly and not visually or symbolically the unconscious movement of the protagonist's erotic project.

The notion of a spiral or circular movement of erotic imagination and desire, moving through various real social settings and geographical locations, remains central to Buñuel's aesthetic programme in the French period. In *Un Crimen*, the world is a subjective universe, seen exclusively from the point of view of the protagonist. This is consistent with a story that has the contrast between imagination and commonsense reality as its main theme and comic-aesthetic device. In the later films, the faculty of the imagination is eliminated or at least not foregrounded. The relationship between desire and reality is not mediated by any conscious psychological process such as feeling, imagination or rational design. Or rather, the rational thoughts, obsessions, character traits, feelings and moral properties that can be ascribed to characters are supervenient upon a structure that is purely erotic. The world of Buñuel provides a space, or, we might say, a home, for this purely erotic structure.

In the fantasy spectacle of the kind discussed earlier, sex and death are coordinated by the trope of danger, which in turn is part of the detective genre. In Buñuel, and in *Tristana* and *Un Crimen* especially, sex and death are so closely intertwined that death itself becomes an object of desire. This reduction of the erotic relation to its most rudimentary, and in a sense metaphysical, coordinates has the price of alienating it from the world.

The primary fantasy, we have seen, on which fantasy spectacle is built and from which it derives its source and pleasure is a fear of personal annihilation and the overcoming of even the most daunting obstacles in the pursuit of one's own survival. Love is part of this fantasy only accidentally, not essentially. Truffaut's *Jules et Jim* is a love film, not a story of escape and survival, but it is a love film narrated in the mode and with the rhythm of escape.

In *Jules et Jim*, and in Truffaut's oeuvre as a whole, melodrama is held at bay only for a certain time, only to return with greater force. *La Femme d'a côté* is this return of melodrama in Truffaut's filmography. In *Jules et Jim* the last part of the film, which purports to explain the heroine and with her the love triangle of the story, returns to a melodramatic psychological mode. The story appears to be 'justified' by the madness of the female character. This sort of melodramatic psychology is given free rein in *Tirez sur le pianiste* and *La peau douce*, in the former through the portrait of a man traumatised by having benefitted from his wife's affair with another man, after which she committed suicide, and in the latter through the depiction of the murderous rage of a jealous wife.

What distinguishes his style from that of classical cinema is not so much to be found in his *mise en scène*, which favours the medium long shot, providing ample space for the characters to move. It is rather the film's focus on *movement* and with it the place that he accords to surprising incidents which distinguish his style from that of classical French cinema. These incidents may carry a strong narrative charge or have a very tenuous and obscure relation to the story, but they always break the rhythm of the film and introduce, within an otherwise rigid narrative frame, an element of unpredictability and vitality.

In this light it is not surprising that Truffaut admired Renoir and Rossellini, two filmmakers who worked with narrative surprise and incident to complicate narrative psychology. Truffaut's narrative focus is on the other hand more psychological than in these predecessors, since after *The 400 Blows* he neither explores the nature of the film medium nor seeks to use the camera to reveal everyday reality. His aesthetic invention resides almost entirely in the creation of a new rhythm. The dramatic problems of his films mostly concern male figures who fail as lovers, who enter love obliquely, or reluctantly, but who are obsessed with discovering, finally, what love is.

The world that love exists in is not made up of obstacles and expectations in Truffaut's universe. Or if there are obstacles, such as shame, timidity, Oedipal fantasies, poverty and political differences, these obstacles are part of desire's trajectory, not fundamentally opposed to it. Truffaut's world is picaresque. It is an arena of adventures and trajectories. The world leaves desire intact, and in return, desire does not alter the world. Truffaut is thus one of the most apolitical of filmmakers.

Prior to this descent into psychology, morality and fatalism, *Jules et Jim* celebrates the power of erotic energy as a relational force, a desire that is factual rather than intentional. Not the desire to do x or to have x or to be x: to make love, to possess sexually a certain person or to be the lover, husband or mistress of a certain person. Rather desire is here a relational energy connecting the two characters Jules and Jim to one woman, Jeanne. Within the parameters of action disclosed by this fact only repetition and permutation are possible. She can be with Jules, with Jim, to some extent with both and betray both, but neither she nor they are able to give up the hope of forming, once and for all, a happy exclusive couple. Only the death of Jules and Jeanne can break the spell, seal the relationship, quench the desire. Desire in this film is thus very close to life itself, pictured within the frame of a fixed border.

The ingeniously chosen title *Jules et Jim* already presents an enigma. Jules and Jim – these names are almost identical. Are these characters rivals, brothers, substitutes or stand-ins for one another? We quickly discover that Truffaut has transposed Henri Roche's autobiographical story into a unique fantasy environment, part history, part psychological exploration permeated by a complex emotional tone, whereas *Tirez sur le pianiste* and *La Peau douce* are caught in dramatic conventions that exclude this kind of tonal complexity. Thus in *Tirez*, a comic orchestral performance in the bar where much of the action takes place stands as a mere counterpoint to the film's principal narrative of moral corruption. In *Peau*, a cruel satire of provincial life stands lamely side by side with the drama of a betrayed wife's revenge. In *Jules et Jim*, on the other hand, Truffaut manages successfully to synthesise the dramatic and the comic strands of the film. As Noël Burch has pointed out, the tone in *Jules et Jim* is carried to some extent by Truffaut's extensive use of long takes that present the unfolding action as a kind of gag or performance (Burch, *Theory and Praxis of Cinema*). The incident in which Jim visits Jeanne and helps her to pack is a good example of this technique. Framed by a marriage and erotic triangle narrative, the scene carries a certain dramatic significance and suspense. Jim arrives, debonair and courteous. Jeanne is flustered, about to make her last preparations. Between practical arrangements and polite conversation she throws a heap of love letters on the floor and sets fire to them. Her dress quickly catches fire. Jim deftly extinguishes the fire and restores order.

An almost mythical clarity emerges from this scene. The Woman sets herself on fire; embodying a primary element of recklessness, temptation and emotional violence, she condenses an ordinary exchange into a drama of self-destruction. The Man, taciturn, tall, efficient and rational, obeys the woman, maintains and communicates order. This mythical sharpness of gender possibilities is never absent from *Jules et Jim*, but it is also never allowed to dictate its tone or narrative content. This is neither an epic nor, of course, an allegorical film. The sharp edges of gender serve, rather, to rid the characters of individual emotional qualities. The Woman is restless, emotional and, as we discover in the last quarter of the film, torn by irresolvable tensions. She is individuated by her psychological history.

The men, Jules and Jim, on the other hand are little but functions or pawns of her erotic scenario. They are like the men in the fictions of Marguerite Duras, entirely substitutable for one another as the objects of female desire. Their qualities are thus essentially sexual. Jules embodies a boyish, non-virile manliness, an attachment to nature and a fundamental spiritual goodness. Jim is the seducer and the *flaneur*. A journalist and a womaniser, he is defined by movement, yet his quiet, tall figure makes him appear as a reassuring speaking statue. He embodies an eroticism of virility and freedom, an attractiveness that lacks only the element of attachment – the element that Jules is fully able to express.

The scene where Jeanne catches fire is, in its choreographic swiftness, told as a silent film comic incident. The speed of exposition and the uncertainty concerning the scene's significance within the narrative produce a particular, fleeting and at the same time all-absorbing focus on the actual movements of the characters. A dramatically more charged scene is also told with a distant camera as a choreographic incident. Jules, Jim and Jeanne walk through Paris at night. Caught in an egomaniacal mood, Jules launches into an interminable misogynist tirade, culminating with long, offensive quotes from Baudelaire detailing the 'abominable' nature of 'woman'. Jeanne does not react to this provocation directly and verbally, but her face takes on a fixed expression as she raises her veil and lets herself fall into the Seine. The two friends run to her rescue and save her.

This incident, although similar in some respects to the previous one, is also fundamentally different. Both are told as surprising, comic episodes. Both involve the portrait of Jeanne as a force of self-destruction. The river scene announces Jeanne's later suicide and encapsulates her strategy of compensation. When she takes Jim as a lover later in the film and discovers what she considers a betrayal on his part she immediately reciprocates by sleeping with a latent lover, in order to start on equal footing, as she explains. In this scene she does not let herself be dragged into a tedious discussion about Baudelaire's misogyny but physically 'changes the subject', forcing the others to do the same.

It is not, however, the scene's dramatic significance that makes it important within the arc of the film. It is a crucial scene within the film's narrative rhythm because it marries the two opposing tonal elements of the film, escape and death. In the beginning of the film, escape is joyous and erotic, whereas towards the end of the film the possibilities of escape are running out, the forces of melancholy take over and death appears to Jeanne as the only remaining escape. Here these two elements are crossed, not as a sequence or as opposing forces, but as parts of the same movement of defiance. This movement of defiance is also, choreographically and architectonically, a movement that brings together different cultural

Love in Motion

spheres. The urban street where the three friends find themselves engrossed in conversation all of a sudden becomes the border of a river that is not only pleasant to watch but in which one can very easily drown.

When we study fantasy spectacle and narrative trajectories of love as escape we are suspended between two aesthetic dimensions, between the archetypal elemental nature of Desire, Woman and Virility and the *subtle* and complex elements of desire and escape. The directors I have compared in this section – Hitchcock, Lang, Buñuel and Truffaut, situate themselves at different points between these two dimensions, but they all have in common the fact that the stations of the lover's trajectory are to some extent without reference, empty forms or borders of a frame. Within the frame is not a picture but a movement. In *Jules et Jim*, this movement is relational. The film, with its distant camera and voice-over narrator, does not espouse the point of view of any of its characters. It narrates the relationship between Jules and Jim and Jeanne – and it narrates it as a relation between Jules-and-Jim-and-Jeanne.

Love in the World

When filmmakers from roughly the mid-1970s onwards have sought new ways of depicting love, they have often developed perspectives that combine meticulous social realism with aesthetic and imaginative freedom.

Withdrawing both from the classical language of moral interpretation and from the sexual politics of the late 1960s, the filmmakers discussed in this section belong to different traditions and do not form one school. Indeed, one could see them as belonging to rival aesthetic movements. What they have in common is that they present original formal means of addressing the dual perspective, the subjective and the cultural, that is constitutive of the love phenomenon, refusing to allow either the subjective perspective of feeling or the cultural perspective of intelligibility to get the upper hand. In each of the films discussed, this encounter with the love phenomenon in its psychological, historical, economic and moral ramifications pushes the films towards a certain inclusiveness: the social world can never be either background or explanation; it cannot just be the stage for an interaction or the set of conditions that makes sense of what the characters do and feel. This inclusiveness also allows these filmmakers to acknowledge the boundariless or transcategorial nature of love, the way that love seems to migrate from one domain of reality to another, and therefore to find a home in no particular discourse. As we shall see it is love's relation to place that characterises it as a phenomenon without boundaries: for the place in which the lovers live is itself both material and social, historical and economic, a limit and a source of identity.

This is a cinema that reflects upon the cultural space in which love is made intelligible, but the love relation is never fully determined by the forces that shape it. Classical elements are employed, but the discursive or allegorical implications of the film's style in each case exceed the borders of classical, character-centred intelligibility. In classical cinema, love was defined as a relationship that makes sense in moral and social terms. It is a relation of sexual reciprocity but one that is embedded in cultural categories that make it rationally intelligible both to the characters and to the spectators. In classical cinema, the character is a centre of intelligibility in the sense of a primary signifier. The character is that which primarily produces meaning, but the character is also a primary content, or signified, that which, above all, the audience is encouraged to enquire about and to speak about. The classical film is not only eminently intelligible. It is also, as we have seen, supremely *interpretable*. Since the psychological character is offered to us as a sort of intellectual spectacle, we are teased and coaxed into an attitude of cultural deliberation. The ideal audience will think about the film in terms of the central character and it will think about this character in terms of the cultural categories that are inscribed within the film's dramatic structure (theme, relations between characters, conflict, resolution). As viewers of the classical love film, we are invited to extend the attitude we have towards the films towards love itself. Love is also presented as a meaningful, interpretable relationship and emotion. The narrative subject in classical film seeks a point of articulation that will enable him or her, finally, to *make sense* of desire.

The reflective form challenges this rational optimism. Unlike fantasy spectacle, the reflective form does not withdraw the relation from rational intelligibility, but it maintains some of the constitutive elements of the love narrative and its intelligibility in a sort of suspense or reflective equilibrium. This state of suspense is reflective in the sense of Kant's reflective judgement: this is a judgement that does not determine a content by the direct application of categories.

Rohmer and Antonioni

Perhaps the two greatest filmmakers of love are Josef von Sternberg and Eric Rohmer. They express in their films both a refined realism and a rigorous aesthetic vision, and both elements, realism and vision, are at the service of love in their films. Rohmer's initial project is moral and philosophical. He analyses the amorous *ego* as a psychological and social fact that can be observed from the outside. The narrative and stylistic aim of his films is to present an aesthetic texture in which this ego, and its delusions, becomes objectified, that is, presented in a way that is not identical to how it appears to itself. This critical presentation of the amorous ego is not, however, objectifying in the sense of framing erotic relationships within pre-given categories. Indeed, many of Rohmer's films have plots based on a pun or a problematisation of a canonical love category, such as seduction, marriage or adultery.

Rohmerian dramatic psychology is indebted to French classical thought. The ego was analysed in the seventeenth century, in authors like La Rochefoucauld, as a complex social and psychological phenomenon. It is social in that the ego fashions itself in the light of social expectations. The ego is psychological in that it is generated from desires that originate in vanity and the wish to increase one's self-esteem.

This moral psychology of the ego is presented by Rohmer within the genre of romantic comedy. Within this genre, a film's plot, or *intrigue* in French, has the double meaning of story and scheming: plots of seduction often involve one character plotting to ensnare another. These plots are comical, in Rohmer, because the scheming character mostly becomes a victim of his or her own machinations. Comedy signifies for Rohmer a screen on which the amorous subject's longings and fantasies are projected for all to see. In Rohmer, comedy puts the subject's most intimate weaknesses and romantic ambitions into the public domain, as the comic plot displays and objectifies the subject's vanity, erotic desires and social aspirations. Romantic, and erotic, comedy is for Rohmer a means of demonstrating the fusion, in the amorous subject, of social ambition and erotic fantasy, or better, the unity of erotic ambition and social fantasy.

Erotic and romantic comedy is in Rohmer a very serious genre. It employs the means of *naturalism* and of philosophical *reflection*. In the filmic space constructed between comic intrigue, naturalist depiction of a social environment and philosophical reflection, Rohmer's cinema establishes a difference between an amorous ego and an erotic subject. The amorous *ego* is self-conscious to the point of self-infatuation. The erotic *subject* is an agency of choice and a source of action. The erotic subject is not necessarily reflected in a self-conscious image that can be attributed to the ego. The ego is charged with the character's self-reflections. The subject on the other hand is devoid of content; it is the voice of desire within the world, and within the realm of action. Of the ego we can say what it is, of the subject what it does.

This dual structure of subject and ego embodied in the same character is filtered, in Rohmer's films, through a sort of *reduction*, where a character is alternately caricatured in its essential traits and rendered as a composite of various inclinations. Dramatic situations serve to bring out the *edge* of a character, that is, its essential and radical possibility, but this radical possibility is at the same time subtly *embedded* in a set of inclinations and other character traits. The Nouvelle Vague is for Rohmer not so much a style – defined by documentary techniques, amateur actors, improvisation, and so on – as it is a programme of cinematic analysis: the characters must be presented in their duality of inclination and radicality, within a place that both motivates their desires and gives them occasions for expressing those desires. In such a circumscribed place, inclinations are in Rohmer's films a kind of rootedness, but this rootedness is only a spring-board or a starting point and never a fatality. In this, he firmly breaks with the psychological style of classical French cinema. Even when his films are carefully situated in a particular town, class or landscape, there is never the suggestion that this environment would somehow *imprison* the characters or script their actions.

Rather there is the superficially similar, but in fact opposed, notion that cinema should be naturalist in its depiction of the relation between erotic desire and social environment. This means concretely, in terms of *mise en scène* and narrative progression, that Rohmer, instead of presenting characters who face a conflict or a dramatic situation, shows them as they are dragged along by the inventiveness of their erotic ambitions; and this process is moulded by place in the manner of a question: what do you do at the beach? What do you do in the new town of the Arc de Triomphe? What do you do if you commute between Mans and Paris, or between Paris and a suburb? There is here the notion that desire is not *caused* by an environment or by circumstances but that it is perceptually *moulded* by the environment and life circumstances of the desiring subject. You can only desire what you see. Desire has at least to be related, even if by contrast and imaginary longing, to one's own actual life with its very specific social-spatial circumstances. Desire is for Rohmer a phenomenon appearing after the fact, filtered through layers of personality, class, language and vanity. The subtlety of his aesthetics resides in the precision with which he depicts both the force of desire and the social circumstances of any erotic relation. This precision is at the same time never reductive – and neither is one allowed, even for a moment, to forget about his characters' sexual interests and social identity. Part of this interest and this identity is age, which is the threshold between a person's biological and sexual identity and her social status and place in society. For the ages of major interest to Rohmer are phases of transition between adolescence and youth or between youth and adulthood.

The act of driving is essential to the flow of events in Rohmer's films. In *Le Beau Mariage* and *Conte d'automne* is a small portion of real time. It is an occasion to be very close to an actual landscape, to enter the real geographical relationships of the characters and of the story. His main characters in the comedies and season stories are mostly women, and those who drive, the woman of *Conte d'automne* and the protagonist of *Le Beau mariage*, drive very ordinary French cars. A point-of-view car-driving sequence begins in *Ma nuit chez Maud* with a chase of the object of desire. The scene displays a strange intimacy. Here one is not reminded of the smells or noise of driving. The car is not a signifier of modernity or anonymity but, on the contrary, an intimate extension of the body. The small trajectories driven in and around towns – often in search of a lover, or in the company of a prospective lover – are invested with the intensity of anticipation and at the same time part of a world of everyday routines. They stage the narrative subject's point of view.

In *La Boulangère*, Rohmer discovers a particular use of the camera, a sort of complicit neutrality in which the implicit subject of enunciation and montage, the ideological point of view that is as if stitched into the fabric of the film, is a particular kind of empathetic yet distant observer. If we compare the distant camera position in Antonioni and Rohmer we find a telling difference on the level of framing. Both directors prefer medium long shots and avoid shot/reverse-shots and other narrative editing conventions within the composition of each scene. Antonioni's camera finds the characters in the midst of geometrically structured spaces that seem to prescribe for them a limited range of movement. The camera often seems just far enough away from the characters to neutralise emotional identification with them. There the subject of enunciation is indeed an observer, and the observing gaze is, if not disinterested, at least *analytical*. The relation between camera and character in Rohmer is more obscure and, we might say, dialectical. Rohmer avoids the direct point-of-view shot, but the literary distinction between narrative voice and narrative point of view applies here: the story always has a character at its point of view. The story unfolds around this character and tracks his or her point of view. This point of view is both physical and emotional. In films like *Pauline a la plage* physical movement organises the space and the plot of the film and the characters display only a limited emotional development. Whether the point of view of the protagonist concerns physical movement or emotional states, the editing and framing of each film are guided by the need to follow the protagonist. A late film that challenges this principle is *Conte d'automne*, in which the narrative point of view is distributed among a series of characters – but even here framing and editing obey the principle of narrative point of view. The protagonist whose point of view the film obeys is at the same time an object of observation. Curiously this structure becomes even clearer when the protagonist himself is a kind of observer. This is the case in *La Boulangère*, *La Collectioneuse* and *Le Genou de Claire*. The observer observed: already the description of this structure provides the idea of dramatic irony, and in fact these three films are plotted around the irony of an observer and seducer whose great cleverness and intricate scheming are revealed in the course of the film to be other than what they seem in the eyes of another observer within the story world of the film. In *La Boulangère* a self-satisfied student is afflicted by some form of lethargy, as the woman he has begun to court suddenly disappears from the streets. As a consolation for this loss he begins a patient and somewhat cynical seduction of a girl in a bakery. The protracted campaign is about to succeed when the first woman suddenly reappears. He flees from the bakery girl and quickly gets together with the original object of his affection. She then reveals to him that from her window she has had the leisure to observe all the steps of his attempted conquest.

This small film is visually modest and relies completely on its carefully crafted plot and the device of irony on which it turns. Rohmer's subsequent films develop more subtle forms of dramatic irony and cover their devices more thoroughly. The observer in Rohmer's early films is usually a male egotist. The egotist observed – this is the narrative principle behind *La Collectioneuse* and *Le Genou de Claire*. These films are genuine psychological studies in erotic desire. They follow directly in the tradition of French eighteenth-century novels such as Laclos's *Les Liaisons dangereuses* with their artificially drawn narrative borders that give to the visual space and the story world of the film an experimental intellectual character. These are not erotic films; they are *intellectual* films about desire, seduction, infatuation and above all the subjectivity of the male seducer. There are thus two objects of psychological analysis in these films: one is the eighteenth-century notion of seduction as a mechanism that can be used by a seducer against the seduced but which also has its own life and is not always within the seducer's control. The other psychological problem is even more classical, as it is the relationship between ego and subject that we saw in La Rochefoucauld. The seducer is very emphatically a *subject*: he initiates action and he does so consciously, but furthermore he is acutely aware of being the one who initiates action. His every action is in fact accompanied by self-consciousness and analysis – analysis of the situation, of his prospects of success, analysis in the manner of Mme de Lafayette of a woman's smallest gestures and reactions. Now, however, we are no longer in the universe of happy transparency of the classical culture. The erotic subject is not always able to read the signs emitted by the object of seduction. On the other hand he is certainly as incapable of reading his own feelings and actions as was the Princesse de Clèves. Being a clever and self-conscious seducer, he is not of course surprised by desire or by an unacknowledged infatuation. His blind spot nests deep within his ego. In his permanent state of self-awareness he is naturally inclined to overestimate his own perspicacity and to ascribe to himself a degree of knowledge that is incompatible with the nature of erotic desire and seduction. The films therefore prove dialectically the life force of erotic communication by showing the failures of seduction. In the two films this dialectic takes different forms.

The seducer in *Genou* is, in a sense, highly successful, but his success depends on an action that he has had to orchestrate in such a way that the young woman who is the object of his desire is unaware that the action is taking place. Or rather she is unaware that an erotic act is taking place. Jerome, the protagonist, is a bearded, rather small, rather nice middle-aged man with an excessive fondness for adolescent girls. He is on holiday at the lake of Anecy and makes contact with his neighbour and old friend, a woman with two young daughters, one dark, one blonde, both adolescent. The dark girl falls in love with him and then avoids him. The object of his interest is the older, blonde girl, who is there with her smart and sporty boyfriend of her age. His erotic *aim*, to use Freud's technical term, is not intercourse, but more simply and more perversely to caress Claire's knee. He orchestrates an elaborate sequence of events which brings about a situation in which he appears as the nice old friend who pats her on the knee in a consoling gesture. Thus the action that he had ponderously worked out in his mind returns to his mind, the satisfaction of his very own desire remains his very own satisfaction. No actual erotic event has taken place, since Claire did not play a part in it. The seducer's gradual self-imprisonment takes a more twisted turn in *La Collectioneuse*. The protagonist is a handsome, vain and much-loved young man. His tall and languid body, his lock of brown hair casually brushed aside from his forehead, his fashionable polo shirts and his melodious soft voice all signal a playboy of some sort. Yet he is far from rich. He is in fact an impoverished art dealer upholding a lifestyle of leisure through the support of wealthier friends. The film narrates his summer holiday in a villa in Southern France. He has planned to spend the summer away from his girlfriend in the company of a painter friend. The pastoral idyll of these male companions is soon disturbed by the intrusion, as he sees it, of a young woman, Haidee, who also benefits from the rich friend's hospitality. The rest of the film depicts a kind of war of seduction between the protagonist and Haidee. A voice-over tells us of the protagonist's thoughts. Well aware of his own near-irresistible effect on women, he is certain that Haidee will fall for him, but he is determined to resist the temptation of an affair and avoid the traps of seduction that he thinks she will put out for him. The events that we see look, on the other hand, somewhat different. We see him eagerly pursuing her in different ways, caressing her body, taking her out at night, putting her down with macho bravado and ridiculing one of her hapless young lovers. This persistent campaign is revealed as such by Haidee late in the film when she says that they have already gone too far in the direction of becoming lovers. Their non-relation takes a different turn, however, in the last episode of the film. After a business deal that he has missed because of her, the ice is broken and they kiss. Before they embark on an affair their car crosses another car with some of her friends. They invite her to join them on a trip to Switzerland. The protagonist just leaves her with her friends, apparently relieved to have escaped the temptation.

The obvious irony of the protagonist believing he is being seduced while acting consistently as the pursuer quickly recedes into the background and is replaced by a different, more interesting problem of seduction. It is in fact not clear who is seducing who or who is trying to seduce who or if anyone is in fact active in the seduction that takes place between the two characters. The film portrays a *situation of seduction*, where the mere spatial coexistence of these two beautiful people seems enough to engender erotic ambitions. The situation not only does not allow the couple to be formed, but also does not allow desire to become articulated as a rational intention or *design*. Seduction remains an unrest, or a tension, a grammar of half-anonymous gestures, waiting to be animated by a more vigorous intentionality.

Place is here referentially non-specific, visually dominant in the composition of each scene and narratively more important than character and motivation. The characters act as they do because they are on holiday in a beautiful place with nothing to do but be troubled by the other's presence. Dramatically more complex versions of the *villeggiatura* story come in other cycles of Rohmer's oeuvre. In the comedies and proverbs *Pauline à la plage* is entirely set in a summer beach resort, while *Le Rayon vert* narrates a woman's holiday adventures. In the comedy cycle intrigue plays a more important role than in the earlier series. The number of characters, scenes and incidents is greater and the protagonists are women rather than men. The comedy cycle explores archetypal character traits and moral flaws arising from a mixture of vanity and indecision. The heroines in *La Femme de l'aviateur*, *Pauline à la plage*, *Les Nuits de la pleine lune*, *Le Beau mariage*, *Le Rayon vert* and *l'Amie de mon amie* seek love and run away from love. They speak about love, and in doing so they miss their amorous opportunities or ensnare themselves in delusions and erroneous self-perceptions.

The woman in *La Femme de l'aviateur* appears unable to get out of her attic flat, stuck between two unsatisfying loves, her distant passion for a pilot who visits her only sporadically and the habitual and unerotic relation she has with a younger man who works night shifts at the post office and is always tired when he sees her. The film juxtaposes her studenty and juvenile attic studio with the larger expanse of Paris. Trapped in a moment of her life that she seems unwilling to leave behind, she speaks in order not to act, in order not to leave her small flat.

The beautiful blonde woman in *Pauline* is a classical comic anti-hero. Styling herself as an expert on love always willing to provide advice on love to her young cousin, Pauline, she is very unsuccessful in her own schemes of seduction. She is courted by a former flame whose intimacy she tolerates. The object of her own interest is a slightly older man, a bohemian type who as it turns out is interested in most women around him. The amorous intrigues that unfold between the beach and the holiday houses are determined by the spatial configuration of the place. There is a limit to what one can do: one can go to the beach or go home or walk along the promenade. In her adolescent earnestness Pauline appears the more mature of the two women, as she observes everything and speaks little, whereas the older woman appears to see nothing and speak too much. The other comedies however do not assign such a clear ironic role to speech. The two most successful and interesting of the films, *Les Nuits de la pleine lune* and *Le Beau mariage*, are both concerned with the logical grammar of decision.

The heroine's indecision, in one case, and precipitate decision, in the other, highlight the structure of erotic choice within the framework of rational deliberation. As this framework has worked its way into the fabric of classical narrative cinema, the decomposition of decision in Rohmer has a moral as well as a meta-cinematic and aesthetic significance.

The protagonist of Antonioni's *Identificazione di una donna* is a filmmaker suffering from a creative and mental block that he thinks he can overcome only if he identifies the right woman to play the main character in his next film. In his search for inspiration he begins a relationship with a young woman from the aristocracy of Rome. He cannot enter her world; he becomes increasingly possessive, aggressive and volatile. She leaves him and he cannot forget her. He looks for her, but she has gone into hiding, having a relationship with another woman. In his search for her, he meets a young woman who offers to help him find her; they start an affair. This affair is lighter in tone, but also ends quickly, as she says that the filmmaker, though interesting, is not the marriable type.

Love in this film is the field of the subject's changing relations to itself and to the world. Love is not dramatically thematised in itself, but love as an erotic relationship is the most important feature of the protagonist's everyday life. Shot mostly in interior medium shots, the film creates an ambivalent sympathy for its characters. We inhabit their world and the claustrophobia of that world, but at the same time we are not invited to identify psychologically with the characters, as the camera keeps a polite distance from what it films. Seen through this distance, the characters, their emotions and other aspects of their subjectivity become objectified.

Love in Motion

The ambivalence between sympathy and critical distance is characteristic of most of Antonioni's films since *l'Avventura*. The earlier films exhibit an unresolved tension between drama and a neorealist style. With the exception of *Zabriskie Point*, which treats its characters like motifs in a fresco of the hippie age rather than as psychological figures, Antonioni's mature style is defined by critical psychological observation, mixing sympathy and distance.

Where *Identificazione* stands out in Antonioni's life work is in its display of speech as an arena where the subject becomes objectified by and in the film, an arena of *self-objectification* similar to, but still fundamentally different from, the self-objectification of characters in early Rohmer. Whereas characters in Rohmer are in love with language and show their infatuation with themselves and with their own ego in interminable monologues, the characters of *Identificazione* all speak a discourse of stilted alienation, as if at the moment of entering speech they lose something of themselves. Language takes on a reality that reflects the subject's relation to itself, but speech is rarely dramatically effective, let alone psychologically revealing. The characters' psychological characteristics are presented rapidly and crudely, in a manner that does not in any way encourage the viewer to enquire into the subtleties of their feelings and motivations. Thus the filmmaker's speech expresses his subjective situation – he is a blocked artist, a middle-aged unmarried egotist, and he suffers from social envy – but none of this adds up to actually explaining or motivating his actions, as he acts largely on whim and impulse. Neither do we see him seducing the two women he has a relationship with. In fact it remains a little mysterious why they fall in love with him at all, given that, apart from being handsome and famous, he seems to have little to recommend him, and when he is with them he seems only to be interested in his own melancholic thoughts.

At the end of *Identificazione* not much has changed in the filmmaker's life. The story presents no robust transformation of the character or of the relations between characters or with regard to what the characters know. A change has, nevertheless, taken place within the protagonist, but this change is intangible and not dramatically explicit. It is a change that can best be described in philosophical terms. *Identificazione* describes the repositioning of a subject. The subject alters his perspective upon the world and his fundamental attitudes of perception and desire. He changes from being mainly related to himself to being related to the world. This change makes it possible for him to break his creative block and begin working as a filmmaker again. The subject's change is described in purely cinematic terms, as it is both a change in perception – at the end of the film he begins to observe things around him – and a change that in fact seems motivated by the act of perception: his relationships with the two women took him out of his flat and brought him around Rome and to different places in Italy. Antonioni does not thereby suggest that the visual world is able to solicit the subject's emotions and interiority in a way that would stir it out of egotism. The change in the subject is gradual and incremental and not located in any specific and discrete moment of intense experience or epiphany. The visual world surrounding the character is merely an antidote to his egotism.

The alienation described by Antonioni in *Identificazione* is not sociological as in *La Notte* or *l'Avventura*. It is not merely a lack of spontaneity or an excess of cunning that Antonioni had portrayed in *Chronaca d'amore* and *Le Amiche*. In *Identificazione*, it appears to be the subject's most intimate processes of reflection as they are expressed in speech that are alienated. He is hit by a kind of ego illness, an egotism that is not even, as in classical film drama, animated by vivid and spontaneous emotions. It is for this reason that the visual world, and in particular nature, becomes an antidote to the ego. Nature resists being absorbed into the ego and its sick ruminations.

Yet, nature is not visually or dramatically presented in sharp contrast with ego psychology, since even the critical objectifying gaze that the film presents on the protagonist and his ego is embedded in a narrative point of view, which is aligned with, and shows sympathy with, his thoughts and movements. Thus the passage of transformation in the subject is a process in which nature is a crucial point of reference, but there are no clear-cut and sharply defined dramatic moments where nature and the ego become thematically opposed. The gradual movement of this passage, which is also the slow and apparently aimless rhythm of the film's narrative, is also a movement that passes through nature in the sense of allowing the ego to pass, imperceptibly, through an alien but cleansing element.

We see where the characters come from socially and geographically, but all these traits are as if subordinated to 'something else' which remains indeterminate. *Identificazione* presents a passage where love is suspended between positions of desire in the world; the passage of the film is a movement through the world, but in itself as a passage it is not determined. The articulation of the events of the story is consumed by the movement through the coordinates that it joins.

In this film, Antonioni thus presents a self whose passage through the world's coordinates displays an ontological gap, separating love from intelligibility. This subject determines itself only in and through its passage through the world's coordinates. The principle of this determination does not coincide with a set of predicates with which the subject or an observer could determine, in thought, what this passage is and thereby make it intelligible.

Love in Motion

Pialat, Lynch, Wong

When cultural categories become reflective and not determining coordinates of an amorous subject, they manifest themselves objectively within the film's narrative and visual world. They appear to the character subject as an external reality. This situation is different from the psychological internalisation of such categories that we find in classical film. In the reflective film, categories appear as something that the subject can pass through. It cannot pretend they are not there but it can neutralize their force.

Pialat's *Loulou* is a classical story of one woman, her boyfriend and her lover, her passage from one relationship to another and the difficulties she encounters in the new relationship. The film is classical in the thematic structure that underlies the plot. One man is a self-employed professional doing editing work. He is cultured and owns a large flat in a good area of Paris; the other is a petty criminal from a working-class and in part criminal family. The film is classical also in its narrative rhythm, both within the logical sequence of the fable and in the subject exposition. Yet, in its visual and dramatic style the film is far from classical. It is furthermore different from intellectual or abstract films of the *Nouvelle Vague* or by filmmakers like Wim Wenders or Jim Jarmusch, who may also treat romantic subjects but who present love from an angle of reflection in relation to the film form (Truffaut, Wenders) or in relation to literary ideas or in virtue of a conceptual self-reflexivity that offers a distancing and ironic gaze on the lovers and their feelings (Jarmusch). There is in Pialat no such distance, but the naked seriousness of emotion and sentiment and the inextricable web of vulnerability and violence emerging from the film's dramatic situations are not really *thematic*; they do not conform to or appeal to a *generic code of intelligibility*. The given lines of social conflict are just starting points, not pegs on which other, moral or psychological, traits and distinctions are hung to frame the dramatic events. The characters are characterised subtly and with extraordinary realism of gesture, but these characterisations still leave the dramatic situations partly underdetermined. In *Loulou* the forward movement of the action is a continuous and logical progression guided by an initial situation. Gerard seduces Nelly. They fall in love, and Nelly leaves to live with Gerard. When she is pregnant the relationship falters. She has an abortion and the end is uncertain. They are still together but the strain of external social pressures that the pregnancy has revealed makes the relation seem fragile. The intentions that we can attribute to the characters are very clear. They are sexual and instinctual. The former boyfriend is possessive and the two lovers affirm their freedom. The differences between Gerard's and Nelly's social and cultural backgrounds create tensions between them. There is an overt conflict between the boyfriend and Gerard and a growing or latent conflict between Nelly and Gerard. But none of these intentions and conflicts are endowed with content. They are not intelligible beyond the brute fact of desire and opposition. The social differences are just conditions of the story and do not illuminate choices or dilemmas. The choices that Nelly goes through and makes arise from the unfolding continuous movement of the drama.

The film is not photorealistic in a documentary sense, since its fable structure is transparent and robust. It is realistic in its momentum of gradual, incremental growth of situations and complexity. The growth of a movement, which involves the characters with each other, places them in situations of conflict that force them to confront simultaneously themselves and dimensions of social reality that would otherwise not have been part of their world.

In *Loulou*, love is involved with a complex web of worldly constraints. It would be reductive to call these constraints social or cultural. They are not just obstacles posed by class differences and beliefs about what love should be. Here love is expressed not from the point of view of feeling, nor from that of external conditions, but from the perspective of erotic desire. From this perspective of desire, everything that the lovers are involved with is either an obstacle or an empowering condition. People, ideas, money: everything has the same status in relation to love. It is enabling if it helps love to flourish and blocking if it impedes love. *Loulou* is as much a film about Paris as it is a film about love. Its main characters are steeped in their local surroundings, their flats, daily walks, regular bars.

In *Jules et Jim* love is romantic and inexplicable, tragic and repetitive. In *Loulou* the perspective that the film presents upon desire consists of a different, less imaginary, more material dynamic between the lovers and between the lovers and the world. Love is here neither tragic nor repetitive, but open-ended: desire cannot be hedged in, but it is not over-determined by structures of power. Desire is articulated in relation to very concrete power relationships, based on class, gender, physical strength, and so on, but the plot does not unfold according to a structure of desire that is gradually revealed. Instead, *Loulou* is a film where the viewer discovers the world of the main characters as they themselves become involved with their surroundings or simply drift through the world.

Loulou is however also a romantic film, in the sense that it affirms love's power to assert itself against the odds of social common sense. This romanticism is not ethereal. It is all the stronger for being immersed in circumstances that spell its imminent death. An enigmatic and beautiful scene in *Lolou* shows the heroine dancing with a friend of her lover, recently released from prison. He is obviously full of the need and desire that prison has produced. She is neither insensitive to this need nor impressed by it. The scene does not fulfil any precise dramatic or narrative role, but it accentuates the sense of drift and need that characterises the whole story.

Pialat depicts the trajectory of subjects who are driven by their desires and only to a limited extent controlled by conscious decisions. The trajectory of desire moves forward but does not have a final goal. Its movement is open-ended, and so are many of the stories in Pialat's films. This material and yet open-ended force of desire is a continuous subject that we can distinguish sharply from a melodramatic subject defined by its relation to its own ego. We can more generally distinguish between two kinds of subject. One is defined by material continuity and a relationship with its environment that is based on involvement and mutual absorption but rarely on decision. The melodramatic subject by contrast is a subject that constitutes itself through a process of rationalisation of its own emotions. This process insulates and isolates the subject from the world. The melodramatic subject relates to the world as representation: it represents to itself emotional and imaginary scenarios which it then enacts and invests in its surroundings. It does not absorb its surroundings since it only selects what it needs for its own imaginary scenarios. It situates love on an internal psychological stage of the ego and it entertains the belief that others, whether actual or potential loves or obstacles to love, are not actual beings that the subject must confront but are figures on this internal stage that can be manipulated by the subject-director, and hence replaced as the subject finds convenient. The melodramatic subject's tears and hope, its shame or sadness relating to the past and its hope of redemption, imply a belief in total self-transformation, total renewal. This belief is correlated with the belief that love itself is at any moment reversible, as it is not grounded in a relation but in the feelings and longings of the ego. Pialat is a fierce opponent of melodramatic psychology in that his films externalise all the protagonist's erotic ambitions and projects, denying the viewer any psychological empathy with his feelings. The trajectory of the continuous subject depicted by Pialat brushes up against real and complex obstacles, opportunities and indeterminate situations. In *Loulou*, a series of sequences connect narrative possibilities into a dense web of interwoven events. This density is attenuated by a realist anti-dramatic narrative style that makes the events flow seemingly naturally one from the other or sometimes one within the other.

Loulou is not an interpretable film in the sense discussed earlier. It does not situate the characters and their acts within a field of cultural categories that we can use to interpret the characters' psychology and motivation. Even the characters themselves seem at a loss, not knowing what to do or why. Hence *Loulou* is, we might say, an *anti-hermeneutic* film, but it is certainly not a superficial film: if there is little to interpret it is not because the characters, as in *The 39 Steps*, are mere narrative-sexual figures devoid of psychological complexity, but because the characters' complexity is always carried out into the world and hence shown through its effects.

In Pialat's films there is an effort to present language as a continuous flow of expression. Within this flow, ruptures and intentions do not appear marked. Speech is a kind of instinctual, gestural action that only minimally extends from the body of the speaker. Speech thus does not actually transform the character into a subject of speech, a subject intentionally using language as a means of action or expression, a subject who would use language to confront difficult situations or to solve problems.

The drama in *Loulou* turns on Nelly's decision to abort the child she has conceived with Gerard because he is unwilling to look for a job. We see her reaching this decision in a long scene depicting a family Sunday lunch with his mother, brother, stepbrother and various other characters. The lunch is jovial and lively but there is a source of unrest. A young woman has a paranoid husband who is kept in the house and not allowed to take part in the meal. One of his friends, just out of prison, has a discreet but irrepressible interest in all women that he sees, and thus also starts a conversation with the crazy man's wife. This leads the madman to enter the courtyard armed with a rifle. He threatens to kill the man. The others relieve him of his gun, and everyone relaxes. The scene is shown from her point of view. As the camera pans around to pick up all the different voices in the family gathering, it always comes back to her and shows her thoughtful expression.

The film follows classical narrative rules in that it builds up, dramatically and psychologically, to the abortion and it clearly shows the psychological and moral motivation behind this choice, but this motivation is never allowed to occupy centre stage. However, as such it is psychologically objective. It leaves nothing left to interpret.

At the centre of Pialat's films is always a series of complex interactions and relationships that release composed feelings of aggression and tenderness in the characters involved in these relationships. These composed feelings and the often very dramatic situations that give rise to them are depicted in a non-classical undramatic form. For even the highly expressive acting out of anger or violence often has the status of mere incidents, of something occurring and which the film describes or puts on record but which is not in itself or on its own the cause of something that follows or itself clearly caused by a prior event. In *Loulou* the two lovers meet at a disco. She is at that time with another man. When she tells her boyfriend that she has met another man he claims that he cannot live without her. Later on in the film, after a series of violent quarrels, he manages to persuade her to come and work with him in his office, even if they will not have a relationship. Throughout this development of the two overlapping and parallel relationships, in the entire arc of the drama, the boyfriend, soon to become ex-boyfriend, is static, or one could say true to himself. He is verbally aggressive, irascible and prone to sudden bouts of physical violence. He is in other ways a cultivated and pleasant character. On the other hand, and this is quite unusual in cinema, he is not depicted as a comical figure, or as a villain, or even as a morally negative person. He is simply possessive and has a quick temper. There is no suggestion in the film as the story unfolds of her definitely ending her relationship with him, nor is there any notion that some acts of abuse would mark a definite limit or create a point of rupture between the characters.

Pialat's use of narrative ellipsis creates an ambivalent sense of continuity. On the one hand disparate dramatic moments are sewn together as if there were no break between them so as to mimic the way in which conflicts are absorbed within the social textures of family and friendship in real life. On the other hand, ellipsis also strengthens the enumerative quality of the film's dramatic moments, and thus contributes to the sharply drawn characterisation of each of the principal characters. We are offered few psychological explanations beyond the basic inclinations that we find in each. These are inclinations that we see acted out again and again in a repetitive but not always identical way, as the characters respond to circumstances, adapt, accept defeat and go on.

In *Blue Velvet* by David Lynch we come to see the narrative subject as part of a fabric or tapestry. The psychoanalytic post-modernism that Lynch excels in problematises the status of cultural categories of love. The notion that the terms which inform how we think of love, terms such as innocence, desire, youth, vice and transgression, could be taken to be 'natural' moral or psychological categories is subjected to a deep-seated scepticism in this film. The film presents a conceptual point of view upon its characters. Within this perspective, their gestures of love and eroticism appear staged, at one remove from any immediate cultural significance. This conceptual construction integrates style, content and narrative within one coherent and complex 'image'. This conceptual image is in turn constituted in part by a multiplicity of cultural quotations. These quotations produce a broken tone, half-way between perversion and adolescent innocence, between a heterosexual and virile world of policemen and a gay, camp world of pimps and sadistic criminals. The film's narrative echoes this broken tone. This is a cinematic bildungsroman of sorts, or at least a journey of discovery. The subject of this journey is a young suburban man in a small town in 1950s America. His journey, like the film, is half perverse, half innocent. Dramatically and thematically this is a journey of love and sexual exploration. It is structured by his desire for two very different women. One is a sweet blonde girl of his own age and neighbourhood. She is the daughter of one of his father's police friends. The other, played by Isabella Rossellini, is dark haired, older, sexually experienced, compromised by vice. His journey towards and between these two women comes to appear to the viewer as one extended image of his desire, subjectivity and longing for love.

The protagonist thus enters two rival relationships in the course of the story, one with the dark mysterious woman and one with the blonde high-school sweetheart. The dark-haired woman is the prisoner and sexual companion of a certain Frank, a perverse criminal who keeps her son as a captive in order to force her to enact erotic fantasies with him. When the protagonist unwittingly becomes the voyeur of one of these scenarios and she discovers him in her cupboard, she reverses the roles, first coercing, then seducing him into becoming her lover.

Apart from Frank, his mistress and his criminal friends, the characters appear in the universe of the film as quotations from a catalogue of ordinary life. This is not to say that the main characters are confined within a static role. The story allows them to evolve and express themselves in a less scripted form, as they are confronted with situations that are not part of their normal identity. A reflective distance and tension arise between the identities that the protagonists seek to sustain, at the outset, and the erotic subjectivity that they gradually come to assert *against this identity*.

The story world of the film is suspended between the moral poles of innocence and vice, but the paths that lead from one pole to the other in the film are many and of different kinds. There is a temporal and narrative path that carries the male protagonist from the normal world to a criminal underworld. There is a symbolic path, suggesting that this underworld corresponds to his unconscious sexual life, or perhaps, more conceptually, to the unconscious world of sexuality in general. There is further a suggestion of pervasiveness and of fluidity, a notion of vice being stronger than innocence, so that even though normality and order are re-established at the end of the story, the elements of the unconscious, of vice and of violence are not actually contained or containable. Hence *mise en scène* is in *Blue Velvet* perfectly continuous. There are no detached objects like the severed hand in *Un Chien andalou*. There are no symbolic structures in space like the tower in Hitchcock's *Vertigo*. The narrative does not – in the manner of the movement of repetition in *Vertigo* – emulate the rhythm of desire. *Mise en scène* is here organised around the expression of specific emotions and moods. These moods and emotions are in part located in the characters and motivated by their narrative situation, but they also permeate the entire visual image of the film as a highly specific tone. This emotional tone is one of perverse regression, or regressive perversion. The film image is permeated by this tone of regression at any instance of the story. This tone has various expressive sources within the aesthetic fabric of the film. Narratively, the film follows, sympathetically, the point of view of the teenage protagonist, who is curious and more than eager to grow up. In the course of the story he encounters various types of sexual violence and criminality. Finally, the film has a nostalgic retro feel. It is set in the mythical universe of small-town America, complete with archetypal stock characters such as the friendly blind brother running the hardware store and the blonde high-school sweetheart who becomes involved in the protagonist's adventures. Thematically, the film contains an enactment of Freud's theory of childhood voyeurism, only the 'child' is no longer a child and he is a voyeur not of his parents but of two strangers. The tone of the film is constructed out of multiple expressive layers – genre convention, camp, self-referentiality, allusions to psychoanalysis, American folklore – each of which is employed to evoke the theme and mood of regression. These different expressive registers are unified chromatically through a consistent use of blue, violet and dark colours. The film generally avoids brownish hues which would have given it a warmer atmosphere. The film creates its own kind of stylised chiaroscuro, which serves to demarcate an autonomous filmic world associated with fear and sexual fantasy. In this dualistic yet ambivalent world, erotic subjectivity asserts itself within the domain of fantasy. Now, the visual enactment of erotic fantasy plays a very complex role in the texture of the film.

The locations of the film are superficially realistic and evoke a small-town world: the suburban house and garden, the high school, the parental car, the diner and then, as the story takes shape, a low-income housing estate, a nightclub, an out-of-town brothel. The social symmetry of these locations, mirroring perfectly the distinction between respectability and a social fringe world, defines them as a set but does not determine their individual aesthetic function. The erotic centre of the film is the apartment of the character played by Isabella Rossellini, a nightclub singer with an ambivalent relationship to the gangster Frank. In this apartment, the protagonist undergoes a sexual education, passing through different roles and sexual personae. The boxed-in apartment looks like an installation from an exhibition of psychoanalytic art. It appears to be itself an unconscious stage, the location of desire and nothing else. It is in fact the location of three different kinds of desire. First, it is the location of Rossellini's and Hopper's sadomasochistic relationship. Second, it is the location of the protagonist's voyeuristic and subsequently reciprocal relationship with Rossellini. Third, it is the location of his fear of Hopper, a fear that the narrative weaves into his desire to the point where the two become inseparable.

This installation technique is also applied to other locations in the film. When the protagonist is kidnapped by Frank, he is taken to a brothel at the outskirts of the provincial town where the film is set. There a friend of Hopper's, a gay pimp, performs a playback croon to a Roy Orbison song. He is 'singing' inside a room, while outside one of the prostitutes lazily and joylessly dances to the beat of the song on top of a parked car. After this musical 'performance', the crooner is given the privilege of hitting the captured young man in his stomach. The scene is filmed in a chromatic register that fits the mood of the song, and which consists in a spectrum that is both shrill and subdued: strong yellows and reds are embedded in a general mood of darkness. The scene evokes the hero's confrontation with his own homosexuality, his fear of a not-improbable imminent death, his youthful excitement at the discovery of a world larger than that of his family. Both of these locations, Rossellini's apartment and the provincial brothel, serve as the stage for the enactment of particular, often quite complicated sexual scenarios and fantasies. These locations are not un-realistic, but their aesthetic function is in no way exhausted by being the locations of particular characters or events in the story; they are not just the place where certain – as it happens, sexual – things happen to the protagonist. Rather, they are used like installation pieces in the sense that within those sequences, location, event, character and tone are integrated into one visual and expressive statement. They form, we might say, using a term from Gilles Deleuze, an aesthetic and emotional block of expression. In his essay on Sacher Masoch, Deleuze associates the aesthetic erotic phenomenon of fantasy with a particular temporal form. Fantasy injects stasis, freezes a situation, imposes a kind of still image on an otherwise dynamic situation. A similar effect of stasis permeates *Blue Velvet*, as it is constructed around these static moments of erotic intensity.

Between these moments of intensity the film creates a fictional space that occupies an ambivalent place between the real and the unconscious, fantasy, social reality and pure emotion. In this fictional space, the moral and social categories that could make desire intelligible are as if turned inside out like in a Moebius strip. They do not disappear and they are not simply, and post-modernistically, reduced to the status of quotations. Rather they appear as the *components of a trajectory of discovery* that is objectified as pure emotional intensity. In this film love disappears as a real erotic relation between two subjects and leaves the scene to the erotic subject as it relates to its own desire.

Other subjects may interact with the principal subject in his exploration of his desire, as figures who introduce new situations, as poles of his imagination, as participants in his activities, but he does not, within the arc of the narrative, form an actual, durable love relation with either the blonde girl or the dark woman. Here desire therefore retreats into the subject, and this subject appears as a continuous unconscious self. Most importantly, unlike in classical cinema, this subject is not trying to make *choices* or to integrate itself into the world. It seeks instead to incorporate people and categories from the world into its own solitary pursuit. In this trajectory, where the conceptual construction of tone through a complex web of quotations produces an image of the subject's unconscious, cultural categories themselves take on a relative status. They appear as quotations or components of quotations, as the social or moral reality of vice in contrast with normality gradually disappears and is replaced by the dominant reality of desire. From the point of view of this desire the world is not, as it was in Pialat, a set of objective coordinates, opportunities and obstacles. The world is in part integrated into the psyche as the map of the coordinates defining desire.

The cinema of Wong Kar-Wai is akin to a kind of phenomenology of love. It is a cinema that seeks to include society, sex, emotion, historical conditions and personal character traits within the *phenomenon* of love, while at the same time suggesting that love in itself as a phenomenon is different in kind from any of these components. The development of Wong Kar-Wai's films from *As Tears Go By* to *2046* is organised by two parallel movements of intensification. One is an increasing focus upon *emotion*, each film pushing further in an aesthetic liberation of emotion from dramatic relationships, giving emotion an ever greater autonomy within the expressive economy of the film image. The other development is autobiographical, charting a movement from adolescence through early adulthood towards maturity. This autobiographical trajectory is mirrored dramatically and erotically in a move from stories of distant infatuation and sexual bewilderment through stories of relationships – unhappy or unrealised – to the meditation on the very *idea* of relationships in *2046*, a meditation that is realised dramatically through frenetic sexual encounters. The first movement is a spiral moving inwards, carving out within the narrative material of emotion an ever more concentrated and pure tonal and expressive quality. The second movement begins in an opposition between imagination and the world and ends in their identification.

We have to consider two questions. The first is the relationship between generic formalism, spectacle, framing and melodrama in Wong's cinema. The second is Wong's relation to two writers that he claims as his models, Manuel Puig and

Haruki Murakami. Let us begin with these two writers. Wong's relation to them is one of elective affinity. Puig is an Argentinian novelist who weaves references to film and popular culture into stories that are strangely hardboiled and sentimental, depicting characters who are less than successful and not quite admirable, but whose longings and sentiments are rendered raw and vivid with a powerful and unironic emotional pathos. This seriousness can at first seem surprising, since the novels are playfully steeped in cultural references, especially to cinema, but these cultural references *do not have a distancing effect*. On the contrary, they serve to *reinforce* the expression and mood of emotional intensity. Thematically, this intermingling of cultural reference and emotional intensity corresponds in Puig's novels to an interest in characters who are neither heroes nor anti-heroes. They are interesting ordinary people whose existential dramas stem from their particular biographic and subjective angle upon reality, with the sorrows and desires this gives rise to. His plots are confined within the range of events that make up these ordinary lives. Yet his characters are not rendered cynically or with a sociological distance, as types. The Japanese writer Murakami equally finds a way of accessing unglamorous lives through a perspective that is not guided by social generalisations. His characters are plainer and more straightforwardly uninteresting than those of Puig. Their uninterestingness is not, on the other hand, exaggerated. There is nothing absurd or bleak about Murakami's characters. They are likeable, charming even. One would like to get to know them. Yet they have extremely little to recommend them in the way of character traits or accomplishments. Murakami's painstaking, deceptively simple prose style manages to create for these characters an aura of suspense, projecting a poetic universe that makes their inner lives mesmerising, like riddles harbouring secrets more significant than the people who embody them. Murakami ambiguously follows the indirect techniques of psychological description cultivated by classical Japanese novelists like Kawabata and Inoue, developing situations of desire in which emotions are symbolised, but his references to popular culture, the light tone of his prose and the absence of moral depth in his characters break the psychological intensity that this technique yielded in his predecessors. Whereas Inoue, for example, analyses his characters' motives and the finer lineaments of their mental life, Murakami's poetics of mental suspense remains, in a certain sense, external, attached to objects and situations, sexual acts, natural landscapes, songs. Murakami's novels are fine-grained psychological studies in their own right, but their psychology is not *analytical*. Transitions, moods and the border between conscious and unconscious states crystallise in his prose within narrative situations and poetic images, but character motivation remains vague.

Love in Motion

Murakami and Puig have three things in common that we can find echoed in the cinema of Wong Kar-Wai: emotional intensity, references to popular culture and ordinary or unexceptional characters. Puig and Murakami are stylistically very different. They develop literary means of accessing emotion that take opposing routes: Puig describes emotions and character traits explicitly and directly, but offsets this psychological realism with an elliptical suddenness of presentation, as if we should get to know the characters suddenly – too suddenly, that is, in relation to the conventions of nineteenth-century realism. Murakami evokes emotion indirectly through flatly described situations rich in mental implications.

Taken together, Puig and Murakami thus present the filmmaker with the alternative between a psychological style bordering on melodrama (Puig) and a situational style close to a realism of everyday life (Murakami). Wong's films in fact incorporate both of these tendencies and oscillate between them. Against this background we can now consider the four terms mentioned above: generic formalism, melodrama, spectacle and framing.

The generic formula of killers, crazy friends, love-sick young women and love impeded by social convention are always only material in Wong's films. They are material for creating an image and a story that *are not completely defined by genre*. This is true already of *As Tears Go By*, which is ostensibly a formulaic gangster, romance and youth film. This film also shows how close-ups of objects constitute a framing technique that can render the visual space plastic and textured and thereby aesthetically permeable, establishing a qualitative continuity with the physical gestures of the characters. In this film, framing of *parts* of rooms, *parts* of the human body and particular objects establishes a particular kind of plasticity, a space always already permeated with gesture. These gestures are always emotionally significant, even if the emotions signified are here, as in most other Wong films, confined within a relatively narrow range: lonely longing and emerging amorous feelings alternating with narcissistic pleasures.

A sequence in *Chungking Express* is interesting in this context. It shows a threat to happy egoism in the domain of sex. The male character lives out a fantasy, seducing a stewardess, but he seems more interested in the fantasy than in its realisation. As the actual woman stands before him playing erotic games, he plays with a toy aeroplane. After lovemaking he caresses her back with the same toy plane: narcissism is resistant and claims its due. Hence loneliness is a rich and ambivalent zone of exploration for Wong. The nightly cyclist in *Fallen Angels* needs little beyond his bicycle, his camera and the city that he traverses. The haunted misogynist in *Days of Being Wild* displays a different, more aggressive and expressive self-sufficiency, a self-sufficiency in relation to others: addicted to seduction and cruelty, he cultivates a display of coldness and distance, serving as a means of humiliating his lovers, but also, we are led to believe, as a defence against feelings of tenderness – given or received, as he carries with him a melodramatic family sub-plot. His mother lives a disgraced life as an ageing beauty clinging to youth through the use of gigolo lovers. A lushly incestuous and high-strung drama is suggested in all the sequences with him and his mother. He is thus, in terms of motivation, cruel in love because he is an emotional cripple. Yet the interest of the film scarcely lies with this dramatic motivation. Rather, in contrasting different locations, each associated with a particular mood, and a particular kind of story, the film moves to the outside of melodrama, containing the melodramatic high temperature within a wider emotional range that relativises its totalising claim to significance. The poetic sequences when a rejected female lover wanders through the Hong Kong streets at night and meets a lonely policeman, who tries to console her, have a very different emotional tone and narrative rhythm to that of family drama. Drawn-out, open-ended and lacking in dramatic intensity, these sequences display a zone of emergent emotions where strangers become friends and friends may become lovers – or not, as in this case, where the two lives that almost intersect in the end fail to do so, as the woman returns to her life and he waits for her to call him, but in vain, for, as his voice-over tells us, he never saw her again.

The aesthetic exploration of erotic loneliness as a phenomenon that takes place in the world is phenomenologically interesting in that it differs from how the lonely person sees him or herself in introspection. This exploration also prepares the more complex depiction of reciprocal love relationships and unfulfilled love relations in *In the Mood for Love* and *2046*. Wong's characters are naturally and obviously subjects who are not defined by middle-class values. Hit men and policemen, fast-food sellers and drifters, none is defined by class, position or gender in a rigid way in the early films, except perhaps negatively, as the absence of a settled middle-class life, which they all have in common, makes it possible for them to live their youthful lives in the mode and mood of travel.

Chungking Express demonstrates another combination of loneliness and love, as the film interweaves two stories, each involving a meeting between two lonely characters: one, an inconsequential encounter, is the meeting of an innocent young policeman and a woman who, unbeknownst to him, is a serial killer; the other is the gradual, protracted falling in love of two young people, she a tomboy working in a fish and chip parlour, he a policeman working night shifts. In this relationship, as in the relationship between the young man and the stewardess earlier, there is a straightforward opposition between love and loneliness, in that both characters are self-absorbed individuals who find it difficult to move beyond themselves. Then again, a certain privacy is also what they have in common. It is the basis of their final encounter, final in the sense that it happens in the very last sequence of the film.

A more sophisticated and abstract conception of the relation between love and loneliness is developed in *Fallen Angels*, where the relation between a young woman and a serial killer that she works for exists largely in her imagination. *Happy Together* on the other hand is a dramatic, almost theatrical drama of domestic power relations between an exiled gay couple. This film gives yet another interpretation of love and loneliness. Here the lovers separate early in the film and we follow one of them, who, consumed with regret and lonely ruminations, lives the relationship retrospectively and on his own. *Happy Together* and *Fallen Angels* seek ways of creating a fast pace that opens up, in its midst, to a very different semiotic and aesthetic dimension of showing and of slowing down. In this narrative slow motion, time is not frozen as in a block – Wong is closer after all to Truffaut than to Tarkovsky – but is aligned with inconclusiveness and repetition. What then is shown? Human subjectivity in its embodied character identity, but also the world in which lives *improbably* cross and combine. The futuristic block in *Fallen Angels* constitutes a space of coolness, a youthful ideal of characters who aspire to exist only for the sake of embodying an image.

In classical French cinema place functions as a vehicle of character analysis, a laboratory of human emotions. In the cinema of reflection that in Wong Kar-Wai resonates with melodrama and with the fantasy spectacles of escape, place is an independent factor of meaning at least as important if not more important than the feelings of the protagonists. *Happy Together* is first of all a film about loneliness in Buenos Aires, only secondarily a psychological portrait of two sensitive young men. *Fallen Angels* is first of all a study in the Hong Kong metro system at night, not a documentary but a phantasmagorical journey where erotic desire is the adjunct of a more basic desire to move and to be constantly on the run. The slightly dumb female assistant and the hit man she loves are both merely caricatures. They are generic figures who gain consistency in and through the spaces they move in as they come to seem, within the cinematic spectacle, consubstantial with those spaces.

The mature film *In the Mood for Love* inscribes amorous loneliness within a specific social and historical as well as autobiographical environment. The Shanghai community in Hong Kong in the early 1960s formed a self-contained and somewhat secluded social environment. The secretary played by Maggie Cheung inhabits an interesting and unstable moral space. As a secretary she is actively complicit in the adulterous life of her boss, administering his relations with wife and mistress. This mixture of establishment propriety and mild sordidness resonates with the political status of Hong Kong as a British outpost with limited freedom and an ethos of permissiveness encouraged by its colonial controllers. She herself maintains or seeks to maintain a moral posture of prim correctness, being obedient to her boss and to her husband even as the husband has an affair with the neighbour's wife.

The protagonist, the neighbour whose wife betrays him, is an office clerk and an aspiring writer of martial arts stories. He is one of those white-collar workers that Siegfried Kracauer described with compassion in his reportage essay *Die Angestellten*: his social opportunities are limited, so his hopes and aspirations are confined to the realm of the imagination. Yet he is not content with day-dreaming. He brings imagination into his life, by writing martial arts stories. At the point in his life where the film takes place, he is at a threshold between different phases of his life. His wife is drifting away, and he is beginning to write. At this point he is susceptible to falling in love with the neighbour's wife, who he discovers is the wife of the man having an affair with his own wife. In this claustrophobic environment of domesticity and adultery, Wong introduces an element of fantasy through the artifice of a game. The two neighbours meet and begin playing a strange game. They pretend to be their respective traitor: he plays her husband, she his wife; they imagine, even play-act the first encounter between the two. In so doing they create a space of experimentation where their confined emotions can find expression and move from frustration to desire and infatuation and hope. The game inevitably ensnares them, inducing them to fall in love.

The 'sequel' *2046* moves on from this carefully crafted balance between erotic freedom and social necessity. In *2046*, the narrative perspective is in solidarity with the main character and we leave the world of the lower middle class to enter that of a *demi-monde* constituted by journalists, courtesans and others who, like the lower middle class of *In the Mood for Love*, live with limited means in small rooms and whose lives take place largely at night. The young girl that the protagonist falls in love with but carefully avoids seducing, the daughter of his landlord, is not part of that world. She is a decent innocent girl fighting with her father to be able to marry her Japanese fiancé. All the characters in the film live for love. They have intense amorous aspirations that are rarely fulfilled or given a release within a relationship. As we follow the protagonist's adventures and get to know a number of women, whose lives run parallel to one another and who all share these same aspirations, we come to perceive the private amorous aspiration as a kind of social event, as the very thing that people have in common and which binds them together but which at the same time keeps them separate, since unrequited love keeps the subject within a self-imposed solitary confinement of longings and regrets.

Love in Motion

In the Mood for Love and *2046* are both reflections on love from a dual perspective, subjective and objective. They fold a subjective point of view into a sociological analysis, which in turn is inscribed within a Proustian evocation of an affective past. The past is remembered as in Proust for the affective significance it has for the self – that is, the psychological significance it would have for a divine observer of that self, and not the consciously felt significance it had in the remembered present of the lived past. The centre of this folded perspective within *In the Mood for Love* is solitude. It is portrayed as a condition in which the subject is ready to fall in love, while at the same time being socially exposed. There is in the narrative universe of this film very little in the lives of the protagonists that makes them stand out from their environment or impose a pattern on it. The man and the woman are both solitary in this way. In *2046*, the dramatic focus is *time* rather than solitude. The amorous subject in the film is constantly in love and each woman he meets has her longings and aspirations that never completely coincide with his. Love exists in this film as a possibility *between* a set of characters, but they each live according to their subjective time-line.

The protagonist experiences three unhappy loves. They are all marked by temporal asymmetries. His relation to the gambler at the beginning of the film is futureless because she appears haunted by a shameful past and is therefore unable to love him. His relation to a sexy neighbour is based on two different temporal assumptions. He sleeps with her to forget himself, to forget his past love, to wait for better times. She on the other hand at first resists his advances, but in the course of their wild sexual encounters she falls in love with him. She then hopes the present is the beginning of a future with him. For him there is no future for them. The third relationship is with a younger woman who has a fiancé living abroad. The girl is Hong Kong Chinese and her fiancé is Japanese. Her father is against their marriage because the fiancé is not Chinese. She still loves him but her camaraderie and friendship with the main character moves to the threshold of a relationship.

In the narrative universe of the film there is no possible point of intersection between these time lines, such that two characters in search of love could become lovers. By presenting love, thus, as a phenomenon of desire, as a longing and a possibility that exists between characters rather than within each, or within actual relationships, Wong presents a fusion of imagination of the world of a different kind from that accomplished by Lynch in *Blue Velvet*. Imagination and regret exist in the world in the form of unactualised possibilities subsisting between different subjective timelines. The world is, as in the philosophy of Leibniz, nothing but the space of coexistence for souls closed around themselves.

Love in the World

Zwartboek

Zwartboek (*Black Book*) is a recent love and war film and a historical blockbuster. *Zwartboek* is significant as an event in film history: it was made by the Dutch filmmaker Paul Verhoeven, who shot it on location in Holland with Dutch actors, after having worked for a number of years in Hollywood and become famous with the sex-and-morality film *Basic Instinct*, among other films. *Zwartboek* deals with moral ambiguity in the context of the Dutch resistance during World War II. This is a difficult topic, since the Dutch resistance was famously brave and the German occupying forces notoriously ruthless in their retaliations against the civilian population. The film is a European World War II action film, perfect in the flow of its action and elegantly filmed historical sets. It is captivating and entertaining according to the sex-and-violence formula – but it is also a sophisticated reflection on the past, and on the notions of heroism, war crime and political innocence ordinarily invoked within historical discourses on World War II. The film is further, like all historical films, a product of the time in which it was made. It is an ego-narrative in the style of the *Bourne* trilogy. It is a tale of survival, cunning and loss of humanity. It is also one of the most significant films about love made in the last decade.

In *Zwartboek*, action spectacle is the justification for a moral reflection, and love is at the centre of that reflection. The structure of the film is like a flower, opening up from the minimal situation of survival and a near-death experience, then extending from there to include ever more characters, places and aspects of life. As the film becomes gradually more complex, it starts to weave a web of relations between sex, morality and the public world.

Central to the film's narrative is a love story. The protagonist is a highly intelligent, beautiful and attractive young Jewish woman. At the beginning of the film, she is in hiding with a Christian family. The house that she lives in is bombed by an Allied plane but she is not in the house and therefore survives. The German authorities are soon on her trail. Together with a young man whom she meets on the way, she makes contact with a family friend and borrows a large sum of money. They join her family and leave on a fishing boat, together with other Jews, in order to escape along the rivers. The captain of the boat belongs to the resistance. Soon the boat is stopped by a German military ship. The Germans shoot all on board and steal their possessions.

Miraculously the protagonist escapes. From this point onwards she is almost entirely alone in the world. She manages to keep alive long enough to re-join the resistance. They give her a new identity. After a few months she is sent on a mission to transport explosives on a train together with another member of the

Love in Motion

resistance, a tall and very able man, a little older than herself. As the passengers are inspected by soldiers she saves her skin and the suitcase with explosives that she is carrying by flirting with a high-ranking German officer. He in fact appears to fall head over heels for her. She is thereafter encouraged by the resistance to have an affair with him in order to give them a foothold at Nazi headquarters. The officer now falls in love with her, and gradually, we are led to believe, she also falls in love with him. He discovers her actual identity but decides not to give her up. She on the other hand finds an opportunity to save him, later in the film. The *chiastic* structure of the plot thus embodies a strong notion of not only erotic but also moral reciprocity. He is portrayed as a courageous, naïve and quite idealistic officer. He accuses a Nazi colleague of stealing properties from Jews – but his act misfires. He is unable to prove his accusation, and the other officer pays him back by accusing him of illegal clemency towards captured enemies. He is imprisoned and the young woman then has the occasion to demonstrate for him the same courage as he had shown to her. As the resistance raids the German headquarters to free prisoners she insists on freeing also the German captured officer. During the raid, she is captured and manages to escape, but only after the Germans have spread the false rumour to other members of her resistance group that she is a traitor who had caught them in a trap. She and the German officer then flee together, but their freedom does not last long. As the war ends, they are both on different 'wanted lists': he as a former high-ranking officer is wanted by the allies and she as a supposed traitor is wanted by the resistance. He ends up in the custody of a Canadian officer who, grotesquely, allows himself to be swayed by a defeated German officer into allowing the Germans to kill him. She is captured by a vengeful mob that drench her in human excrement. She is saved by the hero from the resistance – only to discover that he has been part of a scheme to steal Jewish wealth and that he is complicit in the murder of her family and all the other passengers on the fishing boat where they were killed. She narrowly escapes his attempt to murder her. With another member of the resistance they then capture and kill him.

Love emerges in this film against the background of inhuman circumstances which intensify the erotic tension and exhilaration of the protagonists while at the same time presenting the moral stakes of their love and its conditions of duration in a problematic light.

The film is thus unusual among war romances in that it stresses, at every turn, the moral stakes and complexity of the lovers' relationship. Love is morally more complex here than in *The Russia House*, for example. It involves a crossing of boundaries, a union between enemies, but it also involves a notion of *involvement*. In *The Russia House*, Yeltsin's Russia is a background tapestry and a shadow over the lovers' humble ambitions and hopes. Here there is no separation between sex and politics. Yet sex is not just sex. The lovers' erotic relationship gains a significance that is not limited to the sexual sphere – since it forms a relation that enables both lovers to act for the other against the ideology of their own camp. The film does not seek to demonstrate that personal relationships matter more than ideology – in general. The characterisation of the protagonists as good and decent people caught up in difficult circumstances suggests, rather, that the morality that love implies is more concrete than the principles of a political camp. From this moral perspective the lovers are empowered and ennobled by love to the extent of being able to expose themselves. They are loyal to one another, but this is not what is decisive. What matters is that their loyalty is not embedded in a network of institutional power. This morality is existential but not existentialist. It is not a morality of risk or tragic passion, but of commitment balanced against survival instincts.

As a Mata Hari character, the protagonist is not supposed to fall in love with him, since that would a) diminish her usefulness and b) expose her to the risk of becoming a double agent. She does, however, fall in love with him. We thus have two moral oppositions that are confronted with one another: friend vs. enemy and the beloved vs. the rest of the world. Since the beloved belongs within the category of the enemy, she is, structurally, a traitor, but she commits no act of betrayal against her cause and her country. She betrays no one. Love is thus here at the centre of a moral and historical debate concerning the distribution of blame in retrospect.

Coppola, Trapero, Sorrentino

We shall end this section on worldly love with a brief discussion of three recent films that depict love negatively against the background of social obstacles that are at the same time manifest as psychological problems in the minds of the protagonists. These are not films about beliefs, expectations and morality, as in classical cinema and melodrama. Neither are they films about love's freedom, as in the cinema of Pialat or in *Zwartboek*. They are films that dissect love's impossibility in circumstances that are simultaneously mental and social – external and internal to the main characters of the film. The three films that I compare are Sofia Coppola's *Lost in Translation*, Pablo Trapero's *El Buonarense* and Paolo Sorrentino's *Le Consequenze dell'amore*.

Love in Motion

This is a type of cinema in which there is very little *reflective* distance in the characters or within the films' narrative point of view regarding cultural and social categories of love. Indeed the amorous subjects in these films are fully and totally social individuals, defined by age, gender, class and historical situation. Yet, these narratives are not classical. They are not concerned with motivation and emotion. They are not concerned with moral character or moral choices. These are *existential* films in which the subject of love confronts the social obstacles of its potential relationship with anguish. Love is defined here by the culturally minimalist, existential and social category of *external necessity*.

The heroine of Sofia Coppola's semi-autobiographical film *Lost in Translation* is a twenty-something, pretty, privileged East Coast woman who does not yet know what to do with her life. She writes, takes photographs and spends time being married to an ambitious and nerdy fashion photographer. She is in Tokyo accompanying him on one of his assignments. She is adrift in her life; the trip and the unfamiliar surroundings only accentuate her sense of disorientation. In the hotel she flirts with a middle-aged man. They construct a friendship of sorts, and almost embark on an affair. Their decision not to, their decision not to have sex, not to expose themselves, and to remain within the realm of words, of reasoning and egotistical confessions, is a realist stroke of genius on Coppola's part. It makes the film emblematic of a *subjectivity that prefers its own ego to the world*, as sex and the lack thereof is only a metonymy in the film of the world in general. Retreating from an erotic relationship, the characters retreat from worldly exposure; they retreat into the synthetic sounds of the Tokyo Hyatt hotel. The subject's desire and its effort to affirm the beginning relationship are here only erotic as a support for its narcissistic interest in its own ego. Erotic desire is only the vehicle for a deepening of the subject's own infatuation with his or her ego, with his or her *interesting* existential problems. The triviality of all the dialogue in the film and the quotational quality of all the film's dramatic situations – they appear to be updated versions of 1980s short stories by Tobias Wolfe – do not weaken the film, since this is a study in contemporary nihilism expressed as narcissism. The categories that the protagonists apply to themselves are cultural, to be sure, but the characters do not apply these categories to a relation of desire, but merely to their own existence. Their erotic non-relation in the film does not acquire enough texture and substance to become an object of reflection. They meet not as potential lovers, but as naked human beings in need of comfort and consolation. They express and live out, to the last dot, the anxieties that are scripted for them by their class and specific location within society.

The protagonist of Trapero's film *El Buonarense* is a male recluse, a quiet and introverted policeman, arriving in Buenos Aires from the country. He is an innocent man at the beginning of the film, but in the manner of a Balzac novel, his innocence is modified in the course of the film by his poverty and his desire to be integrated within the society of the metropolis, and this means, since he is a policeman, within the police force of the city. The film in fact depicts a double movement of social ascendance and moral corruption reminiscent of Balzac's tale of Rastignac in *Le Père Goriot*. The young policeman gradually enters an inner circle of power within the district police unit that he is assigned to. This career is accompanied by a *steady decline in his moral sensibility*. The city does not educate him or enlarge his vision but makes him accustomed to performing acts of violence and intimidation. At the centre of this story of negative education is a love relationship. A single woman with a child, also working in the police force, falls in love with him. She is a few years older than him and seeks to steer him in a direction that is different from that of his senior colleagues, different, that is, from the logic of corruption and deal-making. She fails and as a demonstration of that failure he enacts his frustrations and contradictory emotions within their love-making in a manner that comes close to rape. Adding to this violence is his insensitivity to the fact that she lives with her young son, who becomes an involuntary witness to their relationship and to their violent sex. As she refuses to see him, he slides further into moral abjection.

Le Consequenze dell'amore (*The Consequences of Love*) by Sorrentino is a moral tale of loneliness. The main character is buried alive – twice – first metaphorically, then literally, and both times by the Mafia. Between these two events lies his experience of love as a possible – or perhaps impossible – interruption of his solitude. In his former job he was an investment banker and had the misfortune of losing a large sum of money belonging to the Sicilian Mafia. As a punishment he was forced to accept a new life in which he would be separated from his wife and children and live on his own, in a hotel in the Italian part of Switzerland. He has but one duty. Once a week a suitcase with money is deposited at his door and he has the task of bringing this suitcase to a bank nearby. The narrative style of the film is very close to that of the French *nouveau roman* in that narration is here almost entirely reducible to *description*. Throughout the film, we track the protagonist's movements, and his little adventures make us gain a rounded portrait of him. We see him in his natural environment within the social microcosm that is the hotel. Sorrentino refrains from gesturing towards any documentary realism in his depiction of the hotel. There are no 'behind the scenes' evocations of cooks and cleaners. The film's narrative perspective is rigorously subjective. Through its spatial and chromatic symbolism, the film suggests an emotional continuum between the psyche of the protagonist and the labyrinthine space of the hotel. The film at the same time stays on the *surface* of the protagonist's trajectories, thereby remaining faithful to his limited perspective, in a sense, endorsing the protagonist's perspective on the world. The film's spatial symbolism therefore does not significantly point *beyond* the horizon of this character's conscious experience. The sinuous staircases and rooms rich in historical reference do not point to anything of significance, anything that the character could search for or discover. Hence the film creates an evocative image of subjective isolation. This state of isolation is not, on the other hand, socially disreputable. The protagonist is not a tramp or some other form of outcast. He has money, dresses well and treats all the people around him with an air of bored superiority.

Love enters the film, and this character's life, as a minimal and disastrous event. After a visit from his gregarious brother, he becomes unhinged and begins a conversation with a young girl in the hotel, a barmaid whom he has silently observed and coveted for months. She, in turn, seems intrigued by this distinguished and mysterious older man. As he sits down on a stool to talk to her he says that this act is perhaps the most dangerous thing he has ever done in his life. He does not realise how true this apparently flippant utterance will turn out to be. As they begin a tentative courtship, consisting largely of him going shopping with her, the regularity and thereby also the balance of his life reveals itself to be fragile. Not knowing how to speak to her, he can only communicate his feelings by giving her a gift: he steals a hundred thousand dollars of Mafia money and buys her a BMW convertible. This transgressive act already puts him off balance, as the Mafia will not fail to notice this theft. Matters are complicated, however, by another twist in the plot. Two Mafia hit men stay with him for a day to complete an assignment. As they discover that he regularly receives a suitcase full of money, they return after a few days to steal one of these suitcases. Summoned to Sicily to explain what has happened, the protagonist then learns to his surprise that his theft of the hundred thousand dollars has been forgiven. He is further able to account for what happened to the suitcase: he outmanoeuvred the two hit men and killed them, we see in flashback. All is well, it would seem, but then he declares that he *will not return the stolen money*. His boss tersely replies: 'if there is no suitcase, there is no life'. He accepts this and the following day he is executed. Love is here a powerful but at the same time evanescent force. He barely speaks to the young girl. They do not have a relationship. They remain at the threshold of an attraction based largely on mutual difference and curiosity – but even this modest manifestation of love is enough to throw the protagonist completely off course and make him reject his former life, and thereby reject life all together.

Conclusion: On Method

The method of this aesthetic enquiry into the history of film form is grounded in ethical, ontological and semiotic considerations that have been spelled out along the way. It was important to the phenomenological premise of this enquiry that the analysis and interpretation of films should both speak for themselves and speak to a set of problems, but that there should be no underlying specification of traits or themes that one would look for in each film.

The analysis of individual directors and films has taken an interpretative form, that is, it was not always exactly the same expressive or signifying parameters that were salient and merited discussion in the interpretation of particular films. As I sought to do justice to the specificity of individual films and to show their contribution both to the history of film form and to the history of love, the analysis emphasised those expressive features that were salient in each case.

At this point of the argument, however, with the analysis now completed, it could be useful to draw together the principles that guided the interpretation, but which in many cases only emerged gradually from the interpretation of successive films and the comparison between them. This might be useful also as an epistemological statement beyond the particular topic of love.

Apart from its discussion of the ontology and ethics of love, this study proposes an aesthetic theory of film and a semiotic method of analysis. This is not a method that can be applied directly to individual films or to scenes in films in the manner of a tool box. Hence, it does not function like Eisenstein's theory of montage or Bordwell's theory of narrative sequence. Nor is this method a prescriptive aesthetic norm like the psychological theory of point of view put forward by Henry James in his essays on French and American literature. I do not argue for a particular conception of film form. Much of film theory, whether in the realist tradition of Bazin or in the post-modern tradition that champions allegorical films, has implicitly or explicitly defended certain kinds of filmmaking. The structure of my historical account does indeed conform to this pattern in that it is based on a dichotomy between classical cinema, in which love is culturally and morally categorised and determined, and non-classical cinema, in which the love relation is shown to be self-determining in the world. Yet, I do not denigrate classical cinema. Films like *Out of the Past*, *In a Lonely Place* and *The Raven* are some of the most complex films of love ever made. If there is a normative aesthetic and ethical claim in this study it is that love flourished in cinema for a certain time. It flourished in the cinema of Buñuel and Truffaut and it continued in some of the filmmakers of the 1970s, 1980s and 1990s that I discuss. I believe that *Zwartboek* by Verhoeven is one of the greatest love films ever made. It is psychologically and morally complex. It is erotic and subtle, political and wise. Its romanticism tempered by cynicism is in tune with our contemporary mores. No doubt, such exceptional films made on love's behalf will still be made as long as there are films. Yet, the last section of this study, on Trapero, Coppola and Sorrentino, suggests that the moment of love in film has passed, for the time being. Our current social situation, torn between the governance of global capital and a search for alternative routes, does not seem to favour love and its claims.

The method of this study is a conceptual framework that singles out a certain number of expressive and signifying elements in film and allows one to discuss how these elements are brought together, how they become part of an aesthetic synthesis. It is not always the same expressive elements that are salient in film. Place, acting style, dialogue, moral themes, rhythm and character psychology may in different instances occupy centre stage and dominate a film's aesthetic form. This notion of a centre that does not have a fixed position but can be filled out in different ways is what the Russian formalists called the 'dominant'. In their investigation of literary genres and their historical development, they began to think of literary expression as a force field where different elements can function as the purpose for the sake of which other elements are crafted the way they are. This notion of the dominant can be taken in two very different ways. One can follow Tynjanov in emphasising the shifting content of the dominant according to period, genre, author and text, or one can pursue the line of Sklowsky and Jakobson and seek to define the 'literary' or literariness, or poetic quality per se. Jakobson's definition of poetry as a form of communication in which the self-referentiality of the message is dominant is the exact opposite of the Tynjanov approach. Bordwell's theory of film narration follows Jakobson's line of enquiry. Film narration is there defined by the dominant function exercised by dramatic exposition, by *sujet* (sequential presentation) as opposed to dramatic and thematic character relationships (fable).

This theory does capture an essential feature of film narration, but its universalism produces a false problem concerning films that are less narratively transparent: all films are in some sense narrative. In this book I have followed Tynjanov's line. The difference in psychological or dramatic transparency is, then, to be seen as *gradual*. Incidentally, Deleuze avoids making a rigid distinction between narrative cinema and abstraction (or art cinema) with his concept of the time image.

In this book I have contrasted classical French and American cinema with films that are not narratively transparent. Films by Wong, Antonioni, Rohmer, Sorrentino, and so on are not, on the other hand, *abstract*. They are explorations of characters and of character relationships. What makes them non-classical is a relationship between character and psychological theme, and between narrative and psychological theme. These non-classical films are *problematic* rather than *thematic*. They present characters who are neither opaque nor transparent, characters who face questions that have significant moral stakes but who do not explicitly express their motives. The method that I present here is Aristotelian in its focus on character. It is formalist in its acknowledgement of the shifting content of the dominant. It is phenomenological in its conception of how aesthetics and ethics are joined.

Film form creates a space in which characters exhibit their moral qualities and the stakes of their actions. Film form is a *moving plasticity*, a dynamic space in which characters are shaped and confronted with cultural categories. These categories may be presented in a more or less rigid, more or less determinative or predicative, way. Characters may emerge thus more or less *categorised*.

In terms of viewing experience, the essence of film is a real encounter with non-existent people. A good film is one in which the character stands out, seems relevant, is presented as captivating. The character can be captivating in more or less categorial ways. He or she can be captivating in virtue of his or her moral transparency or, on the contrary, in virtue of his or her moral opacity.

Ontology, phenomenology and semiotics form a nexus in this account. In ontology I follow Aristotle and Heidegger. The strict criterion of predictability that Aristotle introduces to define what is determinable, what is identifiable as something discreet and intelligible, negatively throws light on the being of love.

As I have tried to show both through the analysis of film history and through examples of how love was categorised in philosophy and literature, love only exists, only manifests itself, within a categorial space. There is no abstract, undetermined love. There is no love that is morally neutral, psychologically void of qualities, unrelated to other social and cultural norms. This concreteness of love is not external to the love relation. It is not alien to the lovers' sense of themselves. The mistake of Romantic writers like the early Goethe or Constant was to pit the agonising lover or lovers in direct opposition to social and cultural norms. Even someone who uses love as a means of rebellion, like Gerard in Pialat's *Loulou*, will have a sense of what this rebellion means. Yet, if love is a relation, and not just an aggregate of separate desires and feelings, the being of love is an entity that eludes the grasp of predication. For as Aristotle says, a relation cannot be a substance.

Heidegger explores the logical properties of *being* considered in contrast with the notion of *substance* or object. The being of the human being is defined by him through self-reflection, or reflexivity. This reflexivity is not conscious. It is not identical to introspection. Yet, the human being always relates to itself implicitly in all its activities. The subject of the love relation possesses its own kind of reflexivity. It is constrained to posit itself in relation to four questions: the nature of its own desire, the nature of the desire of the other, the duration of the relation and the relation of the relation to other social relations.

Phenomenology entails, for Heidegger, but also for Husserl and Hegel, that one seeks to capture a phenomenon *from the inside*, to make explicit the articulations and relationships that govern a phenomenon in itself and then, subsequently, to unfold that phenomenon within discourse. Thus, in his phenomenology, Hegel intends for consciousness, in its experience of knowledge, to *display* itself in its projects and failures. In this book I have sought to make love display itself, to present love from the inside according to its *eidos*, or invariant structure.

The phenomenology that I practise is informed by Heidegger's ontology but it is also shaped by Foucault's histories of concepts. Common to Heidegger and Foucault is a principle that they share with Husserl, a scepticism regarding *causal* explanations. In my account of love, I have distanced myself from two types of causal explanation: psychological accounts that categorise love as a biological phenomenon and historical accounts that categorise love as a web of beliefs that may be explained contextually.

There are structural invariants in any phenomenon and there are structural invariants in the phenomenon of love. Such invariants function as framing conditions within experience. Conditions are not causes. One does not *explain* a desire, a gesture, an amorous interest or a relationship by pointing to this structural invariant.

There is an aesthetic as well as an ethical dimension to this phenomenological notion of conditions as opposed to causes. I have sought to identify historical ideal types of film form that are not universal structural invariants but which shape conditions for the capturing of love in different periods. This semiotic historical analysis is phenomenological in the sense that it seeks to move from the inside outwards; it seeks to articulate in language the salient semiotic relationships of a given film of a group of films rather than to situate a film in relation to a context that would causally inform how we think about that film.

Ethically, the phenomenological rejection of causal explanation marks a distinction in relation to current explanatory discourses on love in popular psychology. For those explanations to work, love has to be categorised quite rigidly as a social relation of interest. I seek to define love transcategorially.

Hegel identifies one of the central questions concerning the experience of love. Plato and La Rochefoucauld posed the question of why lovers find pleasure in each other's company beyond the satisfaction of sexual desire. Hegel pushes this question further and asks: why is the love relation *binding* if it is neither a rule of law nor the product of desires and inclinations? The binding power of love is indeed one of its secrets. The being of love as relation entails a binding power that is not reducible to need, feeling or contract. Love is therefore a claim against materialism and against the cynicism of psychological self-interest. This claim is neither moral nor spiritual. Love is neither duty nor faith. The love relation may be binding but remain alien to dominant moral categories.

The pre-Socratics theorised eros as a union. They thought the bond was physical, a force of mutual attraction, the same force that is active in fertility and reproduction throughout nature. Their notion of what is physical is vastly different from ours. They did not have a mechanical or mathematical notion of nature and they did not, like Aristotle, classify causes and causal processes. Hence Empedocles, Heraclitus and Parmenides share a conception of philosophical knowledge that is intuitive and esoteric, bordering on mysticism. The beautiful poetic style of their texts, as we have them, embodies this intuitionism.

The path that I have undertaken from the ontology of the erotic relation, through a phenomenology of the amorous *cogito*, via a phenomenological history of categorisations of love in Western culture, to an interpretative and semiotic, historical and comparative analysis of film has been guided by one intuition and is justified in the epistemological terms of intuitionism. The object of this intuition is three-fold. One the one hand, I have identified an *eidos*, or invariant essence, of love. Love is a reciprocal relation of desire existing in time such that the lovers address in language a question as to the duration of their relation.

On the other hand, I have pursued two lines of thought, one ethical and one aesthetic. Love carries an ethical potential of freedom. This potential is only realised in the world, when the love relation manifests itself within and in relation to other social relations. When it does so, the lovers' view of their relation and the views on their relation held by third parties brush up against each other, and this is what gives an edge to love and demonstrates its power of self-determination.

Love in Motion

The aesthetic thought that guided my analysis of film history is that film can narrate a passage through the world in which self-determination, and hence freedom, is demonstrated through the (partial) opacity of characters and their motivations.

In the background of this worldly, as opposed to psychological, conception of love is not only the analysis of amorous behaviour in the French tradition (La Rochefoucauld and Stendhal), but also two modern philosophers who do not theorise love, but who theorise the public nature of our mental activity: Hannah Arendt and John McDowell. It did not seem fruitful to include a lengthy discussion of their conception of the world and of worldliness, since the contexts of those conceptions are far removed from the philosophy of love — a political theory of totalitarianism in Arendt, and a general epistemology in the case of McDowell. The context of the present conception of worldliness is semiotic.

For Arendt worldliness means that the tenor and reality of one's beliefs and aspirations need to be asserted and demonstrated before others in a space where one risks something by exposing oneself. Schlegel idealises his erotic relationship with his wife Dorothea in the short novel *Luzinde*, which I discussed earlier. Arendt is disparaging about Dorothea and her love relationship, seeing it as a plan b in relation to her desire to assert herself in the public sphere. In her analysis of Varnhagen's amorous relationships, Arendt categorises love in terms of existential feelings and historically specific class relationships. Love is thus not something in itself. It is a need that comes from the subject's existential relation to itself, and this need seeks fulfilment in the social world. Love is in any case incapable of authentic and public self-assertion. Through film one can, by contrast, arrive at an understanding of the worldliness of love itself. In the films of Lynch and Antonioni and Wong, love is not a private feeling that seeks to integrate itself within the social strictures of class. Love is a passage through the world, a passage through a categorial space in which it is measured.

McDowell has in many of his writings, especially in his treatise *Mind and World*, pursued the thought that epistemology involves two quite separate notions, both of which are necessary constituents of a picture of knowledge, but which do not exist on a conceptual continuum. One notion is the self-sufficiency of intuitive evidence; another notion is the referential or intentional, and that means *otherdependent*, nature of thought and language. In his reflections on the balance of these two considerations, McDowell also indirectly spells out a psychological condition of love: the lovers are always confined to some extent within their thoughts and feelings and they constantly return to them and cherish them; yet the love relation becomes what it is, determines itself in time, only through its relation to

Conclusion

other relations within a cultural space. It is not easy for the lovers to balance these two considerations against each other.

The aesthetic space of film is not just a spectacle or the site of a narrative. It is an embodied categorial space where characters become culturally concrete. This space is an extended presence where characters pass through a constellation of determining forces. The psychological *underdetermination of relationships*, which is a defining semiotic trait of film narrative, makes film uniquely suited to capturing the binding power and the being of the love relation.

The films by Antonioni, Rohmer, Verhoeven, Lynch and Wong that I analyse in the last and concluding chapter capture love as a passage through a categorial space. Film's temporal plasticity, its capacity to create a temporal continuum in space and to present characters within that space, such that they gradually gain texture and substance, offers a point of view upon cultural predication and categoriality that is different from that of literature, in which categories are expressed directly, linguistically. Hence, characters in film are not necessarily and immediately categorised. Film offers the possibility of presenting characters who are concrete and determinate but who nevertheless remain culturally *opaque* in relation to dominant moral categories and in terms of their motivations and interests. Love's ontological freedom resides in this opacity. *The resilience and persistence of the love relation are all the more powerful for not being reducible to affect, desire, duty or convention.*

The lovers' independence from moral categorisation, as they assert their relation in the world, is their freedom. The passage through a categorial space, in which the character remains partly opaque, is thus film's effort at grasping the freedom of the love relation. This is a freedom of confrontation. In its worldly manifestation, the love relation asserts itself in relation to social constraints and cultural categories while seeking to maintain an autonomy, a capacity for self-determination in time. It is in the ontological gap that separates the love relation from its cultural coordinates that freedom becomes manifest, and film narratives are able to inhabit that gap.

Like Hegel, I believe that love is a relation. Like Stendhal I believe that love is a fluid and dynamic interaction in which it is impossible to disentangle what is desire, what is imagination, what is cultural expectation. Like Heraclitus, Empedocles and other ancient writers I believe that eros is a trace of nature within subjectivity and that this natural trace always commands its due. Like Arendt and McDowell I think that this due is measured in a relation of mutual appreciation which they call the 'world' and which, in the history of discourses on love, was articulated first by seventeenth-century philosophers like Scudéry and La Rochefoucauld.

Love in Motion

My account is opposed to two modernist notions, one rational, the other Romantic. The rational account as presented by Hegel, Freud and their followers contends that love is a sort of transaction or contract or structure. Hence love is intelligible. The Romantic notion is that love is nested deep within the folds and meanders of the human soul, ineffable and deep and worthy – worthy that is for the subject of love, but it is not love itself as relation that is praised. To think of love as a relation and as an erotic force in the world, on the other hand, means that love is social but not intelligible. It is not buried in the subject and not sanctioned by social norms. The freedom of love is, to put it crudely, tied to its *irrationality*, but this irrationality is not simply passion or rapture or spontaneity. It is an epistemic irrationality, the absence of grounds to justify, for the lovers, their love.

Love is intrinsic to itself in the sense that even if we can use moral and other cultural categories to describe a relation – we can talk of happiness and abuse, about passion and dullness – ultimately love finds its own criteria of evaluation and no one is to say that the lovers do not know what they do.

But what is it that makes love desirable? Why is it that human beings are miserable without love? What is it that makes us empowered to do great deeds and wicked deeds on account of love? Love will always maintain its sexual-spiritual Janus face and we shall probably never understand its binding and motivating power. In its spirituality love has an absurd quality. The lover seeking truth and the absolute is like the innocent citizen seeking justice in Kafka or like the man in Borges, discovering the Aleph, the essence of all metaphysical truth, in a mundane cellar. The lover is caught in a labyrinth where what she seeks is always around the next corner.

I would like to end this book on a Nietzschean note, with a series of aphorisms or paradoxes that perhaps express best what I think love is.

The lover is
Herself and
Her shadow,
A compendium
Of unlived
Potential –
Were it not thus,
The present tense
Would be everything.

•

Love is not
Incompatible
With happiness –
Only,
Living together
Has no name.

•

If love is freedom
And freedom
Is individual,
Love is individual,
Hence one can
Only love oneself,
Or there is no love.

•

In love,
Nothing matters
That is not
Related to sex,
And anything
Merely physical
Is trivial.

•

In leaving
The stomach,
Desire
Takes the risk
Of entering
Language –
At its peril.

•

The lover's words
Are but
The clumsy translation
Of acts
And a future tense.

•

In love,
Words
Make sense
Only when superfluous.

•

The language
Of love
Mimics other idioms,
It speaks, ironically,
Of justice
Truth
Work
And all the other things
That love itself ignores.

•

It is sweet
To be free
To submit
To be a slave
It is sour
To reason
To negotiate
Meddle
Mingle
Seek
The just.

•

Lovers love
To be unjust
That is their
Right.

•

Compromise
Is the lowest
Condition,
But
Nature
Tells society
Of submission –
When is submission
Not a compromise?

FILMOGRAPHY

Pedro Almodovar
Que he hecho yo para merecer esto!!, 1984
Matador, 1986

Michelangelo Antonioni
Cronaca di un amore, 1950
Le Amiche, 1955
Il grido, 1957
L'Avventura, 1960
La Notte, 1961
L'Eclisse, 1962
Blowup, 1966
Zabriskie Point, 1970
Professione: Reporter, 1975
Identificazione di una donna, 1982

Jacques Becker
Casque d'or, 1952

Ingmar Bergman
Sommaren med Monica, 1953
Sommarnattens leende, 1955
Smultrånstället, 1957

Bernardo Bertolucci
Il Conformista, 1970
Ultimo tango a parigi, 1972

Frank Borzage
A Farewell to Arms, 1932

Love in Motion

Luis Buñuel
Ensayo de un crimen, 1955
Viridiana, 1961
Belle de jour, 1967
Tristana, 1970
Cet obscur objet du desir, 1977

Frank Capra
It Happened One Night, 1934

Marcel Carné
Le Quai des brumes, 1938
Hôtel du Nord, 1938
Le Jour se lève, 1938

Claude Chabrol
Le Boucher, 1970
Les Noces rouges, 1973
La Demoiselle d'honneur, 2004

René Clair
A nous la liberté, 1931

Henri-Georges Clouzot
Le Corbeau, 1943

Sophia Coppola
Lost in Translation, 2003

Michael Curtiz
Casablanca, 1943

R.W. Fassbinder
Warum lauft Herr R, Amok, 1970
Händler der vier Jahreszeiten, 1971
Effi Briest, 1974
Die Ehe der Maria Braun, 1979
Lili Marleen, 1981

Jean-Luc Godard
Vivre sa vie, 1962
Passion, 1982

Filmography

Peter Greenaway
The Draughtsman's Contract, 1982

Howard Hawks
The Big Sleep, 1946

Alfred Hitchcock
The Lodger, 1927
The 39 Steps, 1935
Vertigo, 1958

Jim Jarmusch
Stranger than Paradise, 1984

Emir Kusturica
Otac na sluzbenom putu (When Father Is Away on Business), 1985
Underground, 1995
Zivot je kudo (Life Is a Miracle), 2004

Fritz Lang
Ministry of Fear, 1944

David Lean
Brief Encounter, 1945

Ernst Lubitsch
Romeo und Julia im Schnee, 1920
Trouble in Paradise, 1932
Design for Living, 1933
To Be or Not To Be, 1942

David Lynch
Blue Velvet, 1986

Louis Malle
Les Amants, 1958

Jiri Menzel
Ostre sledované vlaky, 1966

Max Ophüls
Liebelei, 1933
Letter from an Unknown Woman, 1948

Love in Motion

G.W. Pabst
Die Liebe der Jeanne Ney, 1927
Die Buchse der Pandora, 1929
Tagebuch einer Verlorenen, 1929

Pier Paolo Pasolini
Accatone, 1961

Maurice Pialat
Loulou, 1980
A nos amours, 1983
Police, 1985

Michael Powell and Emeric Pressburger
A Matter of Life and Death, 1946

Otto Preminger
Laura, 1944

Nicholas Ray
In a Lonely Place, 1950

Jean Renoir
La Bête humaine, 1938
The woman on the Beach, 1947

Fred Scepisi
The Russia House, 1990

Paolo Sorrentino
Le Consequenze dell'amore, 2004

Jacques Tourneur
Out of the Past, 1947

Pablo Trapero
El Buonarense, 2002

François Truffaut
Les 400 coups, 1959
Tirez sur le pianiste, 1960
Jules et Jim, 1962

Filmography

La Peau douce, 1964
Les Deux anglaises et le continent, 1971
Le Dernier métro, 1980
La Femme d'à côté, 1981

Agnés Varda
Cléo de 5 a 7, 1962

Paul Verhoeven
Zwartboek, 2006

Charles Vidor
Gilda, 1946

Jean Vigo
L'Atalante, 1934

Josef von Sternberg
Morocco, 1930
Shanghai Express, 1932
Blonde Venus, 1932
The Devil Is a Woman, 1935

Wim Wenders
Der Amerikanische Freund, 1977

Billy Wilder
Double Indemnity, 1944

Wong Kar-Wai
Wong gok ka moon (As Tears Go By), 1988
A Fei jingjyuhn (Days of Being Wild), 1990
Chungking Express, 1994
Fallen Angels, 1995
Happy Together, 1997
In the Mood for Love, 2000
2046, 2004

BIBLIOGRAPHY

Allen, Richard and Ishii-Gonzalès, S., *Alfred Hitchcock: centenary essays*, London: BFI, 1999
Arendt, Hannah, *Der Liebesbegriff bei Augustin* (1929), Berlin: Philo, 2003
____ *Rahel Varnhagen: Lebensgeschichte einer deutschen Jüdin aus der Romantik*, Munich: Piper, 1957
Aristarco, Guido, *I sussurri e le grida: dieci letture critiche di film*, Palermo: Sellerio, 1988
Aristotle, *Poetics*, trans. Stephen Halliwell, London: Duckworth, 1986
____ *Le categorie*, trans. Narcello Zanatta, Milan: Rizzoli, 1989
____ *Metafisica*, trans. G. Reale, Bompiani, 2000
____ *Etica nichomachea*, trans. C. Mazzarelli, Bompiani, 2000
____ *Nicomachean ethics: translation, introduction, and commentary*, ed. Sarah Broadie and Christopher Rowe, Oxford: Oxford University Press, 2002
Aubenque, Pierre, *Le problème de l'être chez Aristote: essai sur la problématique aristotélicienne de l'être* (1962), Paris: Presses universitaires de France, 1983
Austen, Jane, *Sense and sensibility* (1811), London: H. Hamilton, 1948
____ *Emma* (1815), Oxford: Oxford University Press, 2008
Balasz, Bela, *Der sichtbare Mensch oder die Kultur des Films* (1924), Frankfurt: Suhrkamp, 2004
____ *Der Geist des Films* (1930), Frankfurt: Suhrkamp, 2001
____ *Der Film: Werden und Wesen einer neuen Kunst*, Vienna: Globus Verlag, 1950
Barthes, Roland, *Fragments d'un discours amoureux*, Paris: Editions du Seuil, 1977
Bataille, Georges, *Histoire de l'œil* (1928), Paris: Pauvert, 1928
____ *La Part maudite, précédé de la Notion de dépense* (1949), Paris: Les Éditions de Minuit, 1980
Bazin, André, *Qu'est-ce que le cinéma? (1958–1962)*, Paris: Editions du Cerf, 1985
Beauvoir, Simone de, *Le deuxième sexe* (1949), Paris: Gallimard, 1976
Bellour, Raymond, *L'analyse du film* (1979), Paris: Calmann-Levy, 1979
Benjamin, Walter, *Ursprung des deutschen Trauerspiels* (1928), Frankfurt: Suhrkamp, 2000

Blumenberg, Hans, *Die Legitimität der Neuzeit*, Frankfurt: Suhrkamp, 1966
_____ *Arbeit am Mythos*, Frankfurt: Suhrkamp, 1979
Bocaccio, Giovanni, *Decamerone, con le xilografie dell'edizione del 1492*, Milan: BUR, 1999
Bonitzer, Pascal, *Eric Rohmer*, Paris: Editions de l'Etoile, 1999
Braad Thomsen, Christian, *Rainer Werner Fassbinder: en rejse mod lyset*, Copenhagen: Lieke, 1988
Brooks, Peter, *The melodramatic imagination: Balzac, Henry James, melodrama, and the mode of excess*, New York: Columbia University Press, 1985
Burch, Noël, *Theory of film practice*, Princeton: Princeton University Press, 1981
_____ *La lucarne de l'infini: naissance du langage cinématographique*, Paris: L'Harmattan, 2007
_____ *To the distant observer: form and meaning in the Japanese cinema*, ed. Annette Michelson, London: Scholar Press, 1979
Carney, Raymond, *American vision: the films of Frank Capra*, Hanover: Wesleyan University Press, 1996
Cave, Terence, *Recognitions: a study in poetics*, Oxford: Clarendon Press, 1988
Cavell, Stanley, *Pursuits of happiness: the Hollywood comedy of remarriage*, Cambridge, Mass.: Harvard University Press, 1981
_____ *Contesting tears: the Hollywood melodrama of the unknown woman*, Chicago: University of Chicago Press, 1996
_____ *Disowning knowledge in seven plays of Shakespeare*, Cambridge: Cambridge University Press, 2003
Constant, Benjamin, *Adolphe: anecdote trouvée dans les papiers d'un inconnu (1816)*, Paris: Le livre de Poche, 1995
Chion, Michel, *David Lynch*, London: BFI, 1995
Chretien de Troyes, *The Project Gutenberg ebook of Cliges: a romance*, trans. L. J. Gardiner, 2000
Dante, *Vita nova*, trans. Mark Musa, Oxford: Oxford University Press, 1992
Deguy, Michel, *La machine matrimoniale, ou, Marivaux*, Paris: Gallimard, 1981
Deleuze, Gilles, *Différence et répétition*, PUF, 1968
_____ *Présentation de Sacher-Masoch suivi de La vénus à la fourrure de Léopold Sacher-Masoch*, Paris: Les Éditions de Minuit, 1971
_____ and Guattari, Felix, *L'anti-Oedipe*, Paris: Les Éditions de Minuit, 1972
_____ *L'image-mouvement*, Paris: Les Éditions de Minuit, 1983
_____ *L'image-temps*, Paris: Les Éditions de Minuit, 1985
Derrida, Jacques, *Glas*, Paris: Galilée, 1974
_____ *De l'esprit*, Paris: Galilée, 1990
Detienne, Marcel, *Dionysos mis à mort*, Paris: Gallimard, 1996
Diels, Hermann (ed.), *Die Fragmente der Vorsokratiker, griechisch und deutsch von Hermann Diels*, Berlin: Walter Kranz, 1954

Bibliography

Eisenstein, Sergei, *Selected Works*, Vol. 1–3, London: BFI, 1988, 1991, 1996
Eisner, Lotte H., *The haunted screen: expressionism in the German cinema and the influence of Max Reinhardt*, Berkeley: University of California Press, 1961
Elsaesser, Thomas, *Filmgeschichte und frühes Kino: Archäologie eines Medienwandels*, Munich: Edition Text + Kritik, 2002
_____ (ed.), *Early cinema: space-frame-narrative*, London: BFI, 1990
Empedocles, *Testimonianze e frammenti*, ed. A. Tonelli, Bompiani, 2002
Epstein, Jean, *Ecrits sur le cinéma*, Paris: L'Herminier, 2005
Fitzgerald, F. Scott, *The last tycoon: an unfinished novel*, New York: Charles Scribner's Sons, 1941
Foucault, Michel, *Histoire de la folie à l'âge classique* (1961), Paris: Gallimard, 1972
_____ *Histoire de la sexualité, vol. 2: l'usage des plaisirs*, Paris: Gallimard, 1984
Freud, Sigmund, *Gesammelte Werke: chronologisch geordnet*, Anna Freud and Marie Bonaparte, London: Imago, 1940–1952
Fumaroli, Marc, *La Diplomatie de l'esprit, de Montaigne à La Fontaine*, Paris: Hermann, 1994
Godard, Jean-Luc, and Narboni, Jean (ed.), *Jean-Luc Godard par Jean-Luc Godard*, Paris: Belfond, 1968
Goethe, Johann Wolfgang von (1981), *Werke*, Vol. 6, ed. Erich Trunz, Hamburg
Graves, Robert, *The Greek Myths*, London: Penguin Books, 1955
Le Guen, Claude, *Dictionnaire Freudien*, Paris: Presses Universitaires de France, 2008
Hegel, *Werke, vol. 1: Frühe Schriften*, Frankfurt: Suhrkamp, 1986
_____ *Phänomenologie des Geistes*, Reclam, 2004
Heidegger, Martin, *Logik: Die Frage nach der Wahrheit* (lecture from winter 1925/26), ed. W. Biemel, Frankfurt: Vittorio Klostermann, 1976
_____ *Sein und Zeit* (1927), Frankfurt: Vittorio Klostermann, 1977
Honnefelder, Ludger, *Ens inquantum ens. Der Begriff des Seienden als solchen als Gegenstand der Metaphysik nach der Lehre des Johannes Duns Scotus*, Münster: Aschendorff, 1979
Huppes, Ivete, *Melodrama: o gênero e sua permanência*, Cotia: Atelie Editorial, 2000
Husserl, Edmund, *Ideen zu einer reinen Phänomenologie und phänomenologischen Philosophie* (1913), The Hague: Martinus Nijhoff, 1950
_____ *Logische Untersuchungen*, Halle: M. Niemeyer, 1922–1928
Illouz, Eva, *Consuming the romantic utopia: love and the cultural contradictions of capitalism*, Berkeley: University of California Press, 1997
Inoue, Yasushi, *Die Eiswand* (1956), Frankfurt: Suhrkamp, 1979
_____ *Meine Mutter* (1975), Frankfurt: Suhrkamp, 1987
_____ *Das Jagdgewaehr* (1949), Frankfurt: Suhrkamp, 1998
Jakobson, Roman, *Language in literature*, Cambridge, Mass.: Harvard University Press, 1987

James, Henry, *Literary criticism, vol 2: European writers and prefaces to the New York edition*, New York, Literary Classics of America, 1984
Kant, Immanuel, *Kritik der praktischen Vernunft*, Felix Meiner, 2003
_____ *Kritik der Urteilskraft*, Felix Meiner, 2009
_____ *Kritik der reinen Vernunft*, Felix Meiner, 2010
Kawabata, Yasunari, *The lake* (1954), Tokyo: Kodanscha, 1974
_____ *Die schlafende schönen* (1960), Frankfurt: Suhrkamp, 1994
Kleist, Heinrich von, *Sämtliche Werke und Briefe*, 3 vol., Munich: Hanser, 2010
Krakauer, Siegfried, *From Caligari to Hitler: a psychological history of the German film*, New York: Princeton University Press, 1947
_____ *Die Angestellten* (1930), Frankfurt: Suhrkamp 1971
_____ *Der Detektiv/Rroman* (1925), Frankfurt: Suhrkamp, 1979
La Rochefoucauld, François, *Réflexions ou sentences et maximes morales suivi de Réflexions diverses*, Paris: Gallimard, 1976
Lebrun, Gérard, *La patience du concept: essai sur le discours hégélien*, Paris: Gallimard, 1972
Lévinas, Emmanuel, *Totalité et infini: essai sur l'extériorité* (1961), The Hague: M. Nijhoff, 1984
Lévi-Strauss, Claude, *Les structures élémentaires de la parenté* (1967), Berlin: Mouton de Gruyter, 2002
Libera, Alain de, *Introduction à la mystique rhénane: d'Albert le Grand à maître Eckhart*, Paris: OELL, 1984
_____ *La Querelle des universaux*, Paris: Editions du Seuil, 1996
Luhman, Nikolas, *Liebe als passion: Zur Codierung von Intimität*, Frankfurt: Suhrkamp, 1994
Lyotard, Jean-François, *Discours, figure* (1971), Paris: Klincksieck, 2002
Mme de Lafayette, *La Princesse De Cleves*, Paris: Folio Gallimard, 1972
_____ *The Princesse de Clèves*, trans. Terence Cave, Oxford: Oxford University Press, 1999
Mme de Sévigné, *Lettres Choisies (1988)*, Paris: Folio Gallimard, 2006
Madeleine de Scudéry, *Cecile ou histoire romaine*, Paris: Folio Gallimard, 2006
McDowell, John, *Mind and world*, Cambridge, Mass.: Harvard University Press, 1996
Magny, Joël, *Maurice Pialat*, Paris: Editions de l'Etoile Cahiers du cinéma, 1992
_____ *Eric Rohmer*, Paris: Rivages, 1995
Matheron, Alexandre, *Individu et communauté chez Spinoza*, Paris: Les Éditions de Minuit, 1988
Merleau-ponty, Maurice, *Phenomenologie de la perception*, Paris: Gallimard, 1943
_____ *Le Visible et l'invisible*, ed. C. Lefort, Paris: Gallimard, 1964
Müller, Jan-Dirk, *Spielregeln für den Untergang: Die Welt des Nibelungenliedes*, Tübingen, 1998
Murakami, Haruki, *The wind-up bird chronicle*, London: Harvill, 1995

Das Niebelungen Lied, trans. Ursula Schulze, Munich, dtv, 2008
Nussbaum, Martha, *Love's knowledge: essays on philosophy and literature*, Oxford: Oxford University Press, 1990
Ollier, Claude, *Souvenirs d'ecran*, Paris: Gallimard, 1981
Pasolini, Pier Paolo, *Empirismo eretico*, Milan: Garzanti, 1972
Plato, *Theaetetus*, trans. John McDowell, Oxford: Clarendon Press, 1973
_____ *Philebus*, trans. D. Frede, Indianapolis: Hacket, 1993
_____ *Simposion*, trans. N. Marziano, Milan: Garzanti, 2001
Propertius, *Elegie*, BUR, 1987
_____ *Elegies*, trans. Kline, Liber online, 2001
Propp, V.Y., *The Russian folktale* (1928), Detroit: Wayne State University Press, 2012
Puig, Manuel, *Les Mystères de Buenos Aires*, trans. Didier Coste, Paris: Editions du Seuil, 1975
_____ *Kiss of the spider woman* (1976), London: Arena, 1984
Ricoeur, Paul, *De l'interprétation: Essai sur Sigmund freud*, Paris: Editions du Seuil, 1965
Rohdie, Sam, *The passion of Pier Paolo Pasolini*, Bloomington: Indiana University Press, 1995
Rohmer, Eric, *Le goût de la beauté*, ed. Jean Narboni, Paris: Cahiers du Cinéma, 1984
_____ *L'organisation de l'espace dans le Faust de Murnau*, Paris: Cahiers du Cinéma, 1997
Rosen, Stanley, *The question of being: a reversal of Heidegger*, New Haven: Yale University Press, 1993
Rosenzweig, Franz, *Hegel und der Staat*, Munich: Heidelberger Akademie der Wissenschaften, 1920
Rougemont, Denis de, *L'amour et l'Occident*, Paris: Plon, 1939
Sappho, ed. Edwin Marion Cox (1925), The Saturday Review, online
Sartre, Jean-Paul, *L'être et le néant*, Paris: Gallimard, 1943
Scherer, Jean Louis, *L'homme ordinaire du cinéma*, Paris: Cahiers du Cinéma, Gallimard, 1997
Schlegel, Friedrich, *Lucinde ein Roman* (1799), Frankfurt: Insel Verlag, 1985
Spaemann, Robert, *Moralische Grundbegriffe*, Munich: Beck Verlag, 1982
Stendhal, *De l'amour* (1822), Paris: Gallimard, 1980
_____ *Le rouge et le noir* (1830), Paris: Gallimard, 2000
Szondi, Peter, *Theorie des modernen Dramas: 1880–1950* (1956), Frankfurt: Suhrkamp, 1970
Tanizaki Jun'ichiro, *Lob des Schattens: Entwurf einer japanischen Ästhetik* (1933), trans. E. Klopfenstein, Zürich: Manesse, 1987
Tesson, Charles, *Luis Buñuel*, Paris: Éditions de l'étoile/Cahiers du Cinéma, 1995
Thompson, David, *Last tango in Paris*, London: BFI, 1998
Todorov, Tzvetan, *Théorie de la littérature*, Paris: Editions du Seuil, 1965

Love in Motion

_____ *Poétique de la prose*, Paris: Editions du Seuil, 1978
Tolstoy, Leo, *Anna Karenina*, trans. Leon Ginzburg (1877, trans. 1929), Einaudi, 1993
Veyne, Paul, *L'Élégie érotique romaine: l'amour, la poésie et l'Occident*, Paris: Editions du Seuil, 1983
Wellbery, David, *The specular moment: Goethe's early lyric and the beginnings of Romanticism*, Stanford: Stanford University Press, 1996
Zink, Michel, *Roman rose et rose rouge: Le Roman de la Rose ou de Guillaume de Dole de Jean Renart*, Paris: Nizet, 1979

Index

allegory 33, 35
Antonioni, Michelangelo 35, 76, 124–33, 157, 160–1
Arendt, Hannah 160
Aristotle 37, 40, 52, 62, 157–9

Balzac, Honore de 153
Barthes, Roland 78
Bazin, Andre 32, 155
Bellour, Raymond 26
Bertolucci, Bernardo 23, 34
Blumenberg, Hans 29, 109, 112
Buñuel, Luis 33, 114–8
Burch, Noel 26, 120

Cavell, Stanley 17, 31, 37
Clouzot, Henri-Georges 96–100
Constant, Benjamin 45

Deleuze, Gilles 26, 141, 157
Derrida, Jacques 71–2
determination 5, 25, 36, 72–4, 105, 159–61
Duras, Marguerite 121

Eisenstein, Sergei 26, 155
Empedocles 52, 159, 161
Eros 1, 49–68, 159
ethics 1–2, 41, 49, 73, 89, 155, 157

fantasy 10–11, 18, 33, 94, 109, 112–14, 120, 124, 140–4, 146–7
Fassbinder, Rainer Werner 23, 34
Foucault, Michel 158
freedom 1, 3, 5–6, 28, 39–40, 46, 52–3, 69–72, 77, 81, 89, 99, 109, 112, 121, 134, 147, 159–62
Freud, Sigmund 4, 69–70, 74, 76

Godard, Jean-Luc 33–4, 50

Hawks, Howard 89
Heidegger, Martin 43, 157–8
Heraclitus 52, 159, 161
Hesiod 50–2
Hitchcock, Alfred 33, 109–22, 139
Husserl, Edmund 158

imagination 38–40, 45, 117–18, 142, 146–8, 161
intelligibility 3–4, 25–7, 33, 43, 47, 58, 77–82, 85, 92–5, 107, 123–4, 133
interpretation 5, 9, 21, 31, 79–81, 112, 121, 146, 155

Kant, Immanuel 16, 40–1, 71, 77, 124
Kawabata, Yasunari 143
Kusturica, Emir 34

Love in Motion

Levi-Strauss, Claude 69

melodrama 6, 9–20, 28, 33, 82–8, 99, 111–14, 118, 136, 142, 144–5
moral corruption 85–6, 92, 97, 100, 120, 153
Murakami, Haruki 143–4

Pabst, Georg 27–9
Parmenides 51–2, 159
Pialat, Maurice 33, 35, 134–8, 158
positionality 32, 70, 74, 76, 78
Propertius, Sextus 53–4
Proust, Marcel 12, 45, 58, 148

realism 18, 28, 33, 86, 105, 118, 123–4, 144, 153
reciprocity 2, 4, 42, 44, 55–6, 65, 72–3, 84–5, 116, 124, 150

reflection 2, 5, 16, 35–7, 44, 53, 63, 73, 125, 133–4, 149, 152, 160
Rohmer, Ernst 35, 124–8, 131, 157, 161
Rosenzweig, Franz 71–2

Sartre, Jean Paul 9, 37, 46
Schlegel, Karl 76–7, 160
Stendhal 4, 39–40, 67, 160–1
Sternberg, Josef von 14–16, 27, 124

Tolstoy, Leo 4
Truffaut, Francois 33, 112, 114–20, 134, 146, 156

unconscious 9–10, 42, 46, 74–5, 91, 114, 117–18, 139–43

GPSR Authorized Representative: Easy Access System Europe, Mustamäe tee 50, 10621 Tallinn, Estonia, gpsr.requests@easproject.com

www.ingramcontent.com/pod-product-compliance
Lightning Source LLC
Chambersburg PA
CBHW051359290426
44108CB00015B/2083